THE PEOPLE VS CATHERINE NEVIN

LIZ WALSH
WITH RITA O'REILLY

Gill & Macmillan

Gill & Macmillan Ltd
Hume Avenue, Park West, Dublin 12
with associated companies throughout the world
www.gillmacmillan.ie
© Liz Walsh and Rita O'Reilly
0 7171 3146 7
Design and print origination by Carole Lynch
Printed by ColourBooks Ltd, Dublin

This book is typeset in 10.5/14.5pt Goudy.

A CIP catalogue reference for this book is available
from the British Library.

1 3 5 4 2

To the memory of Michael, my father
and life-long friend

And to the memory of Rita's father, also Michael.

Lady Macbeth

'Bear welcome in your eye,
Your hand, your tongue: look like th'innocent flower
But be the serpent under't. He that's coming
Must be provided for; and you shall put
This great night's business into my dispatch;
Which shall to all our nights and days to come
Give solely sovereign sway and masterdom.'

Macbeth, Act I, Scene V, 64–70

CONTENTS

ACKNOWLEDGMENTS

Thank you Martin for your love and support. Thanks to my mother Pauline for her love and unfailing faith in her offspring. Thanks to my daughter Niamh and my two sons Stephen and Alan, my sister Alison and brother Michael.

Thank you Rita O'Reilly for your superb contribution to this book. Thanks to my barrister-friend GSH, who was always on the end of a phone when I needed him. Thanks to Mike Hogan, publisher of *Magill* and editor Harry McGee for their support and to all my colleagues at the Hoson group, particularly Katherine Smyth. And to my fellow law students, particularly my friend Noreen McCusker and Aileen who ensured I was always kept up to speed. Thanks to all those who gave interviews or information, especially Liz Hudson and Eileen Byrne, who were kind.

Thanks to my friends for their support and encouragement: Susan McKay of the *Sunday Tribune*, Emma Counihan of INN, and also the many journalists who sent kind messages of support, including Ed Moloney and Fionnuala O'Connor. And to Jonathan Williams, to Martina, Sarah, Tom and Anne. Finally, thank you, Dr John Flynn and Imelda, for your many kindnesses during my stay in Gweesalia, Co. Mayo when writing this book. You made a stranger feel like a friend.

Liz Walsh

Thanks to Hilkka, my mother Rita and all my family; Diarmaid Mac Dermott and the late Tom McPhail of Ireland International News Agency; Michael O'Toole, Mary Carolan, Suzanne MacManus and all the Four Courts reporters, and Judy Walsh.

Rita O'Reilly

We jointly want to thank the family of Tom Nevin who, in the middle of their private grief, so kindly agreed to talk to us for this book. Finally, thanks to all those people who helped in so many ways but who, for obvious reasons, would not appreciate an individual 'thank you' here. They are: members of the gardaí, the legal profession, individual members of the republican movement and other sources. Without your help this book may never have been written.

Thanks too to RTE's Mary Wilson, Charlie Mallon and the indefatigable Miriam Lord of the *Irish Independent* whose unique sense of humour kept us going during those last tedious days of the trial.

PROLOGUE

❧

I t was one of those balmy end-of-September days when the
scent of summer lingered and had not yet given way to the
cold October chill. The courts had resumed after the summer
break and were in the middle of what is known in the legal
profession as Michaelmas term.

The district courthouse in Gorey, Co. Wexford is a drab grey
building at the top of Main Street, a long narrow road that runs
the length of the town. It was sitting that day, 26 September
1997. The presiding judge was from Arklow, Donnchadh
Ó Buachalla, a dapper, silver-haired former solicitor in his early
fifties.

A licence application was before the court that morning for
Jack White's Inn, a popular landmark on the N11, the main route
between Dublin and the Wexford port of Rosslare. It was a three-
fold application for a restaurant certificate, early-morning and St
Patrick's Day exemption.

Inspector Peter Finn from Gorey was there, his blue garda
uniform a stark contrast to the sombre-suited lawyers for the
applicant, Catherine Nevin, the surviving joint licensee of Jack

White's Inn. In the hushed, near-empty courthouse Finn and Mr O'Gorman, a solicitor acting for Mrs Nevin, waited for the application to be called.

Finn had earlier let it be known that he was objecting to the three-fold application on the grounds that there was no main publican's licence in force. The newly widowed Mrs Nevin had not renewed the annual licence when it fell due the previous October, seven months after her husband Tom was shot dead in the kitchen of Jack White's. When the application was called, Mr O'Gorman asked Judge Ó Buachalla to adjourn the proceedings and a new date was set for three days' later, 29 September, this time at Wexford District Court.

The clock was ticking. If 30 September passed and still no main licence had been issued, Catherine Nevin would no longer be in a position to apply for a renewal or a transfer of the licence. It would have lapsed entirely. Her only options would be either to apply to the Circuit Court for a 'revival' of the licence, or to make an entirely fresh application, and by this time she would stand charged with her husband's murder.

The district court in Wexford is in the town hall, a beautiful old stone building overlooking the Slaney River at the edge of Wexford town. Inspector Finn arrived bright and early with the intention of renewing his objections to the three-fold application for Jack White's. At approximately 11 a.m., just before the court started, Finn was asked to go to the judge's chambers. It is a small anteroom, at the back of the courtroom, just to the right of the judge's bench, containing five or six chairs, a long table, a kettle and a few cups and saucers and some legal texts.

Judge Donnchadh Ó Buachalla was sitting on a chair at the long table, alongside the court clerks, Andy Cullen and Olive

Steward. Standing beside them were Donnchadh Lehane, solicitor, and Seamus Ó Tuathail, barrister, both acting for Catherine Nevin.

Donnchadh Lehane then informed the gathering that he was applying for an order in support for a publican's licence for Catherine Nevin. Inspector Finn was taken aback. He said he had no notice or indication that such an application would be made at that court, and that the relevant notices had not been placed in newspapers. Seamus Ó Tuathail then told those present it was an *ex-parte* application to have the name of Tom Nevin deleted and have the licence issued in the sole name of his widow, Catherine.

Finn turned towards Lehane and Ó Tuathail with a startled look. 'Why then am I present?' asked Finn, 'I'm not on notice.'

Seamus Ó Tuathail is a very affable lawyer, tall and grey-haired. He explained patiently and in some detail the nature of the application and what he wanted the court to grant. Finn retorted that in his opinion, the required application should be one of 'confirmation of transfer' of the licence.

'You cannot confirm something that is already confirmed,' replied Ó Tuathail. 'My client was confirmed in 1988, when she and her husband were licensed.'

It was now approaching midday. At this point, Ó Buachalla halted the proceedings until 1 p.m.

Peter Finn rushed out and telephoned Dan Prenderville, a senior officer in Customs and Excise in Nenagh, Co. Tipperary, the body responsible for the actual issuing of licences. Finn explained the situation that had developed and what was about to happen. He faxed a copy of the proposed order to Prenderville.

At exactly 12.45 p.m. Finn's phone rang. The caller was a Ms Etain Croasdell, solicitor for Customs and Excise. Customs 'would accept the order the judge was about to make', she told him. Finn's hands were tied.

At 2 p.m., the solicitor, the clerks, the lawyer and the inspector began to troop back into the judge's chambers. At 2.15 p.m., when the application was called in chambers, Judge Ó Buachalla issued the order. The following day, Catherine Nevin paid duties of £900 to Customs and Excise in Waterford. They issued her with publican's licence number 461868.

Catherine Nevin was now the sole licensee of Jack White's Inn.

1

THE BLACK BERET

～～◆◆◆～～

Northern Ireland, June 1969. Seven months since the Civil Rights Movement was founded in the Bogside, then a Catholic slum in the heart of the historic city of Derry. Tens of thousands of nationalists had begun to take to the streets to demand equal civil and political rights for the minority population. In January, a civil rights march from Belfast to Derry had been ambushed at Burntollet Bridge just outside Derry city and the marchers beaten off the bridge by a loyalist mob.

By August, the civil unrest had spread to Belfast. In Bombay Street, entire rows of houses were petrol bombed by loyalist gangs, the occupants forced to flee with whatever possessions they could load into prams or wheelbarrows before their homes were engulfed by fire. Flames from burning buildings illuminated the night skies over Belfast and Derry: the street violence had its own momentum, forcing the pace of events on the republican movement.

Catholics were now beginning to pour over the border to seek refuge in the south. Northern Ireland was going up in flames.

The IRA had lain dormant since the beginning of the decade and was now in deep disarray. When Northern nationalists went looking for arms, they discovered that the IRA arsenal had disappeared; rumour had it that it had been sold off to Welsh nationalists. It was then that the slogan 'IRA – I Ran Away' started to appear on walls in the ghettos of Belfast and Derry.

The chief of staff of the IRA at that time was Cathal Goulding. Goulding was an erudite socialist republican who had, by then, moved away from the traditional republican position of a 32-county Republic in favour of a Marxist, pluralist state. Joe Cahill, a small, bald man often seen wearing a pork pie hat, was an unreconstructed republican from Belfast. Cahill had been convicted of the murder of an RUC constable in the forties and had barely escaped the gallows.

By the spring of 1969, the seeds of the Provisional/Official IRA split had been well and truly sown. It came with the first meeting of the IRA Provisional Army Council on 28 December. But the parting of the ways was not complete until Sinn Féin, the political wing of the IRA, split along the same lines. It happened a fortnight later at the Sinn Féin Ard Fheis at the Intercontinental Hotel in Dublin on 11 January.

Cathal Goulding became Chief of Staff of what was to become the Official IRA. Its political wing metamorphosed into 'Sinn Féin The Worker's Party'. Joe Cahill would shortly afterwards become a member of the Provisional Army Council and Officer Commanding (OC), Belfast Brigade. Cahill left Belfast and came south of the border after internment was introduced in 1971. Internment – imprisonment without trial – was a great recruiting agent for the Provisionals. Among the hundreds who joined up around 1971 were two young Dublin men called Gerry Heapes and John Jones.

Up until the split, Sinn Féin's headquarters had been located in Gardiner Place in Dublin, at the end of a large, run-down street, bordered on either side by row upon row of filthy tenements, boarded up and derelict buildings and desolate and abandoned sites. It runs from the south side of Mountjoy Square along the periphery of the north inner city slums, then regarded as among the worst in Europe. Sinn Féin headquarters was situated a short distance from the Castle Hotel in Gardiner Row, which had a large republican clientele; many republicans from outside Dublin would stay there if they were in the city overnight. It was a place where activists like Cahill and Goulding and Sinn Féin's Christy Burke got together for a drink, to talk politics and generally socialise. After the split, the Officials stopped frequenting the Castle but the Provos remained.

Fifty miles from Dublin and a world removed from the Northern conflict, a young student named Catherine Scully was preparing to sit her Leaving Cert exams in June 1969. The young Scully was a pupil of Presentation College in Nurney, a tiny crossroads village several miles south of Kildare town. She was then 18.

Catherine Scully was born on 28 February 1951, the eldest of three children, in Kilboggan, a townland outside Nurney. She went to the little national school there when she was five. Her mother, Mary, was a seamstress who supplemented the family's income by taking in work at the family home, a modest cottage on a small, 32-acre farm. Catherine's father, Patrick, who died in September 1996, worked the farm all his life. When times were hard – and they often were – he would take on extra work with local farmers to make ends meet. Catherine walked around on the day of his funeral with a single rose held up to her face.

They were a close family: Catherine, her parents, sister Betty and brother Vincent. Vincent had been struck down with polio when he was two and although he recovered fairly well he still walks with a limp. He worked abroad for years and has returned to Ireland only within the last 18 months to two years. He is now working as an engineer in Dublin. Betty Scully became an aroma-therapist. She married a successful local builder named Paddy White and now has a family of her own. Since Catherine's father died, Mary Scully has lived alone in the family cottage in Nurney.

By all accounts, the young Catherine was a bright child and a good, diligent student, far ahead of her classmates in many subjects, particularly maths. A former teacher remembers her with fondness: 'Catherine was an excellent student, very con-scientious; you never had to push her to get her to study.'

The nuns at Presentation College in Kildare said the Catherine that the country knew from the murder trial was not the girl they had known all those years ago. As one says: 'Poor Catherine, what happened to her at all? She was so good for our girls.'

Catherine Scully was what is called a 'grafter'. If she wanted something she would work for it. A close relative of Catherine's says she, 'always worked hard; she'd never ask her mother for anything, she'd work for it. If she was going to a dance, she'd run up a dress for herself and she cycled everywhere.'

This relative now feels only contempt for Catherine and asked not to be named. However, there is nothing in Catherine Scully's background or upbringing that would point to the type of socio-pathic behaviour that would later mark her out as a woman apart. 'She was a normal child, no trouble at all,' the same relative says. 'She was born a bit premature but she was fine. And she was a normal teenager. There was no hint of trouble at that stage; that came later.'

'Pretty' is not an adjective that could ever have been ascribed to the young Catherine Scully. Yet an early photograph shows a fairly good-looking young woman with short brown hair, warm eyes and a soft, gentle smile. Someone, somewhere, said she had a kind of Doris Day look about her. The smiling face in the photograph is almost unrecognisable as the brittle blonde who appeared in the Central Criminal Court on a charge of murdering her husband almost three decades later.

But even then, Catherine Scully had ambitions that would take her far beyond the confined world of a small rural backwater. Not for her the daily drudge of life on a small farm, the grinding toil, the muck, the fight for survival, the compromises. She wanted more than that – much, much more. She craved money, status, she liked men and she wanted to look well, to be noticed. In short, Catherine Scully wanted to be somebody and she couldn't do that in Nurney. She needed to leave the 'small-town girl' behind for good.

Her first step along that road was to find a job in Dublin as soon as she got her Leaving Cert. She found one in the Castle Hotel, one of Dublin's oldest hotels and the place where she was to meet Cathal Goulding and some of the other IRA men whose names would later feature in the murder trial.

Mr and Mrs O'Connor owned the Castle Hotel. They were a well-liked, staunchly republican couple. Catherine started working for them as a receptionist in the main office. In common with many country girls at that time, she lived-in, in a room above the main floor. After about a year, she became dining-room supervisor and also helped Mr O'Connor with the accounts, her aptitude for maths coming in handy.

Her time in the Castle took in the period around and after the IRA split. She was young, just up from the country and was very impressionable. A male republican remembers her as being fascinated by some of the people who came in and out of the Castle. The perceived 'glamour' that was somehow attached to the IRA, the armed struggle and all the paraphernalia that went with it, provided a magnetic attraction for certain kinds of people. The kind who hung around on the fringes of republicanism, or flirted with it, for those very reasons, rather then from any ideological position or political persuasion. They were sometimes used by the IRA if it suited the organisation, but more times not.

Another republican vaguely recalls her being in and around the company of IRA men. But, as he said, she could not have made much of an impression on him, because he couldn't remember too much about her.

For most of her adult life, Catherine Scully, the village girl from Nurney, seemed to be in awe of the hard men of the republican movement. It was to them that she turned when she went looking for a pub to buy, instead of an estate agent. And it was to the IRA that she looked when she sought a hired killer to murder her husband, Tom Nevin.

'Some people like (Catherine Nevin) were attracted to what they saw as the glamour of the whole IRA thing,' is how one IRA man put it, looking back. 'You used to get that a lot with some women; they were kind of IRA groupies. It was like the black beret was some kind of sexual turn-on. Believe it or not it wasn't that uncommon, particularly in those years.'

There is no denying that the IRA and the Northern conflict held a lifelong interest for Catherine Scully. 'She was always talking about Provos and the North, she was obsessed with it,' recalls a garda who knew her. 'Even when she had relatives staying, she'd go on about it incessantly. She'd talk about it to customers, even the ones she didn't know too well.'

When it suited the occasion, Catherine Nevin was not averse to threatening people with the IRA. One republican source recalled an incident in Jack White's when Catherine had some work done on the pub. It was while Tom was still alive. She didn't know it, but two of the workmen happened to be republicans. The work did not live up to her expectations. 'She went mad, she threw the head and threatened the men she'd have them "done" by the IRA,' said the source. 'They just stood there, grinning at her.'

A member of staff at Jack White's recalls Catherine's frequent visits to the North from 1986 on. 'Catherine used to go up to the North twice a year for three or four days. She said she had friends up there,' said Jane Murphy. Later, Catherine Scully's stories would concern attacks by strange men in her Dublin flat, IRA men arriving in the middle of the night for clandestine meetings and Provo money-laundering.

Names of senior republicans dropped off her tongue with remarkable ease. One of them was John Noonan, a former IRA man from Tallaght who served five years in Portlaoise Prison for a paramilitary-related offence. She talked of Dickie O'Neill, a senior Belfast republican who was then living in Dublin.

'I've never met the woman in my life, never,' John Noonan told these authors. 'And I speak for Dickie O'Neill as well when I say that. Neither of us have ever met that woman in connection with anything whatsoever.'

One man Catherine Scully *did* know was Cathal Goulding. Goulding had been an occasional visitor to the Castle Hotel until sometime in 1970 and it was there that he met her. Although she leaned towards the Provisionals, her friendship with Goulding was to endure for at least 16 years. She would later describe Goulding as 'my very good friend'.

Catherine's close relative remembers her talking a lot about 'Sinn Féin people' and in particular, Cathal Goulding. 'I remembered that name, I don't remember any other names but I remember that one. She was always going on about Sinn Féin people. She used to bring them down here to the pubs, that would have been years ago, maybe 1983–4.'

The years 1969–70 saw a series of sensational developments on the Southern political front in relation to Northern Ireland. A young cabinet minister named Charles Haughey was charged with plotting to import arms for use by Northern nationalists. His fellow cabinet minister, Neil Blaney, was also charged, as were a number of others. The arms trial that followed resulted in the acquittal of all the accused but provoked a political crisis that almost brought down the Fianna Fáil government of the day under Taoiseach Jack Lynch.

Haughey and his co-accused were subsequently acquitted of gun-running but Jack Lynch sacked him and Blaney from his cabinet. Haughey's nemesis at the time was Peter Berry, Secretary to the Department of Justice, the most powerful department in the State. Berry, who was well known for his anti-republican views, started out as a clerical officer in the department in January 1927 and spent his entire career there until he retired in January 1971. In one incident during the 1960s, when Haughey was Minister for Justice, Berry came to complain about five of his junior staff. He hauled them up in front of Haughey, who signalled Berry to leave the room. As soon as the door was shut, Haughey turned to the five with a wide grin: 'That one's a right bollox, isn't he?' he remarked.

The department's assistant secretary at the time was a man called Sean Ó Buachalla, a supporter of Fianna Fáil and of Charles Haughey. Ó Buachalla began his career as an administrative officer in the department in May 1939 and retired in July 1971, just six months after Berry. Ó Buachalla and Berry did not get along well. They were at opposite ends of the political axis, particularly in relation to Northern Ireland. They had many a clash.

Peter Berry had very sinister habits; one of them entailed writing cryptic notes on the sides of memos to his subservients in Justice. One well-placed source remembers the notes as being 'totally outrageous'. Berry also rifled other people's filing cabinets. He went through Sean Ó Buachalla's one day and what he found written on one of the files there incensed him. After that, Berry couldn't get rid of him fast enough. Ó Buachalla was moved from the Department of Justice in July 1970. Haughey was not pleased at Berry's treatment of Ó Buachalla.

Sean Ó Buachalla had a son, Donnchadh Ó Buachalla, who went on to become a solicitor. Many years later, in April 1989, Charles Haughey, as Taoiseach, would appoint Donnchadh Ó Buachalla a district court judge.

Four years on, Donnchadh Ó Buachalla's path was to cross with Catherine Nevin's. And his name was to surface alongside that of Cathal Goulding, Joe Cahill, John Noonan and Dickie O'Neill in one of the most sensational murder trials in Irish legal history.

Catherine Scully was a man's woman. There was no question about it. She seemed to have a notion that she was sexually alluring, sophisticated and clever. She flattered men, whether by accident or design. She had the knack of making them feel important, particularly middle-aged men. And they loved it.

'You could tell by the way they responded to Catherine that they were flattered,' says a former friend. 'She made them feel she was interested in them as people. And they lapped it up. Maybe it was the old case of Catherine providing something they weren't getting at home and I don't mean just sex.'

Liz Hudson was a long-time member of staff at Jack White's and one of the few who enjoyed a good relationship with

Catherine. Liz knew Catherine more than most but even she couldn't figure out what made the woman tick. 'You can't explain what kind of a person she was, she wasn't affectionate, but you could have a bit of a laugh with her sometimes. But she used to sit on the stool with the split in her skirts going all the way up her leg; it was like she was trying to create an impression.'

Catherine Nevin made sure there was only one exhibitionist in Jack White's – herself. Her rules on dress code for the female staff were positively prissy. She had them written on a notice pinned to the wall in case they'd miss the point: 'Skirts no more than one-and-a-half inches above the knee.'

This mixture of outward exhibitionism versus old-maidish, almost puritanical regulations, is another clue to the complex personality that is Catherine Nevin. If any of the female staff stepped out of line on the dress code – particularly the younger ones – she was quick to pull them up. 'She reprimanded me shortly after my arrival about my dress,' Ciara Tallon remembers. Tallon was 19 when she waitressed at Jack White's. 'My dress was too short. I stayed clear of her, keeping out of her way. She was difficult to work for. She said she was going to watch me.'

'I didn't get on well with Mrs Nevin, sometimes she was hard to work for and would shout at you in the presence of other customers,' says Caroline Strahan, another youngster who worked at the pub. 'I got on all right with Tom. He wasn't like her.'

'She didn't like women, you know,' recalls Eileen Byrne, an elderly cleaner who worked at Jack White's between 1993 and 1994. 'And she hated kids, she would always moan if there were kids in the lounge, she'd tell the parents to leave. The kids always went into Tom in the bar. No time at all for children or women; she'd *plámás* women all right but she didn't like them. She hadn't a woman friend in the parish.'

14

Catherine had sexual affairs, lots of them – some of them with republicans. One affair was with a republican who would come into her life when she was landlady of Jack White's Inn. It is more than likely that some of her lovers were mere opportunists – freeloaders on the make. It is also more than likely that Catherine was using them for her own ends. The sex was just an added bonus.

But even if she had slept her way through the entire Irish Republican Army it would not have made her a killer. And it should not have made her a suspect for murder. It was something deeper and darker in her psyche that did that.

In Catherine Nevin, we have the modern-day version of Lady Macbeth, the anti-heroine in Shakespeare's tale of evil and deception. She certainly displayed all the base characteristics of Lady Macbeth: ruthlessness, a liking for scheming, a lust for power, naked ambition, a sense of omnipotence. And greed. Half an empire was no good to Catherine Scully, the girl from Nurney. She wanted it all.

While Lady Macbeth's husband was weak and vacillating, she was dominant, determined, totally self-possessed. And she had the future all worked out. Lady Macbeth conspired with others to murder the King – leaving Macbeth free to take power – but it was she who would actually be in control. Like the lady in question, Catherine Nevin never intended to do the actual deed, merely to manage the whole affair. And the payoff – 'masterdom'. With Tom Nevin out of the picture, Catherine would be empress of a mini property kingdom in her own right.

As we know from the trial, money, property and status were hugely important to the young Catherine. And so it was when she met Tom Nevin in the Castle Hotel.

She was 21. He was a decade older, a six-foot-three, friendly Galway barman who loved hurling. He was also married, although he was in the process of getting that marriage annulled. And he owned property, a house set in flats off the South Circular Road in the heart of Dublin's flatland. He had just bought 6 Mayfield Road when he met Catherine. He wanted his own pub, more property. But more importantly, he seemed to want her.

'I got to know him well,' Catherine would later tell the court. 'I didn't really officially go out with him I suppose until about late seventy-four, the beginning of seventy-five, sometime perhaps before Christmas seventy-four.'

Tom Nevin came from a farming background in Nutgrove, Tynagh – pronounced Teenah – a sleepy little village halfway between Portumna and Loughrea in south Galway. It is home to Tynagh mines, which have never been very profitable or very big. Tynagh is mainly farming territory. The village's closest links are with Loughrea rather than the nearer Portumna. Tynagh's most famous ancestral son is Paul Keating, the former Labour Prime Minister of Australia. When he visited it with his wife in the 1990s, the village and the hinterland turned out to welcome them.

The Nevin family as a unit agreed to speak to the authors about their murdered brother as they remembered him. Tom Nevin was born in Tynagh on 22 September 1941, the eldest in a family of six boys and three girls. Hurling was his passion. He played it, watched it, talked about little else in those early years. Patsy Nevin, now the eldest, was the closest in age to Tom: 'He was regarded as a county-class hurler at that time.' Tom played centre-field or half-back, first for the school team in Tynagh and then the Vocational School team in Portumna. 'That team combined Tipperary and Galway hurlers, so they were a very good side.'

In 1956, Tom won a scholarship to a Gaeltacht school in Rosmuc but he didn't take it up. There was too much work to be done on the farm. After completing the Group Cert, he went to Mountbellew Agricultural College for six months.

At 16, Tom Nevin left for Dublin. 'There were no teenage years in those days,' recalls his sister, Mary Glennon. 'Once you left school you were an adult straight away. You were a child and the next thing you were in a job.' It was the late 1950s. He got a job as an apprentice barman in Nally's pub in Ballyfermot. As an apprentice he worked a full week, and then joined the publicans' favourite club, the Grocer's Hurling Club, for training in the Phoenix Park on Sunday mornings.

At the time he was living in his 'Uncle Willie's' house on the Naas Road. Willie Frehill was Tom's mother's brother and Tom would later manage Frehill's pub, the Barn House. 'He was part of the family, he used to babysit for them. Tom used to cycle from the Naas Road to Ballyfermot,' says Margaret Lavelle, Tom's youngest sister.

'He had a great sense of humour,' recalls another sister, Nora Finnerty. 'He would be always out for a laugh, anything for a laugh. He liked music and dancing; he used to go to Clery's on his night off. He was a Country and Western man. When he was in Dublin he was a great man for the dress dances. Tom was always there if somebody had no partner. You'd just give him a little ring . . . He didn't mind dressing up into the monkey suits whereas other lads would. He was game for those sorts of things.'

Tom Nevin had a car of his own from a young age, but before that, he would hire out a car to drive home to Tynagh. It was a very close community; whenever Tom came home 'all the neighbours would gather for the hurling and the jokes'.

Mary Glennon remembers one occasion when they were all going to a dance in Kiltomer, a village near Tynagh:

'We were all packed in, and we got stuck in a lot of water. Tom was driving, and I said, "How are we going to get out?" "Well, I'm not going to get my feet wet anyway," he said, "so you can all get out and push me out." A man was passing with a pair of wellingtons on him and sure, one push and we were out. But there was no way Tom was getting his feet wet.'

Tom was a few years in Dublin when he met a Mayo woman, June O'Flanagan. They married on 26 April 1962 and the couple moved into a flat at 609 South Circular Road. They left for England shortly afterwards where they managed a pub as husband and wife. An Irish woman owned it: she later returned to Ireland and bought a boutique in Gorey. Many years in the future she would turn up at Tom Nevin's funeral.

When Tom and June came back to Dublin, Tom got a job in a pub in Inchicore; it is now called the Emmet House. By 1971, when his sister Mary was getting married, Tom's own marriage to June O'Flanagan had broken down irretrievably. 'We were wondering if Tom would show up,' said Mary of her wedding day. 'He showed up. He never let us down. He always came, no matter how bad things were.'

June O'Flanagan took complete responsibility for the marriage break-up. 'It was entirely my fault,' she said. Tom was a quiet, gentle soul. Her family had a pet nickname for him. 'They called him the gentle giant.' The Church annulment came first and then the civil annulment came through.

When he met her, Tom told Catherine about his marital position, the name of his previous wife and the fact that he'd gone through a Church annulment. 'He was going through a State annulment at that particular time,' she would later tell the court at her trial. She did not tell the jury that during that time, posing as a social worker, she paid a visit to June O'Flanagan and tried to elicit details of June's relationship with Tom from her. Tom did not know it.

With the State annulment in his back pocket, Tom was free to marry Catherine Scully. She became the second Mrs Nevin at a ceremony in the Church of St John Lateran in Rome on 13 January 1977.

The wedding photographs are similar to those of countless thousands of couples in love everywhere. Catherine is wearing a Queen-Anne-style headdress with a full-length veil and a white, high-necked bridal gown. Her hair is short, brown and slightly curly.

Tom is standing beside her, wearing a dark suit, waistcoat and top hat, his left arm looped protectively around his new wife's slim waist. He looks relaxed and very happy. Catherine's left hand with its new gold wedding band is resting on his right one and both their hands are pressing down on a knife cutting into the bottom layer of a four-tiered wedding cake. Her wedding bouquet is lying in front of the cake stand. The couple is smiling.

Before she married Tom, while she was still working at the Castle Hotel, Catherine moved out of the hotel accommodation and into a bedsit in a house named 'Esmerelle' on the North Circular Road. In 1973, she left the Castle after three-and-a-half years. She was then 22. In 1974, she moved into Mayfield Road with Tom. Around this time she took a course in grooming and deportment at the University of Ulster at Coleraine.

Ever with an eye to the main chance, the young Catherine was always immaculately turned out and she reckoned there was money to be made in teaching others the tricks of the trade. She saw an opportunity for travelling around schools advising students on interview techniques, how to sit properly, how to put gloves on and take them off correctly and so on. There were no career guidance teachers in those days so Catherine was pushing an open door. The business took off. She'd travel around the west of Ireland with three or four suits hanging up in the car. 'If you get a job in Dublin and you've any problems, make sure you call me,' she'd say to her students. Sister Rose, a nun in Portumna, was very fond of her. She thought she was a 'princess coming to visit'.

However, this entrepreneurial venture eventually fizzled out: times were changing and so were employment patterns. Female school-leavers were no longer interested in taking up traditional roles as secretaries or receptionists to the same extent, and by now, career guidance teachers had arrived on the scene. The result was that there wasn't too much of a market for teaching 'young ladies' techniques anymore.

On her return from her wedding in Rome, the new Mrs Nevin moved back into Mayfield Road. Number 6 is a red brick two-storey end-of-terrace house, with two long, sash windows on the upper floor and a large bay window downstairs. The upper floor was set in six flats so the newlyweds lived in a flat in the bottom section of the house. It had one bedroom, a living room cum dining room and a small kitchen. Tom's younger sister, Margaret, was nursing in Dublin at the time and she would visit her brother and his new wife from time to time. Cathal Goulding was also an occasional visitor to Mayfield Road. He had kept in contact with Catherine Nevin since her time at the Castle Hotel.

It was from this house that Catherine set up and ran a modelling agency, which she named the 'Catherine Scully Model Agency and Beauty Grooming School'. Soft-focus publicity shots for the agency show a smiling Catherine wearing a smart striped shirt, her left arm weighed down with chunky gold jewellery and one painted, manicured fingernail pressed into her chin. The agency never took off.

With the school visits at an end and no modelling school, Catherine's mind turned to more mundane matters – decorating the flats at Mayfield Road. She spent her time painting and making curtains – she was pretty nifty with the sewing machine.

By then she had property in her own right. The year after they married, Catherine got a mortgage and bought a house in her maiden name, Catherine Scully, at 446 South Circular Road. She secured the loan through the Allied Irish Bank in Dolphin's Barn. The deposit was £1,000. She took possession of the house in July 1978.

The property-buying continued. This time it was a pre-1963 house at Mountshannon Road, again off the South Circular Road. Mountshannon was in Tom's name and it was let in seven flats. The significance of the pre-1963 designation is that it qualified for rent relief from earned income. It is clear that Tom Nevin was nobody's fool when it came to money. He was an astute man who was taking this landlord business seriously.

While Catherine was flirting with the precarious world of modelling, Tom was managing the Barn House, his uncle's licensed premises on the left-hand side of the Grand Canal separating Parnell Road from Dolphin House flats. The black-fronted pub faces onto Dolphin House, a large corporation flats complex with a reputation as being one of the toughest in Dublin.

Drugs were, and are, endemic in Dolphin House flats. It was here that the first anti-drugs movement, Concerned Parents Against Drugs, was formed in the early 1980s. Some of its leading lights were prominent republicans. John Noonan, who Catherine Nevin would later name in the trial, was among them.

Six years rolled by. They appeared pretty uneventful with little outward sign that the Nevin marriage was in trouble. In fact, events indicated the contrary. In April 1984, Tom and

Catherine renewed their wedding vows at a civil ceremony in the State Registry Office in Molesworth Street in Dublin.

In truth, the marriage was already starting to unravel. Tom Nevin loved children but he was never going to have a child of his own by Catherine Nevin. A few years into the marriage Catherine had herself sterilised. She had also undergone an abortion in England, the result of an affair with a much older man, before she met Tom. He was a well-known solicitor in Dublin at that time of the affair, which happened in the early 1970s before she married Tom Nevin. The solicitor had pressurised her into having a termination. He died some years ago, but at the time of the affair he had a thriving practice, with offices in Dublin city centre.

One year after the State ceremony, Catherine began an affair with a man named Willie McClean. She told McClean about the abortion and sterilisation. 'Tom found out; I think it was during a row. She told me he went mad, he took it very badly,' says McClean.

Catherine Nevin also told a close relative of hers about the sterilisation:

'Tom loved children but she made sure she'd never have any. She told me about it, she told me she'd had it done. She showed me one day (on her body) where she'd had it done.' This relative is unsure whether Tom Nevin knew about the sterilisation at the time, or not. But if Catherine was telling the truth to McClean, that Tom found out in a row, he did not know up to that point.

Catherine's affair with Willie McClean was to last 18 months. It was to be one of many. As far back as 1985, it seemed the marriage was heading for the rocks.

Financially though, the Nevins' stock was on the up. They were able to afford another house, this time a semi-, number 376

22

Greenpark, in the Dublin suburb of Clondalkin. They left Mayfield and moved into Greenpark. But as things turned out, their time there was to be relatively short.

In the spring of 1984 Willie Frehill sold the pub at Dolphin's Barn. Tom had had some kind of an arrangement with him over stocktaking, but apart from that, Tom was out of a job. They began looking around for a pub of their own.

The Nevin family remember them, 'down in Galway, Galway city and county, looking'. From the time she met Tom, Catherine would arrive in Galway 'all glamour' like the Queen Bee. By all accounts, she was always 'up in the clouds', living in a world of her own. The firm impression she gave the Nevin family was that she really hadn't much in common with them. She certainly never wanted to buy a pub in the west: as she said in court – property-buying was all about 'location, location, location'. The west, in Catherine's eyes, was a 'bad location'.

It was after this that the lease on a pub in west Finglas became available. It was an ugly, two-storey building on Barry Road, in the middle of a tough local-authority area with all of the socio-economic problems associated with the large housing schemes of the late 1970s and early 1980s. It had a reputation in the early part of the Troubles as being an IRA pub. It was monitored like clockwork by the Garda Special Branch, so much so that locals would wonder what was up if the 'Branch car' failed to show up of an evening.

The pub was called the Barry House, although locals knew it as the Cappagh House. For a time back in the early to mid 1970s a young Provo worked on the door as a security man. He lived just around the corner in Barry Park. His name was Gerry Heapes.

2

IRRECONCILABLE
DIFFERENCES

Something was up with Peter Charleton. The normally unruffled prosecution lawyer had a bee in his bonnet. In the tense quiet of the courtroom, you could hear the tap, tap, tap of his pen as he flicked the nib on the bench in front of him. He was glancing darkly at the woman in the dock and you could hear the slight swish of his black robe as he shifted in his seat. It was as though he couldn't wait to jump to his feet.

When he did, minutes later, he made clear the source of his agitation. It was the happy marriage story that Catherine Nevin had been busily telling. It was too much for Peter Charleton. 'I must protest,' he said as he rose. 'The entire case has been thrown into chaos by the way this matter has been handled.'

And with the jury safely out of the room, he challenged the defence to call retired Garda Inspector Tom Kennedy, so that he might be cross-examined on his evidence. 'I take it, that as a matter of honour, Tom Kennedy is now going to be called by the defence.' Charleton's outburst came at the end of Catherine Nevin's evidence. It was Wednesday, 22 March 2000, Day 26 of the trial.

'. . . The case is now being made that Mr and Mrs Nevin had a loving relationship,' Charleton continued. That it was so, 'comes as a total shock'. He didn't believe it. Neither did the witnesses, the gardaí, the reporters or the day-trippers – those curious onlookers who clogged up the court each day like contemporary versions of Madame Defarge. By then, nobody believed it.

The state of the Nevin marriage was a recurrent theme of the trial. It went to the heart of the prosecution case. By the time Catherine Nevin got around to spinning her happy marriage story, a succession of witnesses had testified that the Nevin marriage was anything but.

They lifted the veil on a hellish marriage, one marred by alcoholism, deception, violent incidents and punctuated by Catherine's many affairs.

The truth is a many-faceted concept and rarely has that been so aptly illustrated as at this trial. From early on it was clear that, at best, only limited amounts of the truth would be revealed. Apart from Catherine Nevin, no living person can say with any degree of certainty when exactly the marriage started to fall apart, where it all began to go wrong. Tom's bitterness over Catherine's sterilisation may have played a part in the souring of the relationship but that apart, the evidence is the only pointer, the only reliable yardstick by which the truth can be measured. Some of it was harrowing.

Tom Nevin drank heavily. Catherine also drank too much – whiskey and ginger was her favourite tipple. She took too many prescription drugs. Greed, recrimination, betrayal were constant companions in this marriage. She wanted him to sell his share of the business to her. He refused. She was too often seen in the company of other men, many men. She had sex with some of them. He saw her in bed with another man. He did nothing to stop it.

Catherine may have had extra-marital affairs before 1985, the year after she and Tom renewed their wedding vows at the civil ceremony. She definitely had one that year, with Willie McClean.

McClean is a big, burly, potbellied conman with a bulbous nose and a reddish face topped by a mop of blond, straight hair. By any standards, he is an unattractive man, although he has a certain rough charm about him. In his heyday he wasn't a bad-looking man, according to sources who knew him back then. 'He was slim, blonde, drove flash cars, very much the man-about-town, you could see why he got the women,' says one.

After the trial Willie McClean reportedly boasted that he was the 'biggest whoremaster' in Ireland and that he'd had so many women he couldn't remember half of them. McClean denies he said this. His family have been hurt by those reports, he says. Nevertheless, Willie McClean has quite a track record with women.

He has four adult children, two daughters by his first wife and 18-year-old twin boys from a different relationship. He is now married again. Then there was Catherine Nevin. In later life, Willie McClean's unprepossessing appearance certainly doesn't seem to have proved an impediment to getting women into bed with him.

McClean was born in Co. Monaghan on 13 June 1951 at Kilmore East, Bellanode, a tiny village about six kilometres from Monaghan town. His criminal record is short and pathetic, three convictions, two up North and one in Dublin. On 26 July 1973, Clogher Magistrates Court in Tyrone found him guilty of theft by deception. He was sentenced to three months. Three months after that, he was convicted of a similar offence and sentenced to two years. He was convicted of a minor public order offence in Dublin on 15 April 1988 and bound to keep the peace.

'Well, I don't think they call it deception down here, they call it fraud,' he said. The deception charges were in fact for 'kiting' and 'embezzlement'. Kiting is writing a cheque knowing there are no funds to cover it. He'd bought a Land Rover with no money to pay for it. The embezzlement part centred on small-time fraud like cattle and drink smuggling across the border.

To the world at large, Willie McClean fitted neatly into the classic Arthur Daley mode, sometimes straying on the wrong side of the law, but never too far on the wrong side of the tracks. He was tagged the 'blond bomber' in Monaghan after an incident in which he wrote off three cars belonging to Customs and Excise, he tells these authors.

McClean was involved in another incident in Monaghan, unrelated, but much more serious. In 1974 he was taken from his home by a number of men who brought him to another location – this side of the border – where they beat him about the head and chest. He came out of it black and blue and with a couple of cracked ribs. He refuses to say why he was attacked or who was responsible, other than to deny reports that he was admitted to Monaghan Hospital with injuries to his groin.

McClean met Catherine Nevin in the Red Cow Inn on the Naas Road in late 1984 or early '85. It was an almost casual encounter. 'We were just talking of an evening and it went on from there,' he said. What went on was a relationship, a sexual one, which lasted from then until sometime in August or September 1986.

That first evening, when McClean and Catherine Nevin met, she invited him back to the house at Greenpark while Tom was at work in Willie Frehill's bar in Dolphin's Barn. They didn't have sex that night but they did shortly afterwards. At the start, it was a sensuous liaison with the added frisson that comes from having illicit sex with a partner who is married to someone else. But that gradually waned, according to McClean's one-sided insight into the affair. 'She was just too much work; she'd wreck your head. I think she lived in another world half the time.'

It was in the middle of the affair that Catherine and Tom Nevin saw a notice for a forthcoming pub auction. 'Famous Roadside Pub' the advert read, 'For Auction on 6 March 1986'. The advert, which was tragically apocryphal, carried a picture of what was then a red-brick, rambling building just outside Brittas Bay approximately seven miles from Arklow town. At that time Jack White's consisted of a bar and small lounge where you could get a cup of coffee and a biscuit. The turnover was very low; it was basically a drinks turnover. The original Jack White was a smuggler – there's a plaque on the wall inside commemorating the old rogue.

Tom Nevin loved Jack White's at first sight. It was his dream come true – a pub of his own in an idyllic country setting with ample living accommodation. This was a place where he felt he could finally hang his hat. The Nevins took it over as a going concern and moved in on Friday, 2 May 1986.

Tom and Catherine bought Jack White's through Tom's bank, AIB, in Dolphin's Barn. With stamp duty and legal fees they paid £270,000 for it. They used the houses at Mayfield Road, Mountshannon and 446 South Circular Road as collateral for the loan.

By then Tom Nevin had met Willie McClean. He helped the Nevins move their furniture into Jack White's. McClean also helped out behind the bar from time to time at weekends, but received no cash for the work. McClean said he was paid in kindness. Tom Nevin knew about the affair, he couldn't but have known. It was happening right under his nose at the Inn.

Catherine's bedroom was next door to the 'blue room,' a room with a sunbed, beside the bathroom. Tom's bedroom was at the opposite end of the pub. Hers was a large, untidy room, with a clothes rail, sink, portable television and two bedside lamps near the head of the double bed. She kept a jewellery box on the floor beside a locker. The bedroom phone was kept on a second locker on the left hand side of the bed facing the wardrobe.

One summer morning in 1986 Tom Nevin was downstairs in the pub rummaging for the keys to one of the Dublin flats. He couldn't find them. Catherine and Willie McClean were upstairs having sex. Tom climbed the stairs to ask Catherine if she knew where the keys were and without knocking, walked into the room.

He saw his wife and McClean together underneath the bed-clothes. Willie McClean was lying on his back under the covers. He was naked and so was Catherine. Tom mumbled something about not being able to find the keys. 'She snapped at him and said the keys were down on the table,' recalls McClean. 'She told him not to disturb us again.'

Tom walked out of the bedroom and closed the door behind him. McClean felt slightly uneasy about what Tom had witnessed. 'It didn't take a feather out of Catherine, she continued on as though it never happened,' he said. 'I felt it. I felt bad; Tom was a nice man.'

Willie McClean ended the affair sometime after that, in August or September 1986. The affair, from McClean's own account of it, seemed to have been a half-hearted one once the initial gloss had worn off. He'd simply lost interest in Catherine Nevin. She took it badly: 'She went mad, she told me she'd get the IRA to kill me,' he said.

In the pre-trial deposition at Dublin District Court on 28 July 1998, prosecution barrister Tom O'Connell asked McClean if he had an affair with Catherine in 1985–86.

29

'I did, yeah.'

'Do you know if her husband knew about it?'

'He did,' McClean replied.

Why Tom Nevin allowed his wife to carry on her adulterous affairs under his nose is a mystery, one that he took to the grave with him. It seemed as though he was trapped in a wretched marriage and by all accounts led a pretty miserable existence. He was also drinking very heavily.

There was other evidence that all was not well.

When Catherine and Tom first arrived in Jack White's in 1986 they were sleeping together. Then, after a few years, they moved into separate bedrooms. Billy Randles was a man who used to help out at the pub from time to time. He was a brother-in-law of Jane Murphy, a cleaner in Jack White's for ten years. Catherine asked Billy to bring down a double bed from the flats in Dublin.

'Catherine told me she was moving down to the room she is sleeping in now,' said Jane Murphy in her statement. She asked Billy Randles to put the bed into her new bedroom. 'Catherine said she wasn't, "going to sleep with that oul fuck anymore",' meaning Tom Nevin.

Liz Hudson remembers the time Tom Nevin moved out of the bedroom, just after he and Catherine returned from holidays in 1991. Tom hadn't wanted to go on the holiday – he hid the passports the morning they were due to fly out. Jane Murphy found them and gave them to Catherine and off they went. 'They went on the holiday to Tenerife together; they brought me back a key holder,' Hudson said, gesturing towards a colourful trinket on the wall. 'It was a few weeks after they came back that Billy Randles brought the double bed down.'

There was talk of other men. There was a Northern Ireland man whom Catherine brought to Mountshannon Road occasionally. Then there was a Scandinavian with whom she used to spend an odd weekend between 1991 and 1992. 'Catherine used to go away for a few days with a man who came over from Sweden or somewhere like that,' said Caroline Strahan in her statement. Strahan was a waitress at Jack White's between 1991 and 1992 and would later give evidence at the trial. 'I remember once she went to Wexford with the man from Sweden or Denmark for the weekend. She'd ring a few times every day when she was away. Terry Keogh was in charge at the time.'

There was also a Dublin republican on the scene by this time. The sexual liaison between Catherine Nevin and this man spanned 18 months. He would later verbally acknowledge the affair to gardaí, but this did not emerge in court and there is no written account of his admission. Obviously, the man in question was anxious to keep the lid on the affair because he was married. The gardaí were relying on his help in the case and, as the prosecution never wanted to turn the case into a sex trial, the extent of Catherine Nevin's relationship with the man was never made public. He was just one of many lovers.

Catherine Nevin had not been promiscuous when she was younger, in the years before she came to work in Dublin. Newspaper headlines calling her the 'Curragh Carpet' – a reference to her sexual life as a teenager – are not accurate, according to a relative. 'That's not true; she was not like that then. Whatever happened to her afterwards, she was not like that when she was young. I think it's the crowd she got in with after.'

In the years in which Caroline Strahan worked at Jack White's, she never once saw Tom and Catherine sitting down and having a laugh or sharing a drink together. 'They were always arguing and she used to give out to Tom in front of the staff,' she recalls. The staff appeared to like Tom Nevin. He was 'nice to us', remembers Catherine McGraynor, another waitress at Jack White's, 'All the younger staff used to call him Daddy.'

When Tom got up out of bed in the morning, he'd come down wearing his jacket and then hang it in the storeroom. He would always wear a shirt, tie and jumper when serving behind the bar and then put the jacket on again if he was going out somewhere, like driving the staff or customers home. He often did that. Then he'd go back into the kitchen or the bar and start drinking alone. Catherine was always putting him down in a perverse kind of way.

She repeatedly denounced her husband to all and sundry – family, friends, the entire staff, sometimes even to a complete stranger. Basically, anyone who was prepared to listen.

'I heard her saying in court that Tom didn't get up until the middle of the day; that wasn't true,' said Liz Hudson. 'She'd get up in the morning at half-eight or nine o'clock. She'd come down in her towelling dressing gown and she'd say, "Make sure you get Tom up". I'd bring him up tea and toast or a glass of orange juice and he'd come down then, maybe about ten o'clock.'

Monday was the one day of the week that Tom Nevin would head to Dublin on business. Usually, he would lodge money in the bank, collect meat for Jack White's from the wholesalers, Kepak, in Clonee and the rents from his houses on the South Circular Road. 'Tom never went out much except on a Monday,' the former cleaner, Eileen Byrne recalled. 'He'd get up at nine o'clock and he'd say, "Have you everything on the list, do you want anything brought back, now where's that young one or that young fella, don't they want a lift?" He was like that, asking everyone if they needed anything brought back from Dublin, he was a very thoughtful man.'

Behind these ordinary, everyday tasks lay constant tension. There were many, many tears shed in Jack White's in the decade between 1986 and Tom's murder on 19 March 1996. Some were shed by Catherine, more were shed by Tom.

There was talk of Catherine bringing male friends back to the Nevins' flats in Dublin, including the Northern Ireland man. Three former tenants at Mountshannon Road gave statements to the gardaí saying that they saw Catherine entertaining male friends at a vacant flat at weekends. This was between 1991 and 1994. The Nevin relationship was in absolute turmoil.

'When she came down in the morning, if there was anyone in the bar she'd give them a smile or a greeting,' said Eileen Byrne. 'All Tom Nevin got was hot tongue and cold shoulder. She was a user, she'd use people and she'd dump them. Tom didn't seem to have much of a life outside the pub as far as I could see. He loved to see people playing football; he used to sponsor the football jerseys for Brittas, Barndarrig and Kilbride. After the matches he'd have them all back in the bar; he enjoyed that, but that was all he had, God love him . . . did Catherine hurt Tom Nevin? Oh, Jesus, yes. He loved her . . . he loved her.'

The Nevin family remember Tom wanting to, 'do a bit of travelling. Only a month or two, I'd say,' says Margaret, but he never got around to doing it.

A local student worked in Jack White's during her school holidays in 1990 and 1991. 'Catherine and Tom never spoke a lot to each other and they slept in separate rooms,' she says. She recalls the day Catherine flew into a temper and threw a knife at her. She was off target and the knife narrowly missed the youngster.

The Nevins' world was full of contradictions, many of them not immediately apparent to those who didn't know this seemingly ordinary couple well. By that time, Catherine was actively trawling the IRA for a hit man to kill her husband. On the face of things, though, the Nevins had a stroke of good fortune.

The European Golf Club opened at nearby Brittas Bay. The clubhouse had no bar licence so Catherine Nevin arranged that she would host the various golfing functions at Jack White's. She was the mover on this initiative – she showed a sure-footedness and drive sometimes lacking in her husband. One European employee remembers her as being 'very shrewd':

'For instance, a coach-party of golfers might play the course. When the first four-ball arrived back at the clubhouse they'd want a drink and she'd be there offering them a lift up the road to Jack White's. Once she had the first batch up in the pub all the rest would follow.'

The lengths Catherine went to secure the approval of polite society didn't always endear her to her staff. One former staffer revealed: 'She'd put on a show, always ordering the staff around. When she said "jump" you asked how high? If a customer complained about a meal she'd turn it into a public exhibition, taking it out on us.' That was the thing about Catherine, she never did anything in half measures – everything she did was over the top. Her marriage was no exception. It was a marriage of extremities: extreme degrees of sadness, despair, lust, of self-delusion and narcissism.

However, in all of this were glimpses, fleeting glimpses, of normality. Like in the photograph taken outside Jack White's sometime after it opened. Tom and Catherine are standing in front of the pub, Tom is a lot heavier than he appeared in the wedding photos, his hair has started to thin slightly and he is now wearing spectacles. Catherine's hair is longer than it was and is now blonde. She has also put on weight. There is no physical closeness, but their smiles betray nothing of the hell that was now their life together.

The line in *Macbeth* – 'False face must hide what the false heart doth know' – seems particularly apt. Lady Macbeth's strength of purpose and leadership are a remarkable contrast to her husband's. As a result, she has nothing but contempt for him and attacks exactly where she knows it will hurt most – his male pride. Catherine Nevin enjoyed rubbing Tom's nose in it.

He was not an expressive man, he was very proud, the kind who kept his feelings pretty much to himself. Elaine Butler started work in 1995 at Jack White's. Before long, she noticed all was not well between her two employers. She got to know Catherine quite well, but found Tom harder to get to know:

'I never heard them have a polite conversation with each other. She used to pass comment about her husband and she did not care whom she spoke to. She said that Tom was an alcoholic, that she was happy she wasn't married to him anymore. I felt uncomfortable with the way Catherine was speaking like this. I was not clear about their marital status but Catherine made it clear to me that they were not together as a married couple. I knew there was arguments and tension between Tom and Catherine.'

Caroline Strahan heard the rows. 'All the time I was there Tom and Catherine Nevin were always arguing and fighting with each other. They never got on. They were sleeping in separate rooms.'

To all who came in contact with them, the relationship between Tom and Catherine appeared cold and uncaring. It functioned only on a business level.

Fiona Lawlor, a part-time employee in the pub, was aware that they were not getting on. They had the odd argument, mainly over Catherine giving out free drinks in the bar – mostly to men. She appeared to relish her femme fatale image, once boasting to Lawlor that she considered herself 'a bitch and proud of it'.

Yet another employee recalls a screaming match between the pair in the early hours of one November morning in 1994. This followed the accidental activation of the Inn's burglar alarm. 'There was a lot of shouting going on and the alarm was going off for about ten minutes,' she said. On the afternoon of the same day, Catherine arrived down with her arm in a sling. She said that Tom had pushed her.

Bernie Fleming, a full-time employee since May 1995, was aware that the relationship between Tom and Catherine Nevin was not good. She was often present during rows. Tom Nevin knew his wife was having affairs with other men, she said.

During this time, Tom's drinking escalated. The murder file states that since around 1990 he had been consuming a half bottle of whiskey at night after work and his drinking showed no sign of slowing down. He would drink by himself, mainly in the kitchen, or sometimes he'd play darts. Apart from the odd darts match, he seemed always to be alone and desperately unhappy.

In March 1993, Tom was admitted to St John of God, a rehabilitation institute in Stillorgan, Co. Dublin, to be treated for his drink problem. He was there for about five or six weeks. A former patient recalls Catherine as having put only minimal effort into the 'Contact Care' element of Tom's treatment and having shown 'no interest in his well-being'. He said Tom Nevin was a very quiet man, not very open or expressive. In the patient's opinion, Catherine treated Tom 'like a piece of shit'; her purpose in visiting him at all was to do the books.

While in St John of God, Tom confided in this patient. He told him that Catherine was having an affair and that, 'anyone could have her but himself'. From conversations Tom Nevin had with this patient, it's clear Tom didn't believe he was an alcoholic (although many alcoholics don't) and he was convinced that his wife was 'trying to get the pub off him'. In a statement, this patient says Tom Nevin was resigned to the fact that his marriage was over and he and Catherine were leading separate lives.

Some of the staff are not convinced that Tom Nevin was an alcoholic – albeit the 'disciplined alcoholic' that Catherine Nevin would later describe to the court. 'I never saw Tom Nevin drinking anything more than a couple of glasses of Guinness,' said Eileen Byrne. 'I think him going in to John of God's had more to do with the strain he was under than anything else. I believe it was more of a nervous breakdown that put him into John of God's.'

'Tom wasn't an alcoholic,' insists Liz Hudson. 'He'd have a glass of Guinness in the bar, although I think he did have a drop of whiskey in the kitchen at night. We used to keep a bottle in the kitchen for making hot whiskeys and sometimes in the morning I'd see there was some gone out of it from the mark in the bottle. It had gone down a bit even though it wouldn't have been used in the bar. But Tom wasn't an alcoholic. No way.'

But whether his drinking, his mental state, or a combination of both, precipitated his admission into St John of God, there is little doubt that his marriage was the primary factor.

Catherine Nevin would later deny all of this. Her version of the marriage was vastly different. They had separate bedrooms that's true, but that didn't prevent them from making love, far from it, she said. She could even recall the last time they were in bed together, 28 February 1996, her 45th birthday. It was 19 days before Tom's death.

Catherine and Tom had disagreements, like any other couple, no more, no less, she said in court. He had hit her just once. 'There was one occasion where the circumstances were pretty unusual and my husband had a lot of drink taken, and he did hit me,' she said in direct evidence. 'I think it was about 1990.'

'Did he damage you?' asked Patrick MacEntee, her defence lawyer.

'Oh no, no, I wasn't damaged, no, I wasn't damaged.' Nevertheless, she went to the casualty unit of St James's Hospital the following morning and was X-rayed there, she claimed. They told her everything was okay. This claim of hospitalisation was never corroborated.

She had told a different story to Assistant Garda Commissioner Jim McHugh, however. She told him Tom had assaulted her on a number of occasions and she repeated the claim that she had had to be hospitalised after one beating. Around 1989 they had considered separating but decided against it: 'Tom wondered if anyone would have either of us at this stage of our lives,' she said.

She disputed the various sworn testimonies that she had many extra-marital affairs. It just didn't happen, she said, none of it. Sure, she had a lot of male friends but she never slept with any of them, never had sex with any man other then her husband. The trouble was, the jury didn't believe her.

If life with Catherine was that bitter and indeed hopeless, it was open to Tom to walk out of the relationship. He could have taken steps to end it. Legal separation was an option and maybe, eventually, even a divorce. There were, after all, no children to consider. The only thing binding the couple together was the business. Yet he did not leave.

Those close to Tom say it wasn't that easy. Patricia Flood, Catherine's step-aunt, was very fond of Tom Nevin. She was the first person on Catherine's side of the family to meet Tom. For a while, Flood, her late husband Mick, and Tom and Catherine would go dancing together, mainly to the Hazel ballroom in Kildare. Tom and Catherine would often call to the Flood home at Suncroft, a little village about three miles from Nurney. Sometimes they'd stay overnight. They always spent Christmas night there after having dinner with Catherine's parents in Nurney. Tom loved pottering about in Mick Flood's shed. If something needed doing to Tom's car, Mick Flood would do it.

'Tom and Catherine were always good to me,' recalls Patricia Flood, particularly around the time of her husband's death in 1989. The first hint she had that Tom Nevin was in trouble was in 1991. From what he told her, she detected that emotionally, he was very hurt. Despite everything that had happened in that marriage, all that had gone before, he still loved Catherine Nevin. Willie McClean was long gone but now there was a new man on the scene, a garda inspector by the name of Tom Kennedy. Tom Nevin was worried.

Patricia Flood first saw Tom Kennedy in 1990 or 1991 in Jack White's. The first time she saw him and Catherine alone together was in Morrin's public house in Suncroft, a long way from Kennedy's home in Wicklow. It was in 1991. She was only in from work one day when she got a call from Catherine asking her to join her in Morrin's. When Flood walked in, Catherine was sitting there with Tom Kennedy. 'He's very high up in the guards,' Catherine told Flood.

In her statement to the gardaí, Flood recalled one emotional episode during Christmas 1994 when Tom Nevin called to see her in Suncroft. He broke down and cried while telling her about Catherine's relationship with Tom Kennedy. 'How would you feel if you saw your wife in bed with another man?' he'd wept. Of all Catherine Nevin's male friends, Kennedy was the only man about whom he spoke to Patricia Flood. It was killing him. He sat on a little brown couch in Patricia Flood's kitchen, put his hands over his face and cried.

Flood was shocked. Tom Nevin went on to say that, 'Catherine was wining and dining Tom Kennedy to the best and that he had to put up with it'.

'Is she trying to drive you mad?' Flood asked him. It appeared suspiciously like that to her. 'She seemed to have some hold over him. It looked like that,' she recalled. 'I got the impression that Tom was afraid of Catherine. He seemed to be afraid to talk.'

Flood advised him to leave, to sell the pub and split the takings. In other words, cut his losses and go. For some reason he didn't think that he could – it was not that simple.

Details of Tom and Catherine Nevin's financial situation at that time show they owed more than owned. That perhaps was what Tom Nevin was hinting at when he said it wasn't that simple – if they had legally separated then there would be very little left for either of them once all of the outstanding creditors had been paid. The bank alone was owed more than £250,000.

Tom and Catherine had sold their home in Greenpark, Clondalkin when they bought Jack White's. She sold 446 South Circular Road in June 1989 and used the proceeds to fund £80,000 worth of new kitchen equipment. The Nevins saw an opening for a lucrative food trade given the pub's location on the busy N11, but the expansion into the food business meant that all their money was now tied up in Jack White's. There was simply no capital left. Tom was trapped.

Pride may have been another reason why Tom Nevin con-tinued to live with Catherine. He was an intensely proud man and he already had one broken marriage behind him. He may have found it difficult to tell his brothers and sisters that his marriage to Catherine was sheer hell and that she was seeing other men. He may have found it easier to pretend things were okay.

By this time, whispers of Catherine's affairs had spread far beyond the confines of Jack White's Inn. The whole of Wicklow was awash with the rumours. The name of one man began to feature prominently – that of Garda Inspector Tom Kennedy.

Tom Kennedy is a 66-year-old man, married with three grown-up children. He lives with his wife, Mary, at 'Hillview,' St Patrick's Road, Wicklow, a neat detached house at the edge of Wicklow town. By the time he met Catherine he had notched up almost 40 years service in the gardaí and was nearing retirement from the force. He had held the rank of Inspector since 1976. His entire garda career was spent in uniform. He is a big man, perhaps six feet tall, with steel-grey, combed-back hair. He has the face of a once handsome man, but these days has a tortured look about him.

The relationship between Kennedy and Catherine Nevin goes back at least a decade. On 20 November 1991, Catherine reported to Pearse Street garda station in Dublin that she had been the victim of a smash-and-grab robbery while driving her car through Dolphin's Barn. The bridge at Dolphin's Barn is notorious for such robberies; the perpetrators are mainly young, mostly drug addicts. She was driving up to the traffic lights at the bridge when a youth jumped in front of her, forcing her to stop. A second youth grabbed two handbags that were lying on the floor of her car. They contained £4,500 in cash and other valuables. The total amount stolen amounted to £5,786. The £4,500 was the cash lodgment from Jack White's Inn.

Catherine told the officer on duty, Garda John McElroy, that she had been on her way to the bank to lodge the money but was late and missed it. So she went to a friend's house instead. It was on her way home that she had been robbed. Garda McElroy confirmed that the car window was smashed. He says that a garda officer collected Catherine from the station. 'This was in fact Inspector Kennedy.'

The insurance company settled the claim for £1,500 and refused to entertain any claim for the theft of the bank lodgment. They cited breaches of the policy for not paying.

Tom Kennedy was a frequent visitor to Jack White's Inn. He was too often seen at Catherine Nevin's side. 'It was like a second home to him,' said Eileen Byrne, one of the former cleaners at Jack White's. At the start, Tom Kennedy's wife, Mary, would occasionally accompany him to the pub. Catherine would give her the VIP treatment. 'She was wined and dined, God love her. At that stage, we all knew what was going on.'

When the pub was quiet, Catherine did not do much work, either behind the bar or in the kitchen. Tom Nevin's family remember seeing Kennedy during one of their visits to Jack White's in the early 1990s. At the time they thought he was Tom's friend; they didn't read anything into it. On one occasion, when they were there, she shouted at Tom to bring more drinks down to Kennedy and herself.

The former staff member, Caroline Strahan, remembers Catherine and Kennedy spending a lot of time in the lounge together and Kennedy often being at the Inn. 'He spent a lot of time there and stayed there sometimes.' Arklow is a small place. Soon enough, tongues started wagging. There was worse to come.

In her statement, Strahan recalls a morning in the summer of 1992 when two gardaí from Wicklow arrived at the front door of Jack White's looking for Tom Kennedy. They felt sure he would be there as he now seemed to spend most of his time at the Inn. His wife, Mary, would later say that she frequently spotted his car parked there as she was driving by. Caroline Strahan was working that day, the day the gardaí called.

'Is he there?' they asked. Strahan knew he was upstairs with Catherine. 'I went up to tell her and when I knocked and opened the door, I saw Tom Kennedy in the bed with her. They were under the covers and Tom had nothing on on top.'

Strahan told Kennedy about the two gardaí waiting downstairs. Catherine started to panic. Caroline Strahan ran back down the stairs. 'She just came down after me and went in behind the bar. Tom Kennedy then came into the lounge from the car park; he was in his ordinary clothes. After this I went back into the kitchen and I can't remember if Tom [Kennedy] went.'

One afternoon in 1993 Catherine rang down from her bedroom for someone to bring up a scotch and a pint of Smithwicks. Debbie Boucher brought it up. 'When I brought it up to her room, Catherine was in bed and Tom Kennedy was sitting in a chair beside the bed,' she said.

In court, Tom Kennedy acknowledged being in Catherine's bedroom but never in her bed. His relationship with her wasn't a sexual one, he said. It was merely platonic.

Linda Evans is a former tenant at Mountshannon Road. In court, she stated that Tom Kennedy accompanied Catherine to the flat.

'Have you ever visited premises that belonged to the Nevins on Mountshannon Road?' the prosecution asked Kennedy.

'I have M'Lord, yes. Catherine Nevin asked me to collect rents.'

'Did you ever stay overnight there?'

'No, never.'

'Tom Kennedy used to help her a lot,' said Jane Murphy in a statement: 'I used to see him counting the money in the store sometimes. He used to get the change from the bank in Wicklow for her. When Tom Nevin would go away on holidays, Tom

Kennedy used to do the banking. He used to be sleeping there and when I'd go to work in the morning around eight or eight-thirty in the morning I'd see his car outside the pub. He used to sneak down the stairs and go out the hall door and come back in through the pub door to let on he was just arriving.'

Eileen Byrne remembers Kennedy being there every morning although she never saw him coming down the stairs of the pub: 'When he'd come in, he'd sit at the end of the counter. When Catherine would come down she'd give him a big smile. There was more chemistry between her and Tom Kennedy than there ever was between her and Tom Nevin. They never talked and when they did they snapped. Apart from Jack White's she used to socialise with [Kennedy] outside. They'd go to the Tap [a public house near Arklow] or Finn's in Conry.'

Tom Kennedy described himself to gardaí as a friend of Tom Nevin, that was why he socialised at Jack White's. Catherine, he said, was the type of person, 'who would give you a pain in the head when she started getting on about things'. He knew about the rumours that were doing the rounds but it wasn't true. At more than 60 years of age, sex would not be a concern of his.

Some of the staff dispute that Kennedy and Tom Nevin were friends. 'That's not true,' insists Liz Hudson. 'Tom never had any time for Tom Kennedy. If he saw him in the bar he'd say, "Oh, that old bollox is in again."'

'Tom would never come into the bar when Catherine and Tom Kennedy were there,' says Eileen Byrne. 'Many's a time I'd bring him up a cup of tea in the bedroom and he'd ask me if Kennedy was there. If I said "yes" he'd make a face. Tom didn't like him, he didn't like him being around the pub.'

Jane Murphy blamed Tom's drinking on Catherine's infidelity. 'One morning, myself and Catherine McGraynor brought up tea to Catherine in the blue room and I nearly died when I saw Tom Kennedy tucked up in bed with her. Tom Nevin knew all this and that's why he went haywire, going off drinking and all.'

Tom Kennedy's own marriage was in serious difficulty. His wife, Mary, blames Catherine Nevin, but a plethora of sources close to Tom Kennedy say his marriage was in trouble long before that. He and Mary Kennedy lived separately in Hillview; she upstairs and he in a little room off the main hall which he normally locked. Mary Kennedy, in an interview with the *Sunday Independent*, confirmed rumours that had been doing the rounds in Wicklow for years – the Kennedys were no longer a couple:

'We were married thirty-four years and the marriage could have worked. I wanted it to work . . . but she destroyed us. I speak to him only if absolutely necessary, but I sleep upstairs and he sleeps in a little room downstairs, which he locks and I can't get in . . .'

When Tom Kennedy was asked in court if he was having a sexual affair with Catherine Nevin, he replied: 'No, My Lord, never. I am not into that, My Lord, I value my family and my marriage.'

Tom Kennedy's statement contained in the murder file gives no hint that he was particularly friendly with Catherine:

'I knew the joint proprietors very well. The late Tom Nevin frequently asked for my advice when recruiting new staff and also in connection with security and cash lodgments. I have accompanied either Mr or Mrs Nevin to AIB bank in Wicklow on a number of occasions. The last time was after Christmas, 1995, when I drove to Wicklow after Mr Nevin and waited until he entered the bank. I also deposited cash lodgments in the bank night safe on his behalf on a number of occasions.'

Other, more personal, documentary evidence suggests that Catherine regarded Tom Kennedy as close to her. So close that she saw him, and not her husband, as her next of kin.

Catherine Nevin was obsessed with her appearance: she saw herself as a successful member of society running around buying property and running pubs. She had to look the part. Whatever their inner turmoil, the Nevins had attained a certain cachet. The pub was doing well and there was the income from the flats.

This allowed her to buy new clothes – which she did, compulsively – and to have regular professional hairstyles and expensive jewellery. She was never a beautiful woman, but she certainly made the best of what nature had given her. She was, in that well-worn Irish term of begrudgery, 'getting a bit above herself'.

Just before her fortieth birthday, Catherine Nevin decided to halt the outward signs of advancing middle age. She resorted to cosmetic surgery. She had three plastic surgery operations between July 1990 and September 1991: liposuction, a tummy tuck and an 'eyelid job' – a technique that removes the tell tale signs of ageing from around the eyes.

It was when she was undergoing the last of these in the Mater Private Hospital on 6 September 1991 that she named Tom Kennedy, and not Tom Nevin, as her closest living relative. His home telephone number is written on the chart beside her medical record sheet, number 1093277. We shall never know what the members of the jury would have made of this piece of potentially influential evidence. It was never put to them.

Nevin denied in court that the relationship between her and Tom Kennedy was sexual; that he'd ever stayed overnight in the Inn or was there at breakfast time. He was sometimes there early in the morning, but he had come from his home, she said.

During the trial, she was put under intense cross-examination by Peter Charleton, who pressed her on a series of dates and dinners with Tom Kennedy in a variety of venues from Naas, Co. Kildare to Ballinaboula in Wexford.

'Did you ever meet Mr Kennedy alone in the Horse and Hound in Wexford and have a meal there?' he asked.

'I'd say the chances are I probably did, yes . . . I would have thought in this day and age two people can have a meal together without people drawing inferences from it,' she retorted. Catherine Nevin denied ever having committed adultery with any man, including Tom Kennedy. At this point she dropped in the name of Superintendent Bill Ryan as having attended a darts match with her one night. Her bottom line was she had many men friends but she wasn't sleeping with any of them.

In December 1993 the Nevins apparently had a break-in. Catherine reported that her engagement ring, wishbone necklace and T-bar bracelet were stolen from a bedroom. Her gold wedding ring was also missing. Tom was upset about the wedding ring. He'd had it specially made by a friend who worked for Weirs jewellers in Grafton Street.

Tom Kennedy was told about the theft. He suggested they report it to Arklow station and he mentioned it to detectives at Wicklow although he never recorded the theft in official garda records. Scully Tyrrell and Co., Merrion Square, acted as loss adjusters for the insurance company, F.B.D. Insurance Ltd. They sent Tom Kennedy a form to verify that the theft had been reported to him. He kept a copy of the claim form among his own personal diaries.

The insurance company settled the claim for £1,685. Three years later, the wedding ring was to turn up in one of the Nevins' Dublin flats. It was in the middle of February 1996, just weeks before Tom Nevin's death. Catherine waved it in front of Tom Kennedy. 'That ring was stolen and Tom recovered it for me,' she said. Tom Nevin had, in fact, found it in one of the flats and returned it to his wife on Valentine's night.

47

'It's extraordinary, the bold Tom recovered it. It's an extraordinary story after that length of time,' Kennedy told Sergeant Fergus O'Brien.

Tom Kennedy had acted honestly when he had liaised with the insurance company on behalf of the Nevins. But a big question mark remains over whether or not the jewellery was actually stolen, or if Catherine Nevin had made a false insurance claim.

'How did a ring supposedly stolen from a bedroom in Jack White's end up months later in a Dublin flat?' wondered a garda based in Wicklow. 'And the fact that she claimed Tom handed it to her on Valentine's night was an attempt to suggest Tom was a romantic husband when the opposite was the case.'

There were other men. On one occasion, it was like a French farce. Towards the end of the summer of 1995 Liz Hudson clocked in for work as usual at around 8 a.m. She let herself in through the hall door using her own set of keys; she was the first one in that morning and she'd closed up the night before, leaving Catherine and her lover in the 'crib' area of the pub.

When she went to pull the curtains that morning Hudson saw the empty wine bottles on the floor. They were Calvet or Chevalier half-bottles. She bent to pick them up and spotted Catherine's shoes by the fire. 'I found Catherine's bra and knickers near the table on the carpet near where they were sitting the night before,' she said in her garda statement.

Liz Hudson put the garments in the laundry basket. Somehow, though, she had missed a pair of men's boxer shorts. Jane Murphy came in to clean an hour later. She found the shorts; they were wine coloured with a little design on them. 'Look what I found,' said Murphy, holding aloft the boxers, 'Underpants in the crib.'

'I don't know how I missed them,' Hudson said.

When Catherine came down that morning, Liz Hudson told her what she'd found. 'I hope Janey didn't see them,' said Catherine.

'Too late,' replied Hudson, 'she found the boxers.'

These lurid goings-on took place against a background of constant rows between Tom and Catherine over staff and the running of the pub. 'I never saw Tom and Catherine hit one another,' recalled Jane Murphy. 'I knew Tom was not pleased with the carry-on down there over the people Catherine was entertaining free in the pub. I heard Catherine say to Tom on several occasions when they were fighting, "Go back to John of God, you old bastard."'

Catherine's barbed taunt had a ring of brutal irony to it, given that she drank too much herself, and took too many prescription drugs. James Smullen, an ambulance attendant with the Eastern Health Board was on duty in the early hours of the morning of 11 December 1993. He got a call to go to Jack White's. When he arrived Tom Nevin was at the door. Catherine was in the pub and very, very drunk. Tom told Smullen he was worried that Catherine had taken a lot of drink and tablets. Smullen spoke to Catherine. Her vituperation shocked him. Fuelled by drink, she let out a string of curses at him. Smullen decided she was more drunk than ill and he drove off.

There were other occasions when the ambulance was summoned to the pub. On a warm summer night, 10 July 1995, Una Doogue, a member of staff, was asleep in her room when she was called downstairs. She ran down to the bar and saw Tom Nevin lying on the floor, blood pumping from a wound on the top of his head. A doctor was with him, Dr Golden, and he was treating the injury.

Smullen was again on duty when the emergency call came through. When he got to the pub, Catherine Nevin let him in and Smullen brought Tom to St Columcille's Hospital in Loughlinstown by ambulance.

Three months later, the ambulance crew was called again. Catherine met them at the door. Tom was lying in his bedroom with a back injury. He told the crew he'd fallen and injured his back. Declan Magee, a consultant at St Columcille's, gave an account of Tom's injuries, but it was never positively established how he had received them.

Over the Christmas of 1995, Catherine's step-aunt, Patricia Flood, was in hospital recovering from an operation. She hadn't seen Catherine Nevin for four years. Out of the blue Catherine dropped in to the hospital to see her. Then she received a Christmas card signed by Tom and Catherine. She thought that was odd because previously it had been Catherine alone who always signed the cards. Looking back, Flood thinks the visit and the card were strange. It could have been an indication that Catherine and Tom were coming closer, or, that Catherine was deliberately trying to create the impression that that was the case.

In that same week, Tom Nevin called to see Patricia Flood. He seemed to be in a rush. She asked him if everything was okay. 'He shrugged his shoulders and said things were just the same.' The relationship between Catherine and Tom Kennedy seemed to have ended but things were just as bad, Tom Nevin told her. She remembers he was, 'feeling miserable and appeared very unhappy. He looked to me to be very depressed. He seemed to me to be a man who didn't care.'

Patricia Flood looked at him as he walked out the door, a broken man. That Christmas was to be Tom Nevin's last.

3

SOLICITOUS BEHAVIOUR
1985–1991

⚜

Lady Macbeth

> 'Only look up clear;
> To alter favour ever is to fear.
> Leave all the rest to me.'

Macbeth, Act I, Scene V.

Catherine Nevin and Gerry Heapes sat in a car near the Wellington monument in the Phoenix Park overlooking Kilmainham. As dusk fell, you could see the streetlamps from Islandbridge twinkling in the distance. Looking down it is possible to make out the road at Islandbridge coming from the direction of the Nevins' flats, just to the right of Kilmainham Jail and the entrance to the memorial park.

From this point it would be easy to monitor a car crossing over the bridge and follow its path from the bridge, along Islandbridge Road. Catherine turned to Gerry Heapes who was sitting beside her in the front passenger seat of her white Opel Vectra. 'Will you do it, will you shoot Tom? We could time his arrival there and his journey back. You could do it in the flats.'

Heapes listened to her proposition: 'Talk to me again about it.' The £25,000 Catherine Nevin was offering for a hired killer was too low, he said. 'I was fobbing her off,' he would later tell the court. She upped it to forty.

It was 1989. Gerry Heapes is a big stocky Dubliner, with puffy facial features, married with five children. Fifteen years had elapsed since he was a young Provo doing security on the door of the Barry House. Eight of those he had spent in jail for an armed robbery carried out on behalf of the Provisional IRA. He had joined an IRA active service unit in 1976, at the age of 26. On 27 November 1977 Gerry Heapes and eight other Provos robbed a wholesale store – Leydon's Cash & Carry in Fairview.

It was an amateurish operation: the IRA gang locked the staff in a room with a telephone. Heapes was the getaway driver. The robbery turned into a débacle for the Provos – one of them phoned the *Evening Herald* to negotiate surrender terms with the gardaí. They called for food, a priest, and Myles Shevlin, a solicitor. The head of the Special Branch, Chief Superintendent John Joy, and three hundred gardaí, some of them armed with Uzi sub-machine guns, laid siege to the premises. The whole unit was captured red-handed.

When he was arrested, Heapes had £500 in cash stuffed up the leg of his trousers. He was keeping that for himself, something the IRA took a dim view of and has never quite forgiven him for. Very occasionally, discrepancies would arise between what was collected at gunpoint and what was handed over to the movement. In this instance, there was no handover, but there was an IRA inquiry. 'We knew beyond doubt that that £500 was for himself,' said a key IRA source. 'He was money mad, that bastard.'

Heapes served his time on the IRA landing in Portlaoise Prison. He was released in April 1985 and like many republican ex-prisoners, hung around in Sinn Féin circles. That's when he first met Catherine Nevin, in the Sinn Féin advice centre in Finglas village.

The advice centre at 2a Church Street doubled as a television and repair shop, which was run under the name Channel Vision Ltd. John Jones, a republican and member of the Finglas Sinn Féin Cumann, owned Channel Vision.

The Jack McCabe Cumann, as it was called, was a fairly large one; at one time it had 14 members. These included Heapes, Tommy Thompson, Pat Russell and Noel Ellis, the father of Dessie Ellis. All these names would surface at the Nevin trial, many years into the future. Dessie Ellis is now a Sinn Féin councillor on Dublin Corporation.

The Nevin jury heard that Ellis was a business partner of John Jones at Channel Vision. He was in prison during the years of Catherine Nevin's contact with the advice centre. In the early 1980s he had been convicted in the Special Criminal Court of possessing parts for explosives and had spent eight years in jail. The jury also knew that later, he was extradited to England to stand trial there as well. What they were not aware of, as it never surfaced, was that in the 1991 trial that followed that extradition, before a jury at the Old Bailey in London, Ellis named his former business partner, John Jones, as the man who had talked him into checking circuit boards for use in IRA bombs destined for the North.

That Old Bailey jury famously acquitted Ellis on a charge of conspiracy to cause explosions and he returned to Ireland a free man. In the course of his evidence, he had said that John Jones was his link to the IRA. In the Nevin trial, Jones said that not alone did he not know anyone in the IRA, he wouldn't even know how to go about contacting it. There is no doubt that, at the time when Catherine Nevin was approaching Jones to get 'the IRA to kill Tom', Jones's attention was focussed on his former colleague.

In the Nevin trial Jones remembered Catherine Nevin approaching him with her bizarre request sometime in 1989, or 1990, or maybe 1991. The period coincided with attempts to extradite Dessie Ellis and his subsequent trial by an English jury.

In the intervening period Ellis had become a cause célèbre, first because of a foiled plot to spring him from jail as he awaited an extradition hearing in June 1989, then for his lengthy hunger strike in protest at the plan to hand him over and finally, for the delays and disputes that prolonged the legal battle before he was eventually tried and acquitted by the Old Bailey jury.

Dessie Ellis was Jones's partner until his arrest in 1982. The advice centre/TV repair shop took up the entire first floor of 2a Church Street. There were six rooms, some of them used as store-rooms. It was well known to the Garda Special Branch. It was raided during the Ellis years and turned upside down. There were never any explosives or other IRA material discovered at 2a. 'By the time the guards had finished with it there would be nothing left,' John Jones later testified in court.

Gerry Heapes used the back room to make the type of hand-kerchiefs and wooden crosses that are sold in Sinn Féin shops. Heapes had fallen from grace with the Provos: he was now also too well known to be of any use to an IRA active service unit. Even if he were not, it is doubtful the Provos would have taken him back. He was effectively 'stood down'.

But he was still an ex-prisoner so they tolerated him for a couple of years after he came out of prison in 1985. In any case, the wooden crosses and other handcrafts he was producing were helping to raise money for 'An Cumann Cabhrach', the republican prisoners' dependents fund. The money was badly

was Cathal Goulding, the Official IRA leader.
ng had remained 'very good friends' in the 16
ad worked at the Castle Hotel.

said he didn't see Joe Cahill or Cathal Goulding
'I wouldn't have known Joe Cahill,' he said.
was a prominent veteran republican and even
on 31 of the Broadcasting Act[2] in force, repub-
een, if not heard, on RTE.

Nevin, meanwhile, had grand plans for Jack
s a great promoter of the business; she always had
ain chance. The N11 was the main autoroute to
ty to Europe. Because it is such a vital arterial
e had plans to turn Jack White's into a major
possibilities were endless.

er the opening celebration Gerry Heapes met
n again in Finglas. Although now ensconced in
as Bay, she kept coming back to Finglas and back
t was lots of different occasions, you know what I
d run into Catherine,' Heapes recalled in his pre-
I think they had only opened Jack White's and she
he said the place was robbed; three fellows robbed
k locals, of some spirits or kegs or something.'
Catherine didn't have a car of her own, she used
apes was to spend a lot of time in that car, a large
ra.

t later, after the opening. I had left Sinn Féin and
d a pool hall up in Finglas and she was up there –
e evening and we went into the Barry House for

evin had sent word that she was looking for Gerry
l she was looking for me; she said she wanted to

needed. At that time in the early 1980s, the IRA had approximately 300 prisoners in jail on both sides of the border – 300
families to be looked after financially.

Gerry Heapes, meanwhile, was doing all right for himself. ' I had
a pool hall up in Finglas,' he said in a pre-trial deposition.[1] It was
called the Classic and it was in Finglas West, near the Barry House
and just around the corner from where Heapes grew up. Sinn Féin
member Tommy Thompson was a regular in the pool hall.

One day in 1986 Gerry Heapes was working in the advice
centre when a blonde, well-dressed woman in her thirties came in
through the entrance to the TV shop. 'Either Tommy Thompson
or John Jones introduced me to her,' he said. The woman was
Catherine Nevin. They stayed chatting for a while and then she
left. She knew she would see Heapes again. 'I received a verbal
invitation to the opening of Jack White's,' he said. He took
advantage of a general invitation to attend.

Catherine and Tom Nevin had bought Jack White's after their
short stint as landlord and landlady of the Barry House in mid
1985. The Barry House was a rough pub in a tough area: its
windows and doors were barred with iron grilles. The Nevins'
early enthusiasm quickly faded.

The guards were frequent visitors to the Barry House. There
was constant confrontation between the local hoods and Provos
about the hoods' anti-social behaviour. Joy-riding was a particular problem. On many an occasion hostilities broke out between
the Provos and the hoods either in the Barry House itself or in the
car park at the side of the pub.

Locals still chuckle when recalling one memorable occasion
back in the mid 1970s. It was after the hoods had fallen foul of
the Provos yet again. A couple of Provos jumped on a gang of
hoods, taking them around the back of the pub and giving them

a hiding and a warning. A few nights later, a couple of local Provos were in the pub having a drink; they had left their cars on the main road outside. The hoods took one of the cars, set it alight, rammed it through the front door of the Barry House and set the pub on fire. Customers had to scatter out the back entrance. There was all out-war for a while after that.

Tom Nevin hated the Barry House – he felt it was just too rough and he couldn't get out of it fast enough. Catherine had another idea – she contacted the republican movement and asked them to 'police' the pub. When the Nevins were *in situ* in the Barry House, the republicans had an open door. The republicans were allowed to use the pub to sell *An Phoblacht*, the Sinn Féin newspaper, and for fund-raising functions.

Years later, the jury in the Catherine Nevin murder trial were to hear that a piece of paper had been found in her bedroom. On it were three telephone numbers. Two of them were bracketed with the name 'John'. They turned out to be the business and home numbers of John Jones. These authors have established that the third number led gardaí to a well-known Dublin republican, who confirmed to them that Catherine Nevin had approached him to provide security for the Barry House. The approach happened when the Nevins first took over the pub.

But the fact that republicans organised security for the Barry House while Tom and Catherine Nevin were its proprietors, as well as being allowed to hold fund-raisers and sell *An Phoblacht* there, indicates a closer relationship than has heretofore been suggested. What is not known is whether Tom Nevin knew of the significance of the people his wife had apparently made a security arrangement with. Garda sources say that they do not know if he did. When this was put to the republican movement they declined all comment.

Tom Nevin was deligh
into Jack White's. Gerry
tation to the opening ni
down and stayed overnig
arrived a bit late. That w
Nevin. It was also the first

At his pre-trial depo
28 July 1998, Heapes was

'At the opening did yo
O'Connell.

'I met him, as far as I r
met Tom.'

'Had you met him prev
'No.'

'Do you know a man ca
'I do, yeah. That was th

The opening of Jack Whit
500 assembled guests. Tw
invitation, the rest, mainly
left an open invitation at
helped out behind the ba
were there, along with som
the night in the Arklow B
them to stay at the Inn.

It was a motley gatheri
guests could hardly have b
the gadfly socialite, was in h
she said to Gerry Heapes b
judge over there and that's a
that the veteran Provision

opening. So to
She and Goul
years since she

Gerry Heap
at the opening
However, Cah
then, with Sec
licans could be

Catherine
White's. She w
her eye on the
Rosslare, gate
route, Catheri
truck stop. Th

Not long
Catherine Ne
picturesque B
to the Provos.
mean, you wo
trial depositio
came down an
the place. I th

At that ti
Tom's. Gerry
white Opel V

'This was
everything. I
she came up
a drink.'

Catherine
Heapes. 'I he

talk to me. She asked me in and we were having a drink and she said she was getting a terrible life off Tom, that he was bashing her up and wouldn't give her any money, and you know, the whole lot.'

It was then Catherine dropped the bombshell; she wanted Tom Nevin shot dead and she wanted Gerry Heapes to do it.

She just came straight out and asked Heapes if he '. . . would be interested in killing him'.

They were in the bar of the Barry House, drinking. The bar is long, with a booth on the left-hand side near the window. Catherine was sipping her favourite tipple, whiskey and ginger, and Gerry Heapes was drinking a glass of cider.

In the dim, dingy interior of the Barry House, Gerry Heapes listened to Catherine as she told how hard done by she was by her husband. She told him she was a battered and abused wife, that she had no money, couldn't go anywhere, do anything, without Tom's say-so. He was watching her all the time. 'She said she couldn't go out. She couldn't have friends,' Heapes remembered. 'That is how the conversation came around.'

At first Heapes thought she was joking. He didn't take her seriously and he said as much. 'If someone asked you, you know, you would think it was a joke, and basically I thought it was a joke,' he said. He went back to the pool hall and told a couple of lads there that, 'this lunatic was looking to bump off her husband'. The 'lads' in question were called Mickser, Redser and Tommo. They all had a good laugh about it. If she mentioned it again, 'get more detail,' the lads advised.

While Catherine was busy trying to arrange her husband's murder, she tried to convince Tom's family that she was killing him with kindness. At around this time, Tom's brother, Michael, died in the United States. Catherine told his family that she was worried about Tom's health and that he was going to get himself checked out in the Blackrock Clinic to see if heart complaints ran 'in the family'. But her contact with the Nevins was to get less and less. Just before Michael's death she visited Tynagh for the second-last time. It was Christmas 1988 and it was also Tom's mother's 80th birthday. She arrived 'jewellery all over the place' but she and Tom did not stay the night. She put the fur coat back on and said they had to return to Wicklow. She came down that summer for a family wedding. It was her last time. She never again set foot in Tynagh while Tom was alive.

Gerry Heapes may or not have been aware that in or about the same year – 1989 – Catherine Nevin tried to solicit another man to murder Tom Nevin. That man was John Jones.

Jones was born on 12 November 1944. He lives with his wife and two children in Balbriggan, a coastal town in north Co. Dublin. When his television business failed, Jones got a job with Crossan Transport at Dublin Airport.

Jones and Heapes were both republicans but that is really pretty much all they have in common. Jones is a quiet, serious type of man and a dedicated republican. 'He's very principled, he's almost moralistic,' said a republican source who knows Jones well. Unlike Heapes, John Jones is held in high regard by the republican movement.

He has one criminal conviction. He pleaded guilty at Dublin Circuit Court on 18 November 1988 to receiving a stolen car. He received a three-year suspended sentence and was ordered to pay £3,000 to the insurance company and £500 to the owner of the car.

Like Heapes, John Jones did not immediately send Catherine Nevin packing when she arrived at his door with her proposition for murder. More to the point, he never informed Tom Nevin that she was planning to end his life. He treated it as exaggerated blather but in retrospect, it acquired a deadly ring.

The first time John Jones met Catherine Nevin was back in 1983–84. She arrived at the advice centre one day out of the blue. She was looking around for a pub to buy. Most prospective purchasers, whether they are looking for a pub or any other property, consult an estate agent. Catherine Nevin consulted Sinn Féin. She told Jones she'd been referred to him by Christy Burke who was then based in the Sinn Féin offices in 5 Blessington Street. Christy Burke, a Dublin city councillor, says he doesn't remember her.

'She requested information on property that was available in Finglas. She specifically mentioned pubs,' said Jones. 'She was in and out of the advice centre quite, you know, quite a lot.'

Even after the Nevins moved to Jack White's, Catherine continued to drop in to 2a Church Street. Jones visited Jack White's once or twice in May 1986, on one occasion in the company of his wife. If Catherine dropped in to the advice centre and Jones was not there, she'd leave a message asking him to join her for coffee in a café across the road.

One day in 1989 she called in and Jones was there alone. They spent 45 minutes making small-talk but it was obvious to Jones that Catherine Nevin had something on her mind. Then she came straight out with it.

'I have a proposition for you,' she said.

'Go ahead,' replied Jones.

'I want you to get the IRA to shoot my husband,' she spluttered.

Jones couldn't believe it. He laughed it off. 'I wasn't sure whether it was her sense of humour or what the hell it was.'

Proposition number two came five or six week later. 'Have you thought about the proposition?' Catherine asked him.

'What are you talking about?' Jones replied.

Catherine went into more detail this time. 'I want you to get the IRA to shoot Tom in what will look like a botched hold-up. There will be £23,000 to £25,000 available if it's after a bank holiday. He always lodges money on Tuesdays.' Tom would always travel to the bank in Dublin, normally in the company of one of the young barmen in Jack White's. 'I'll ensure that Tom is on his own. The IRA could get him en route to the bank.'

Jones said it was out of the question. 'How she could expect members of Óglaigh na hÉireann to act in such a fashion baffles me, you know,' he said during his pre-trial deposition.

Jones told two people in the republican movement about the proposition. One was Pat Russell, the secretary of the Cumann. The other, a 'superior member' of the republican movement, he refused to name.

When giving his deposition in Dublin's District Court, Judge Mary Malone directed John Jones to name the senior republican. 'I don't recall the other person's name,' he said.

'You should give the name of the person that you spoke to,' the judge ordered. 'You said you spoke to two people. You have given the name of one. You should give the name of the other person.'

Jones turned to the judge. 'And just a question to yourself. If I am not at liberty to give that name, that's the scenario I am raising.'

'You either know the name or you don't.'

'No, I don't know the name,' Jones replied.

Most people, if solicited to commit murder, might feel compelled to alert the gardaí. Obviously, Jones felt no such compulsion. If he did, his 'bitterness' towards the gardaí prevented him from approaching them, he later told the trial. He discussed with fellow republican Pat Russell his suspicions that the proposition might have been a set-up. 'I didn't know who Catherine Nevin had come from; maybe she was trying to infiltrate our movement because of her relationship with the guards,' said Jones, 'I didn't know if herself and Tom had been asked to do it.'

Four attempted solicitations followed, the last in 1990. Catherine Nevin asked Jones if he had thought about the proposition. He told her it was not something, 'we should get involved in'. It was beyond thinking about. 'It is all nonsense,' he told her.

Some time in 1990–91 – Jones cannot be sure of the date – she arrived back in the advice centre. Her eyes were hidden by dark glasses; both her hands were bandaged around her palms and on the back of her hands. She removed the glasses to show Jones her black eyes.

'What do you think of that?' she asked. 'That's what Tom has done to me; you don't know Tom like I do. If you and his garda drinking buddy knew him when the pub was closed you wouldn't be so friendly with him.' Jones didn't know what to make of it. But Nevin knew that her attempt to solicit Jones was doomed. With John Jones a non-starter she now switched her attention fully towards Gerry Heapes.

Gerry Heapes sees himself as a mover and shaker. Some people see him as a bit of a rogue, but a likeable one for all that. Others, particularly his former comrades in the republican movement, can't stand the sight of him.

The authors spoke to many republican sources in the course of researching this book. They are from different 'factions' within the movement: some are past members, more present; some Northern, most based in the South. All knew Gerry Heapes at one time or another, or knew of him. Not one had a kind word to say about him. During the course of the trial and after Heapes gave evidence for the prosecution, a number of republicans approached members of the IRA. They asked the organisation to issue a statement disassociating the republican movement from Gerry Heapes, and to state exactly when this association ceased, back in the 1980s.

The IRA refused. At this juncture in the Northern political process, there was an awful lot of politics being played. After the trial the idea was floated in a number of newspapers, including the *Sunday Times*, that the IRA took the unprecedented step of 'sanctioning' Heapes and Jones as State witnesses in a newfound spirit of peace and reconciliation – something the IRA privately concedes is rubbish.

But the organisation does maintain that it didn't want to prejudice 'an ordinary domestic' murder trial through its intervention. This is the line the IRA took when asked by individual members to drop Heapes in it. Anyway, the organisation reasoned, if P. O'Neill[3] was to issue a statement disassociating the republican movement from everyone claiming to be a member, the IRA would be up to its eyes in faxes all day.

'That's what we were told, but I'll tell you everyone is hopping mad. Even in Belfast they're talking about him,' said one republican. Gerry Heapes was no fond favourite.

He was born in 1950 on the North Strand, an old part of Dublin less than three miles north of the city centre. The family moved to Finglas in the 1960s at a time when Dublin Corporation was beginning to house families in the new suburbs of north-west Dublin.

After his release from jail, he and his wife and children lived in Ballygall Crescent in Finglas East. By the time he met Catherine Nevin they had moved to Harristown Lane, in St Margaret's, a rural part of north Co. Dublin on the back roads between Finglas and Dublin Airport. Heapes has a varied history of employment. Over the years he worked as a hospital porter at the Rotunda Maternity Hospital and the old Jervis Street Hospital. On his release from Portlaoise he switched to the more lucrative security industry and got himself a job as a doorman in the Black Sheep pub in Coolock. For two years he worked on the door of the Columbia Bar, the short-lived lap dancing venture on Sir John Rogerson's Quay.

Heapes then got an offer from a man called Brian Cappagh who owned a company called On the Spot Security. Cappagh provided security on a range of pubs and Heapes reckoned there would be better pickings with him. As soon as he got the nod he was gone from the Columbia like a shot.

During his time with Cappagh he was put on the door of three Finglas pubs: The Bottom of the Hill, Martin's in Finglas East and the Fingal Inn. He worked in The Penthouse in Ballymun, which had a reputation as being one of Dublin's toughest pubs. He then moved upmarket, doing security on the clubs on the Leeson Street strip.

In 1989, when Catherine Nevin first tried to solicit Gerry Heapes, he had changed career and was working for Willie Adams, a north Co. Dublin haulier who had a warehouse at Kilnamona, on the Ashbourne Road. She was to meet Heapes ten or 12 times between January 1989 and 4 September 1990, picking him up in her car.

'The way it basically worked was she could only get the car when Tom wasn't using it,' recalled Heapes. 'So if Tom was going to Dublin on a Monday with the take, she could have the car on the Tuesday.'

At the next meeting, she said: 'He has to be killed. Not robbed, he has to be killed.' Heapes mentioned to her that it costs money to get someone killed. There would have to be money up front. It wasn't a problem, she replied. 'There would be £10,000 up front and £25,000 takings if the shooting was done over a bank holiday weekend.'

Heapes was intrigued. He didn't knock the idea on the head: he strung her along to see how far she would take it. 'When someone says 'it to you, I don't know, maybe it's just me, but I just wanted to see how far she was going down the road with this; was she serious or was it just a big joke?' said Heapes.

They would meet again within a fortnight. There was another trip to the park, a slip road near the Wellington Monument:

'She drove me back to the Phoenix Park and showed me a view of Islandbridge. From this point you could see the road at Islandbridge coming from the direction of their flats. She said from this point you could see Tom's car crossing the bridge and follow it and that we could time his arrival there and his journey from there. She used to pick me up, either in Finglas or if there was a pre-arranged meeting at the park, she would pick me up there in this big white car.'

The third meeting took place shortly afterwards. This time she drove to the South Circular Road: 'She brought me over and she showed me this particular house. She said Tom owned it and another property. And that when Tom came from Dublin on a Monday he would come with a barman and they would collect money out of the house, and the money from the pub would be in the boot of the car. He would do odds and ends and then shoot over to Blanchardstown. That is where the bank was.'

Catherine drove Heapes to the bank. He now knew she was deadly serious about having her husband murdered. He still never told her to go to hell – he asked if she had the money to do it.

'How do I know you have this money to give up front?' Heapes asked her. 'Well, I will see you in two weeks,' she replied.

Two weeks to the day, she and Heapes met again. This time she drove him straight to the bank in Blanchardstown – AIB beside the garda station. She showed Heapes her bank book; it was one of the small, old-fashioned lodgment books. It was later discovered that it was held in her maiden name of Catherine Scully. Deposit account number 35329163 had been opened at Blanchardstown on 23 June 1989 with an opening balance of approximately £8,000. 'She opened it, there was X amount of thousands in it,' said Heapes.

That £8,000 would quickly swell over the next 19 months. By the time the account was transferred to the AIB in Drumcondra on 21 February 1991, Catherine Nevin's bank balance was a healthy £21,823.[4] Each time Catherine Nevin met Gerry Heapes the two would discuss a fee for shooting Tom Nevin: 'She said that on a bank holiday weekend the money from Jack White's would be given to the police in Arklow. There were two guards there that used to keep it in their locker and then Tom would collect this on Monday. If it was a bank holiday he would collect it on a Tuesday off the guards and then head for Dublin for the houses to collect the money there and then on to the bank.'

During one of their meetings, Catherine Nevin also told Gerry Heapes about the double insurance policy on Tom's life.

Insurance details were never heard in court, as the insurance witness was known to one of the jurors, but the murder file shows that at the time Catherine Nevin solicited Heapes two insurance policies were in existence worth a quarter of a million pounds. One, an ordinary life policy on Tom taken out with Irish Life on 1 May 1983 was valued at £77,874. The second, a mortgage protection policy with Irish Progressive Life Assurance was worth £185,700 if Tom died. In that event, the outstanding mortgage on Jack White's would be cleared; the life insurance policy of

£77,000 would clear Catherine's bank overdraft, leaving about £17,000 outstanding. She would then be the sole owner of a property that would be expected to make at least one million pounds at auction. Clearly, by having her husband murdered, Catherine Nevin stood to become a millionairess. Furthermore, a sudden despatch would bring into effect the legal principle of accelerated inheritance: Tom had made no will, and without one, his wife would get everything.

When he saw the bank book, Heapes was impressed, he knew the money was for real. She suggested that Heapes 'do' Tom when he was at the houses on the South Circular Road. 'I'll give you a key so you can wait inside for him,' she said.

Heapes knew it would be hard to pull off. 'Well, the street, it's a very narrow street and there are cars parked on both sides . . .,' he said. The door also posed a problem; it was a half-glass door. 'No, sure he would see, when he's walking in, he would see behind the door. And if there was something happening in the street, it's too narrow, anything could happen, a car could pull out or you would get blocked in.' That plan was knocked on the head.

Undaunted, Catherine Nevin began exploring other possibilities, other locations and then she'd put it to him. Another meeting followed in quick succession. Gerry Heapes had still not told her that the murder plan was a non-starter. By his own admission, he was stringing her along, keeping her sweet.

This time she drove him to the Grasshopper Inn in Clonee, on the outskirts of Blanchardstown. It was where Tom sometimes stopped off for lunch on the way to pick up meat in the nearby Kepak meat factory. They had taken the route that Tom would take.

They sat in the white Vectra and talked about how the killing could be done. She knew her husband's route like the back of her hand: Tom Nevin would cut through the Phoenix Park and come out the Castleknock gates. But if for any reason he was running late and he knew he'd miss the bank to lodge the takings, he would drive on, collect his meat from Kepak and then go up to the Grasshopper Inn for lunch. She was even able to say where he sat: at a table just inside the window where he could sit and watch his car. At this meeting Catherine Nevin mentioned St Patrick's Day weekend as the ideal time to stage the robbery.

'He has to stop here and I will make sure that he will be late for the bank,' she told Heapes.

When he was leaving the Grasshopper, she suggested, Heapes could shoot him and take the money, which would be in the boot of the car. Tom would have his keys in his hand coming out of the pub and they could be taken from him. Alternatively, she would supply Heapes with a spare key to get the money out of the boot.

That day in Blanchardstown, Heapes turned to her and said that he could not rely on Tom being there. 'What I will do is I will go with him,' she said. 'I will make an excuse that I will have to come to Dublin with him and make sure he misses the bank and go in and sit down. When he comes out, you can shoot him.'

'You can't do that, because if I shoot him and you are behind him you could end up getting shot.'

'Well, it would look great,' countered Catherine, with a dramatic flourish, 'with him dying in my arms.'

'There's not enough time to arrange it,' said Heapes.

Gerry Heapes makes an interesting study of human psychology. Time after time he wasn't able to remember vital information, yet he had total recall of the minutiae of conversations he'd had with Catherine Nevin.

At the trial, dates particularly confounded him. He couldn't even remember what decade it was that Catherine Nevin propositioned him to kill her husband. 'Would you settle for the century?' he asked in court when pressed to come up with them. He eventually settled for the late 1980s, early 1990s. It was only through documentation from a local garage that the dates were pinned down. Tom Nevin bought the Vectra from Hills Garage in Arklow on 3 January 1989 and he traded it in to Hills on 5 September 1990. If Heapes is correct in saying she always picked him up in the white Vectra, the solicitations had to have taken place between these dates.

Throughout all of these approaches, not once did it occur to him to go to the gardaí. Why, defence counsel Paddy MacEntee asked in the formal stuffiness of the courtroom, did he not immediately tell the guards this woman was plotting to bump off her husband? 'Why didn't you say, "Sorry for your troubles but killing him is out of the question?" Instead you're saying: "I'll see you again about it."'

The one other person who might have found this information useful was Tom Nevin. He was busily running a pub 48 miles away in Brittas Bay, completely unaware that a former IRA man was walking around Finglas telling 'the lads' that Catherine Nevin wanted him shot dead.

Heapes had no answer for Paddy MacEntee.

It was later, much later, when Tom Nevin had been murdered, that Gerry Heapes was able to shed a little more light on the IRA's reaction to the murder proposition. He claimed to detectives that he had 'reported' to his 'organisation' – i.e. the IRA – what Catherine Nevin was up to. He was told that not alone would they not sanction it, but they would take measures to prevent it. 'I later heard that some of the organisation had gone to Catherine

Nevin and told her they knew about her plans and told her to desist,' said Heapes. If she didn't they would deal with her and anyone she contracted to do the killing.

Given that the IRA's motives are never purely altruistic, Heapes's story suggests that the organisation had something to gain by Tom Nevin staying alive, and, possibly, much to lose by his death. No further evidence was offered to back up Heapes's claim that he ever brought Catherine Nevin's murder plan to the IRA.

Whatever transpired between Gerry Heapes and Catherine Nevin at that last meeting, she suspected that her attempts to solicit him as a hired gun were running into the sand. She had tried to charm, cajole and pay someone to kill her husband but so far her efforts had not proved fruitful. For now, Heapes was out of the picture, although his path was again to cross with Catherine Nevin's four years down the line, in late 1994.

Heapes and John Jones were dead ducks as far as her plans were concerned. As it turned out, Catherine Nevin had already turned her mind towards another possibility – to a third man. She looked to her old friend and lover, Willie McClean.

Of all the men rumoured to have had sexual affairs with Catherine Nevin, Willie McClean was the only one to acknowledge it. He is also the only man who sent her packing when she asked him to kill Tom Nevin. This was in 1990.

There was a lacuna of four years between the last time Willie McClean had seen her – at the end of the affair – and January 1990. The 1990 New Year festivities were still underway when he bumped into her again in Jack White's Inn.

McClean and his new girlfriend had dropped in for a bite to eat. He spotted his old lover behind the bar but he did not acknowledge her. But Catherine Nevin had spotted him. As he was going to the toilet, she buttonholed him. After a brief exchange of pleasantries, she asked him for a contact number. 'You can contact me in the Irish House,' McClean told her. The Irish House is a pub in Harold's Cross, quite close to where he has a piano shop. He was in the pub one night and he got a phone call. Catherine Nevin was on the other end. She was calling from St Vincent's Hospital where she was a patient. Would he go up to see her?

He arrived at the hospital the following day and was ushered into a private room. Catherine was sitting by the side of the bed. He enquired about her health and Catherine mumbled something about her heart. Convicted criminal as he was, Willie McClean was not prepared for what happened next. She came straight to the point. She and Tom weren't getting on together and she wanted someone 'to get rid of him'. And she wanted to rekindle the affair with Willie McClean.

She said to him baldly: 'There is £20,000 there to get rid of Tom and you and I could get back together.'

McClean was incredulous. 'Where is this to happen?'

Well, there were a variety of possibilities; at the bank or the flats, Catherine responded. 'You have the contacts to do it,' she added helpfully.

'Why would you want to do that?'

'I'd get the insurance money, the lot, everything.'

Taken aback, he said equally baldly: 'No fucking way.' He got up to walk out.

'You blond Protestant bastard,' she roared after him, 'You were always a bastard.'

'I was shocked,' McClean recalled. 'I just said no fucking way. I said it was a non-starter, no way.' Just before she came out with her bombshell, Catherine had started to flutter her eyelashes at him, he remembered. 'When I told her I was no murderer and no way was I doing that, the eyes started to roll around in her head. They just kept rolling and rolling. I just walked out and she started calling me a bastard.'

The next time Willie McClean saw Catherine Nevin was St Patrick's Day 1993. He was on his way to Rosslare with his nephew; they were catching the ferry to France and they stopped off at Jack White's for a drink on the way. He never saw her again in Jack White's after that.

Catherine Nevin was playing a very dangerous game. She was flirting with the IRA, consorting with a criminal element – she had even acquired a proclivity for slang; thieves from Dolphin's Barn became 'tea leaves on the barn' – and so on. And she was telling anyone prepared to listen the most intimate details about her and Tom's private life, more importantly, their financial details. At the very least, she risked leaving them both open to blackmail or extortion. At the same time she was playing the part of the chic, refined lady of the manor in Jack White's. By this stage, she saw herself as a fully-fledged member of the social elite; totally pretentious, she enjoyed rubbing shoulders with the judiciary, businessmen, senior gardaí and the well-heeled golfing fraternity in Co. Wicklow.

It has been suggested that Catherine Nevin was passing low-level intelligence on the IRA to certain members of the gardaí. She definitely had information on certain individuals. This could account for her name-checking republicans in connection with an IRA plan to buy the Killinarden Inn and to install Tom Nevin as a frontman.

Her allegation related to 1988, long after the Provos had moved into real estate and when they already had a portfolio of licensed premises. She claimed that £100,000 of the £500,000 asking price was to have been put up by John Jones, acting as a silent partner. The money was coming from the North. Catherine Nevin claimed that it was lodged in a Dublin bank account. At the time she made the claim – during her trial – it was dismissed as another of her fantasy trips. But these authors have established that there was some truth in it.

The IRA refuses to shed light on any dealings they may or may not have had with Catherine Nevin. After going through the 'channels' and meeting a wall of silence, the authors were left with the distinct impression that the Republican Movement was acutely embarrassed by the whole affair. Individual activists were prepared to help, however, and what they had to say was very interesting. A key republican source revealed that the Provisional IRA *had* planned to buy the Killinarden Inn and had set a sum of money aside for that very purpose. The sum was in fact £100,000, the exact figure Nevin claimed had been put up.

The IRA has had involvement in 20 pubs in the greater Dublin area since 1980. The authors have established the names of the individuals at the top of the command structure responsible for securing the pubs.

There *was* a Provo banker. His name and other details the authors have verified from both senior security and republican sources. By all accounts, this person had a very successful career. He worked in the national and big commercial banks and was promoted wherever he went. And wherever he went, the accounts went with him.

The unlikely source of ex-Sinn Féin member Pat Russell also lends some credence to the Killinarden claim. According to Russell's evidence in court, 'It was well known around Finglas that the Nevins were looking at the Killinarden Inn.' In addition, the key republican source revealed that senior IRA personnel travelled to a meeting that involved Catherine Nevin in connection with the purchase of the Killinarden Inn. What is not known and was not confirmed is whether Tom Nevin was there or indeed, whether he ever knew about the matter.

This new information means Mrs Nevin's story now begins to sound less like a flight of fancy. Except that it still has one major flaw. For her to suggest, as she did, that Tom Nevin was a member of the IRA, and in the same breath claim the IRA was using him as a front man, is nonsensical, and betrays how little she actually knows about the workings of the IRA. Anyone used in that capacity had to be 'clean'; for them to do otherwise would be counter-productive. There is no evidence to suggest that Tom Nevin was ever a member of the IRA. And what is known about Catherine Nevin suggests that the republican connections were hers, not her husband's.

There is no Special Branch file on either Tom or Catherine Nevin. Informed sources suggest that she appears only as a cross-reference on other Provo files. At the time when the Nevins were running the Barry House, Sinn Féin had the use of a room upstairs where they held the odd cumann meeting. Because the pub was so closely monitored, the Special Branch took note of who was coming and going. It was in that context, coupled with her visits to 2a Church Street, that she would have appeared on the files. Those are just the known sources of references.

But what is beyond doubt is that when it came to the Provos, Catherine was the mover and shaker, not Tom. She was the one who sought out Jones and Heapes and hung around IRA circles. When the Provos were looking around for a frontman, as they were, it's quite possible they looked at Catherine Nevin.

1. A 'deposition' is a statement, on oath, of a witness in a judicial proceeding. The examining justice usually signs a certificate listing each

witness who gave oral evidence. The deposition can be used by the prosecution or defence instead of calling the witness.

2. Ministerial directives under Section 31 of the Broadcasting Act banned interviews or reports of interviews with members of Sinn Féin, the IRA and other republican and loyalist paramilitary groups on national TV and radio. Although their voices could not be heard, RTE television was allowed to screen their faces. In January 1994, the Fianna Fáil/Labour coalition dropped the ban.

3. All statements issued by the IRA are signed 'P. O'Neill'.

4. The following are the transactions in Catherine Scully's bank account no. 35329163. *Lodgments:* 6/11/1989, £3,000; 27/11/1989, £1,000; 30/3/1990, £5,000; 13/9/1990, £2,400; 3/12/1990, £1,500. *Withdrawals:* 23/7/1990, £200; 19/12/1990, £500.

4

THE JUDGE
FROM ARKLOW

❧

For four years, the photograph took pride of place on Catherine Nevin's cabinet. The colour snapshot shows a burly, greying man with a broad smile and a microphone in his hand. Around him, beneath a balloon-festooned ceiling, crowd a throng of well-wishers. The man with the mike is Inspector Tom Kennedy. At his left shoulder is another man with silver-grey hair, distinguished-looking in his dark, tailored suit. He is the judge from Arklow, Judge Donnchadh Ó Buachalla.

The pair are surrounded by Kennedy's garda colleagues and assorted local dignitaries. The photo was taken in a function room in Jack White's in 1994 at Tom Kennedy's retirement party. It was his second party: he'd already had one in the Grand Hotel in Wicklow. At the back of the photo is the cheery figure of Catherine Nevin. She baked the celebration cake and it was she who made the speech. At the end of it she presented Kennedy with two airline tickets to the US. 'For you and your lovely wife,' she announced with a flourish. Tom Kennedy's wife, Mary, sat quietly in the corner of the pub with a couple of friends.

At first glance it is an innocuous enough snapshot but that photo would have strong and emotive resonance six years on. By the time it was taken Catherine Nevin and Tom Kennedy had come through a relationship: sexual, according to the staff – platonic, according to her and Kennedy. Her relationship with her husband was the stuff of nightmares and she was actively trawling the underbelly of society for someone, anyone, prepared to shoot Tom Nevin dead. The morning after Tom Kennedy's retirement party, Eileen Byrne was cleaning up and Tom Nevin was in the bar. He turned to her and remarked: 'This will all end in tears.'

It was into this volatile situation that Donnchadh Ó Buachalla walked in 1993. Ó Buachalla is a dapper figure, with a slight frame and narrow, slightly pinched, features. He lives with his wife, Therese, and teenage children in a detached house in Stillorgan Wood, Co. Dublin. Ó Buachalla was assigned to District Area 23 in 1993, four years after his appointment to the bench by Charles Haughey. District 23 encompasses the towns of Arklow, Wicklow, Enniscorthy, Gorey, Rathdrum, Wexford and stretches as far as Tullow in Co. Carlow. It was shortly after his arrival as district court judge in Arklow that Donnchadh Ó Buachalla met Catherine and Tom Nevin.

Catherine thought that having a judge about the place gave her a certain social standing. She would always treat Ó Buachalla as a VIP when he called, as he often did, en route to or from the nearby European golf course. Ó Buachalla is an avid golfer. He was an honorary member of the European and captain of his own golf club, the Old Conna in Bray. 'Jack White's became my half way house on my travels in work and I would call there on average two or three times a week,' Ó Buachalla said in a statement to gardaí after the murder.

The staff at Jack White's were not always happy to see the distinguished guest coming. His visits always precipitated a bout of nit-picking from Catherine, and as a result they regarded him as a bit of a pain in the neck. They resented the deference with which Catherine treated him. Their annoyance comes across in a plethora of staff statements:

'He used to come in in the evening and we would all be on our toes,' said Ciara Tallon, a former staffer at Jack White's. 'He was a VIP; we dropped everything and looked after him. He used to have his own menu and his own seat in the conservatory. A few times the judge used to rest upstairs in the evening time. I remember one occasion when I was at the dishwasher with Elaine and Michelle and Catherine called us aside and told us to be quiet going upstairs that night. When the judge arrived, Catherine would sit down with him.'

If Catherine was napping, she was to be alerted when the judge arrived. She instructed the staff that only seniors should serve the judge. 'I did serve him on one occasion, but one of the more senior girls would normally serve him,' said Tallon.

Debbie Boucher, who worked for two summers in Jack White's, remembers the judge as being a regular visitor to the pub:

'Himself and Catherine used to sit in the conservatory most of the time,' she said in her statement. 'Tom Nevin would ignore all this and he used to stay in the bar, maybe playing darts.' The judge would have a drink with Catherine when he was there, usually a Harp. 'He used to have wine with his dinner,' said Boucher. 'Catherine made a very big fuss of him. Sometimes the judge would have his wife, and a girl and a boy with him for Sunday lunch.'

'The staff were nervous in serving the judge as they were terrified if they did anything wrong Catherine would be furious,' recounted Elaine Butler, a younger member of staff. 'When the judge arrived he would stay for quite a while and there were times he rested upstairs. We were warned by Catherine not to disturb him.'

The task of serving the judge his dinner would normally fall to Liz Hudson. The staff thought him courteous but felt he had an air of superiority about him. 'Oh the judge, he was classed as a VIP,' said Hudson. 'Well you knew he was a judge. He used to have his own tray and his own doilies. Catherine would say, "I want you to serve the judge." He always called me Mrs Hudson, never Liz. He was never charged for his meals and Tom went mad over that too.'

Judge Ó Buachalla liked the title 'judge'. He insisted on being called 'Judge Ó Buachalla' as soon as he was elevated to the bench in 1989, even on social occasions. One man, who frequently came across Ó Buachalla during the course of his work, found him a very charming man. 'He was the epitome of the old-style gentleman. He was very sensitive in family law cases. I remember one case when it was over and he thanked everyone for their patience and their sensitivity.'

Another who came across him in his judicial function described him as a 'very compassionate judge, very sympathetic to battered wives and parents of youngsters who are starting to get into trouble with the law'.

Before the Nevin trial, he came to notice during the memorable invasion of Arklow courthouse by dozens of mice in 1999. Ó Buachalla stuffed his trousers into his socks to prevent the little rodents from running up his legs, before declaring the court session abandoned and heading for the comparative safety of his chambers.

Ó Buachalla's appointment raised a few eyebrows at the time and it might never have occurred had he not managed to overcome the financial difficulties in the mid 1970s that had threatened to ruin him.

Like many district court judges, Donnchadh Ó Buachalla is a former solicitor. (Judges of the superior courts are drawn from the ranks of barristers.) He started out as a young solicitor in 1968 with the firm Porter Morris in Dublin. He got into financial difficulty when he went into private practice under his own name and opened registered offices in Dublin's Merrion Square.

The cause of his trouble was a man called Tom Cawley. Cawley launched scores of companies but the one that was to lead to Ó Buachalla losing money was called Invest of Ireland Ltd with an address at Fitzwilliam Square. Through Invest, Cawley offered mortgage funds for commercial buildings but the prospective mortgagees were first required to deposit £3,500 with Cawley's solicitor, Donnchadh Ó Buachalla, while the valuation was being carried out. In the event, no finance was forthcoming and the depositors lost funds, through no fault of Ó Buachalla's.

Subsequently, two High Court judgments were registered against Ó Buachalla from two separate companies and a third was satisfied. The first company, Brendan James of Amiens Street, was granted a judgment of £1,400 in July 1972. The second was Irish International Bank for £1,458 in February 1973, the month after he was declared a bankrupt. A third creditor also sought a judgment but it was settled out of court in 1970.

Because he was now a bankrupt, the Law Society, the governing body for solicitors, suspended his licence to practise. It was restored in 1978 by which time he had discharged all outstanding debts. He was back in business, this time with his friend and fellow solicitor Paddy Kevans.

Donnchadh Ó Buachalla's career trajectory started in the sensible, secure way of the legal profession, nice, middle-class surroundings, good schools. He was born on 28 March 1945 and reared in leafy

Villiers Road in upmarket Rathgar. Sources interviewed for this book recall that his parents' relationship was not an entirely harmonious one.

The Ó Buachalla home was close to where Peter Berry, the secretary of the Department of Justice, lived, in St Kevin's Gardens. His father Sean and Peter Berry were at daggers drawn for most of their careers. Ó Buachalla's mother, Máirín Ní Glasáin, had a drapery business, just off Cathedral Street in Dublin city centre.

The young Ó Buachalla was sent to the best schools: Gonzaga College, then onto UCD and finally, the Law Society in Blackhall Place, where he qualified as a solicitor.

When Judge Ó Buachalla arrived in Arklow, he became a regular visitor at Jack White's Inn. Tom Nevin noticed the friendship with Catherine first, then the staff. Judge Ó Buachalla denied in court that he'd had 'an irregular sexual affair' with Catherine Nevin. She denied it also.

Eileen Byrne's reading of the situation was: 'She was a user. She used Kennedy and Ó Buachalla because they were respectable to be seen with – that was the only reason.'

Another staff member, Jane Murphy, remembers a row between Tom Nevin and the judge a few weeks before Tom Nevin was killed, which is recorded in her garda statement. It was on a Monday morning in early March and Murphy had arrived at the pub at 8.30 a.m. to start work. There was a huge argument going on between Tom and Catherine. Catherine was sitting on the bottom of the stairs. She was crying.

'Bernie (Fleming) told me, "say nothing, there's a row going on",' said Murphy. 'She said Tom was fighting with her. I think it was over the judge.' Tom Nevin instructed the staff that if this man rang for Catherine they were to fetch Tom. 'The judge rang and I told Tom.'

'Put it through to the hall,' he ordered. He took the phone and let out a string of expletives at the man on the other end. 'You oul bollox,' he roared.

'I heard Tom fucking and blinding the judge, telling him to fuck off,' said Murphy.

Judge Ó Buachalla was expected to call in to Jack White's later that day. He didn't arrive. It was the following day, Tuesday, before he turned up.

Liz Hudson testified in court that the 'Judge from Arklow' had visited and stayed there. She said Judge Ó Buachalla was so well known at the Inn that at one stage Catherine told her he had a set of keys. It was on this crucial point that Judge Ó Buachalla was called as a witness: the prosecution had intended not putting him on the stand.

According to Liz Hudson's version of events, Catherine Nevin had asked her, sometime in February or March 1996, for a loan of her staff keys because someone else had Catherine's. 'And I think that was somebody who was well known on the premises?' asked Peter Charleton in court. 'That's right. Judge Ó Buachalla,' Liz Hudson replied.

Hudson told these authors that she was surprised when Catherine asked her for the loan of her keys to Jack White's. 'When I said, "Sure haven't you got your own?" she told me the judge had hers. That's what she said and I'll stand over it.'

Judge Ó Buachalla gave a statement to the gardaí on 29 April 1996 at the Glenview Hotel, Co. Wicklow. This is the full text of the statement:

'I have known the late Tom Nevin and his wife Catherine for more than three years, having been introduced to Jack White's pub and restaurant by Inspector Tom Kennedy. In

1993 I was captain of my own golf club in Dublin and had established many friends through golf in Dublin, Wicklow and Wexford.

'The European Golf Club had opened around that time in Brittas Bay and I developed links with that club, its members and guests. It had no clubhouse and Jack White's was used as the official 19th hole. Many members not only used it as the nearest hostelry but also used the bed and breakfast facilities and the shower and dining facilities after golf. I was made an honorary life member and took part in prize giving occasions and presentations at various functions over the years.

'Jack White's became my half way house on my travels in work and I would call there on average two or three times a week. I would often leave my car there when playing golf with friends at the European or other golf clubs.

'I had an excellent relationship with both the late Tom and his wife Catherine. They were both very hospitable and would regularly sit with me, depending on which of them was not working at the counter.

'From time to time there would be late nights and if I felt tired before driving, which did happen on about three occasions, I would rest in the living room, have a shower and let myself out the front door and drive home. I never stayed overnight and I never had occasion to have a key to any part of the premises and never had sight of any keys.

'I have no idea as to what procedures were in place for closing time or who locked the premises. It was common knowledge that Tom spent many hours late at night doing books and handling cash matters. Over time I did become aware from both Tom and Catherine about this great apprehension and that of many members of the local community in relation to certain members of the local gardaí. I do know that Tom was greatly troubled by these ongoing matters and both he and his wife firmly believed that there was serious garda harassment over the years and that it was futile to make complaints.

'I last saw Tom on the night of Saturday, 15 March [*sic*] when I brought my wife, parents-in-law and my youngest daughter to Jack White's for a very pleasant meal which we had in the conservatory between 8.15 p.m. and 10.30 p.m., during which time Tom came and joined us for about ten minutes in general conversation.'

Signed: Donnchadh Ó Buachalla

Witnessed: John McElligott, D. Superintendent

Liz Hudson was on duty the night of Saturday, 16 March when the judge and his family were having their meal. 'I didn't see Tom Nevin sitting talking to the judge. I'm not saying he didn't, just that I didn't see it. But I would be surprised to see Tom Nevin joining in a social conversation with him, because Tom didn't really like the judge. He had no time for him.'

Hudson did see Catherine sitting down at the judge's table. 'They had their meal and then the wife and the others left and went into the bar or somewhere. Then Catherine sat down and was talking to him. They were talking for a while when someone – I think it was one of the judge's kids – called him to say the family were waiting in the car, they were ready to go.'

Judge Ó Buachalla did not enjoy a good relationship with the gardaí in Arklow. By 1996, when Tom Nevin was killed, it was positively poisonous. The judge's statement, in which he mentions the Nevins' concern about 'certain members of the local gardaí', is a reflection of the volatility of this relationship.

It has its roots in a dispute between the Nevins and two Arklow-based gardaí that pre-dates Ó Buachalla's arrival in Wicklow. The complex series of events began in 1991 with a row between Catherine and Tom Nevin in Jack White's. Her version of events was that Tom, in a temper, threw her down the stairs. Garda Mick Murphy was in the pub that night but he left before the argument. He said he didn't see anything. Catherine reported to Tom Kennedy that Tom Nevin had assaulted her, but there were no witnesses.

That same year, 1991, the pub was raided for after-hours drinking, although no prosecution followed. On 13 July 1992, Catherine and Tom Nevin made a total of 16 complaints against Mick Murphy and one against his patrol-car colleague, Vincent Whelan. The complaints relate to incidents alleged to have occurred two years earlier.

Murphy and Whelan were suspended from duty in January 1993 while the complaints were being investigated. The Director of Public Prosecutions' office reported back in 1994: 'Proceedings should not be taken against these men. The witnesses are lacking in credibility and reliability.'

Mick Murphy and Vincent Whelan were reinstated but they were subsequently confined to indoor duties. A report on their case appeared in the *Wicklow People*. The staff left it open on the table in front of Catherine so she couldn't miss it. 'She took one look at it', said Eileen Byrne, 'and she said to us, "I have friends in high places, they'll never work again."' But Catherine was not as powerful as she thought because Murphy and Whelan did indeed work again – in fact they are still serving in the area.

By the time they were re-instated, Judge Ó Buachalla was on the bench in District Area 23 and Mick Murphy and Vincent Whelan were now bringing cases before him on a regular basis. Murphy, Whelan and three other officers were unhappy with decisions on a list of cases adjudicated on by Judge Ó Buachalla. The five complained to the Garda Representative Association although two later withdrew their complaints. The Department of Justice was informed.

It was only after the Nevin trial had concluded that the Department of Justice publicly acknowledged that a problem exists between the gardaí and the judiciary in Wicklow. On 18 April 2000, the Minister for Justice, John O'Donoghue, ordered a formal inquiry under Mr Justice Frank Murphy of the Supreme Court.

The Murphy inquiry got underway a full three years after the Department of Justice had become aware of the tensions in Arklow. For all of that time it was allowed to fester.

5

'THIS IS
JOHN FERGUSON'

⁂

J ust after 9 a.m. on 13 March 1996 the phone rang in the
hallway of Jack White's. Bernie Fleming answered it. The
caller had a cultured accent and spoke in a clipped, business-
like manner. 'This is John Ferguson,' said the voice at the
other end of the phone.

Fleming ran to tell Catherine Nevin. Catherine made a dash
for the phone – she had warned the staff that they were to call her
immediately if a man by that name rang the pub. On no account
were they to tell anyone else who was calling.

'Catherine used to tell us to make sure and get her if a John
Ferguson rang for her. She told us to get her no matter what and
no-one else was to be got,' said the cleaner, Jane Murphy, in a
statement. The 'no-one else' was Tom Nevin.

Liz Hudson remembers the calls – and Catherine Nevin's reaction. 'He'd say, "This is John Ferguson, can I speak to Catherine?"
She'd jump out of the bed when I'd tell her who was on the
phone.'

There were two telephone lines into Jack White's – a public
one in the hall of the pub which could also be answered from the

living quarters, and a private number. The public line rings in the hallway of the bar beside the toilets, and upstairs on the landing across from Catherine's bedroom. It was this number – 0404 47106 – that John Ferguson used to call.

Once, when Ferguson rang, Murphy stood by the phone extension in the hall near the kitchen door and waited for Catherine to finish speaking to him from the extension in her bedroom. 'I had to stand by the phone for half an hour,' she recalled. When Catherine finished talking she rang down from her bedroom. Lots of times, when it would be other callers, Catherine would order the staff to say, 'I'm not in.'

The man on the phone was not 'John Ferguson'. His real name is Patrick Russell, a financial consultant who ran a business trading as Royal Irish Group with registered offices in Dublin city centre. Catherine Nevin knew him in another life; she'd met him in 1984 when he was secretary of the Sinn Féin Cumann in Finglas and was John Jones's sidekick.

By the time of Nevin's trial, Russell was 37, a big, stocky man with a receding hairline. If image means anything, then Patrick Russell seems to have prospered in the years since 1984, when Catherine Nevin first knew him. Gone was the youthful, slightly rakish look; Russell is now every inch the man-about-town with tailored suits and a mobile phone. By 1995, when he re-entered Catherine Nevin's life as the ubiquitous John Ferguson, he lived in a fine house at Castletown in Leixlip, Co. Kildare and had offices in Merrion Square.

Patrick Russell has described himself in various publications as an established financial consultant. He is not accredited to any of the regulated accountants organisations in Ireland. He is a busy man these days. His business dealings are international and he has, or had, interests in companies with impressive names like

Royal Irish Financial Services Ltd, Royal Irish Group, Garrard International Holdings and Universal Management Consultants.

Universal is an investment trust formed in Jersey on 27 October 1998. In March 1999, Universal had three development projects for sale in London, Manchester and Liverpool worth a combined £1.213 million. The company is currently being sued in the High Court by the Derry-based firm, O'Neill Brothers Ltd, for the return of £500,000 for projects which did not go ahead. The former Taoiseach, Albert Reynolds is being sued along with Russell. In a May 2000 hearing, Reynolds was represented in court, but Russell is not.

Another of Russell's companies, Garrard International Holdings, has an exotic address. It is registered in the British Virgin Isles. In 1998, it had head offices at 17 Berkeley Street, Dublin 1, Nortexmill in Bolton, and Old Hall Street in Liverpool.

Patrick Russell's Irish base was at the Royal Irish Group's offices at 11 Merrion Square in Dublin. This company was formed on 5 February 1996, just a few weeks before Catherine Nevin would start calling him there. Its parent company is Royal Irish Financial Services Ltd, 78 North King Street, which was incorporated in September 1995. Russell was appointed director the same month and Muriel Russell, with the same home address of Castletown, Leixlip, is named as co-director. At the date the company was dissolved – 7 January 2000 – Royal Irish Financial Services Ltd had an issued share capital of £2. Eight judgments have been registered against Russell at 78 North King Streeet since 1993.

Patrick Russell's hectic schedule didn't prevent him from keeping in touch with Catherine Nevin. He would often stop at Jack White's on his way back to Dublin from Waterford, where at one time he had the lease of a pub. Occasionally, Russell would see Tom Nevin there. Russell knew that Catherine Nevin had tried to get someone to kill her husband – Jones had told him back in 1989–1990. 'I wasn't aware of the full details of the approach,' he would later tell gardaí while he was in custody, 'but the organisation with which I was then involved wouldn't sanction the killing.' Catherine Nevin would have been made aware of her approach being rejected, he said.

Like fellow republicans John Jones and Gerry Heapes, Patrick Russell, too, neglected to tell Tom Nevin that his wife had been trawling the IRA looking for a hit man to kill him. Apart from the gardaí, this was the one man who might gainfully have used this little nugget of information.

Sometime towards the end of 1994, Gerry Heapes reappeared in Jack White's. Heapes and his wife Breda had 'fallen out'. In fact, she had thrown him out of the house and he was on the lookout for a roof to put over his head. He hit on the idea that the Nevins might rent him a flat in one of their Dublin houses. When he went into the pub first, Catherine wasn't there, Tom was. Catherine came in on the tail-end of the conversation. Heapes told Tom Nevin his tale of woe. 'Any chance of a bedsit?' asked Heapes. As far as he knew there were two country lads that might be moving out at Christmas, Tom replied. Heapes never took him up on the offer – he patched things up with his wife and went back home.

Heapes returned to Jack White's about a year later – he couldn't give precise dates: it's his memory, it's not what it used to be, he says. This time he saw Catherine. He intended to black-mail her.

The version Heapes gave to the court is that he was 'bumming around with nothing to do' when he hit on a great plan for making a quick buck. He would, 'go up to the Nevin one and see if she still wants her husband killed. She wouldn't want me to go to the guards.' Catherine was behind the bar when he went in. Heapes asked if she still wanted the old man killed. He was hoping to con her out of £10,000. 'Oh no,' said Catherine. 'Everything is okay now, we've had a reconciliation.' She didn't want it done. Gerry Heapes smelled a rat and thought Catherine Nevin was up to something. His plan was scuttled and he headed back to Dublin empty-handed.

There was no such reconciliation. If anything, the rows became more frequent and more intense in late 1995 and early 1996.

In August, a niece of Tom Nevin's came to visit. Anne Marie Finnerty got talking to Catherine and during the course of the conversation, Catherine told her that she and Tom were separating. They were also thinking of selling the business, she told her, and it would be done before Christmas. Tom Kennedy and Catherine had earlier joined her for a drink, and Anne Marie took Kennedy to be a customer.

Catherine had harboured plans to sell Jack White's as far back as 1990. On 31 January that year she contacted an auctioneer called Tony Morrissey to value the pub for the purpose of a sale. There was another call on 15 February. Two years later, Morrissey received a further call about Jack White's on behalf of Catherine Nevin, made by Inspector Tom Kennedy. She called herself the following day.

Tony Morrissey – who was not called as a witness – prepared a memo detailing his discussions and contacts with Catherine Nevin. She told Morrissey she was negotiating with an oil company about installing a fuel depot and petrol station on the site, and that was the reason she was considering selling the pub.

Another year went by. On 27 July 1993 Catherine Nevin again contacted Tony Morrissey. 'I've completed a deal on a pub in Dublin and I want to sell Jack White's,' she told him. Tom Nevin was at the third meeting with Tony Morrissey. Morrissey presumed Tom knew it was Catherine's intention to sell up. However, Tom didn't know about the previous contacts and it now transpires that he was interested in getting a valuation but had no intention of selling up.

Around Christmas time 1995, the calls from 'John Ferguson' began coming more frequently. By then, he had been phoning for about three months. It was around the same time that Catherine stepped up the pressure on her husband to sell out to her. She wanted to buy Tom's share of the pub. She kept after him. He kept saying 'no'.

Russell also knew about Catherine's plans to buy her husband out. She'd told him so. Russell was trying to interest her in some property deal that was going down in Dublin. She didn't seem that interested. Her first priority was to buy Tom Nevin out, she'd have no problem raising the finance but she knew he wouldn't agree to it. She was stuck.

It led to many rows in Jack White's. Jane Murphy recalls a particularly bad argument between Catherine and Tom in the lounge about a year before he was murdered. 'She wanted to buy Tom's share of the pub and he said "no". Tom Nevin and Catherine were always arguing and fighting even up to his death.'

The calls from John Ferguson continued. Bernie Fleming took many of them. 'Since he began calling it would happen once or twice a week, usually in the morning before Tom got up. After his call, Catherine would leave saying she was going to Dublin or somewhere.'

Later, Russell had a simple explanation for phoning. Catherine Nevin said she'd had a revenue audit the previous year and she wasn't happy with her accountants. Around 17 February 1996, Russell met Catherine Nevin in the Davenport Hotel in Dublin, near Russell's Merrion Square offices. Catherine asked him to do the accounts for the pub. He told her he couldn't, but he'd get her fixed up with someone who could – Noel Murphy of the firm Parffrey Murphy in Cork.

Murphy travelled to Wicklow and met Catherine and Tom Nevin in Jack White's on 14 March. He openly discussed financial arrangements with them. In court, Catherine Nevin said the reason she asked Russell to use the alias John Ferguson was because she didn't want Tom to know about these dealings. Russell agreed. Yet Noel Murphy had no problem talking to Tom about this very matter on 14 March.

There were other strange goings-on in Jack White's in the weeks before Tom Nevin's murder. 'The telephone would ring and when it would be answered there would be nobody on the other end of it,' according to Bernie Fleming. 'This would start about 8.10 a.m. and would be over by 9 a.m. This would happen on both the private and public telephones about three mornings a week.' On 8 March at around 6.30 p.m. a customer, Michael Kelly, dropped into the pub. It was a cold evening, typical for early March and only a few customers were in the pub. Tom Nevin was behind the bar, pulling a pint for another man when Catherine came out from behind the counter:

'Tom was followed the other night,' she said to Kelly.

'Yeah,' Tom Nevin agreed. 'I was coming from the Cash and Carry and I had stuff in the car which I was worried about.'

'Your car is a fast car, you should have been able to lose them,' said Catherine.

From the general conversation, Kelly got the distinct impression that Tom and Catherine Nevin were not getting on together.

There were other times when Tom Nevin suspected that he was being followed. He told Eileen Godkin in December 1995 that he thought he was being tailed when returning to Arklow from Dublin one Monday night. Catherine mentioned to Inspector Fintan Fanning in Jack White's on 3 March that she was worried about the crime scene in Ireland. She was arranging for someone to accompany Tom when he was collecting the rents, she said.

She also told Tom Kennedy she was concerned that Tom had been followed. 'No problem,' said Kennedy, 'I'll mention it to Pat Carroll, he'll keep an eye.' He asked Garda Pat Carroll to patrol the route to make sure there was nothing suspicious. He did so the following day, 4 March, and reported nothing of a suspicious nature.

The month before Tom Nevin was killed Jane Murphy was working in the storeroom just off the kitchen of the pub. It was about 11 a.m. when an unmerciful row broke out between Catherine and Tom in another corner of the store. Murphy heard them cursing at each other. Catherine shouted at Tom that she wanted to buy him out. 'No, I'm not going,' he roared back, his face contorted with rage. 'Fuck off wherever you want, I'm not selling out.'

Murphy had to pass both of them to come out of the store. They didn't even notice her. She recalls it vividly: 'both of them were very vexed. They were still shouting at one another.'

Murphy finished work just after midday. 'I got a packet of fags from Tom before I left that day. I did not see Catherine at all before I left. There were constant rows going on down there between Tom and Catherine over the running of the pub. I knew Tom was not pleased with the carry-on down there over the people Catherine was entertaining free.'

Bernie Fleming remembers arguments in the months before Tom Nevin's death: 'I was often present when there were disputes between the two of them. Tom would never hit her. Tom was well aware that Catherine was having affairs with other men. She did this openly and these men would sleep in her room with her.' It didn't stop Tom Nevin lavishing gifts on his errant wife, however. He mentioned to Patricia Flood, the last time she saw him, at a family funeral in January 1996, that he had a new car on order for Catherine. Catherine was with him on that occasion. It was two months before the murder.

At the end of the second week of March 1996, Catherine Nevin took her last known phonecall from Patrick Russell, alias John Ferguson. It was the week that Donnchadh Long, a carpet fitter from Dunboyne in Co. Meath, arrived with a couple of workmen to do some work in Jack White's.

In between laying carpets, Long found himself regaled with tales of just how decadent Tom Nevin was – in Catherine Nevin's eyes. She had barely known Long five minutes when she began denouncing her husband as an alcoholic, a wife-beater and a 'queer' who was making off on holiday with one of the barmen. Lunchtime was her best opportunity; Catherine would give the men a meal and a drink and she'd bombard Long with stories of how awful her life was with this man, while tippling away at her favourite drink. Long would later give this evidence on behalf of the prosecution. Incredibly, Catherine Nevin seemed incapable of keeping her plans to herself. She broadcast to all and sundry that she wanted Tom out of her life and out of the business.

This series of one-sided glimpses into the Nevin marriage occurred one week before Tom Nevin was killed. By that time all the elements of the tragedy were in place.

6

DANCING QUEENS

~~~~~

The disco in Arklow on St Patrick's weekend was to be the high point of the month. The staff of Jack White's had been looking forward to it for weeks beforehand. It was about 11.30 p.m. on 9 March 1996 when Genesa Phelan finished work for the night at the Inn. The lounge and bar were empty. She sat down at the bar and had a drink with two other workers, two brothers, Alan and Brendan McGraynor. Tom Nevin and Catherine Nevin were there also. Someone mentioned the disco on St Patrick's weekend.

'We were sitting chatting about who was going to the disco on the bank holiday Monday night,' is how Phelan later put it. 'Alan asked was any of the staff going to be staying in the pub after the disco on the bank holiday because he usually had the key to let us in after the disco.'

Catherine Nevin's ears pricked up. 'All the staff will be going back to their own homes because there's no key,' she butted in. It would appear that Tom Nevin was not party to this remark.

This struck Genesa Phelan as strange. 'We usually go back to the pub after a disco when a crowd of us go out,' she later recalled.

In Liz Hudson's experience, nobody was allowed to return late to the pub from discos and sleep in the upstairs rooms unless Alan McGraynor or Bernie Fleming were with them to let them in and make sure everything was properly locked. McGraynor was letting the staff know he was available to let them back in but Catherine was allowing none of them back to the pub that night. They were going to have to make other sleeping arrangements. As it turned out, Alan McGraynor had a road accident on 12 March and ended up in hospital the week of the murder.

St Patrick's weekend began quietly. Business in the bar was brisk enough that Thursday, the takings £1,500.

Tom did not get to the AIB branch in Wicklow with his customary lodgment that Friday. Catherine went there at 11.30 a.m. to get coinage for the busy weekend ahead. She then made a 60-minute journey to a meat factory in Clohamon, Bunclody to collect meat. She left there at 1.08 p.m. She told gardaí that she dropped in to Toss Byrne's pub on the way back and stayed awhile.

That day, Catherine had a problem with her eyes. When she arrived back at the pub she rang her local GP, Dr Pippet, for an appointment. She knew Tom had to make a cash lodgment at the bank. He had at least £3,000 to lodge, the takings for Monday to Thursday of that week. He may also have had taken £4,500 – a payment from an advertising company for hoarding space outside the pub – and £2,000 sterling. However, Tom offered to drive Catherine to the doctor's surgery where a Dr Collins saw her. Tom missed the bank in Wicklow. He'd made no lodgment in the AIB since that Monday. According to Catherine Nevin, Tom was waiting in the car for her when she came out of the doctor's surgery.

The following day, Saturday, was busy in the pub. There was a steady flow of customers all day. That night there was a

50th birthday party for a local woman. The staff noticed nothing untoward in Catherine either that day or the following day, Sunday.

The bank holiday fell on Monday, 18 March. Bernie Fleming arrived bright and early at 8 a.m. The cleaner, Jane Murphy, clocked in shortly afterwards, in good time to get the pub spick and span for what was expected to be one of the busiest days of the year. Tom and Catherine were in their separate bedrooms at opposite ends of the pub.

Fleming opened the restaurant for business at 10 a.m. A middle-aged couple arrived for breakfast shortly afterwards. There was a steady flow of customers all morning. Five or six of the younger staff members had stayed in the pub overnight and they started coming down in dribs and drabs around midday. More of the staff trickled in within the next half an hour.

By now the pub was buzzing. Catherine McGraynor arrived for work at midday. After a brief 'good morning' to Tom Nevin, she went straight upstairs to do the ironing. Catherine Nevin arrived down at 12.30 p.m. and had her hair styled in the hair salon. When the hairdresser, Janice Breen, had finished, Catherine swanned back upstairs for a leisurely bath. There was a steady trade in the bar and lounge during the day. Tom was serving behind the bar, sipping a cup of coffee as he served. He seemed in good form.

At around 2.30 p.m. Catherine asked two customers to leave and take their crying child with them. The only odd thing that happened during the day was in the early evening. Bernie Fleming was serving behind the counter when she noticed a strange man coming in to the lounge. He was carrying a bag and wearing a long black coat. He ordered a coffee and sat drinking. Then he went to make a call at the public phone and Fleming thought she heard him muttering into it. Another customer noticed the stranger speaking with Tom Nevin in a business-like manner.

Bord Telecom would later reveal that the call had been made at 6.50 p.m. After 20 minutes the stranger left the pub. To this date he has never been located or identified.

Bernie Fleming finished around that time – about 7 p.m. She sat down in the lounge and had a drink with a couple of customers. Catherine joined her there. 'Are you going out tonight?' she asked Fleming. Fleming reminded her she was going to the disco in Arklow, the one they'd been talking about for days. Bernie Fleming remembers Catherine running up and down to her bedroom a lot that night. At about 9.30 p.m. the two women sat down to have a cigarette and a chat but Catherine had to get up when more customers filed into the pub.

There were a couple of departures from the norm in Jack White's that night – the staff were paid by cheque instead of the usual cash, seemingly without Tom Nevin's knowledge. Catherine Nevin told Fiona Lawlor there was not enough cash on the premises to pay them so it was a cheque or nothing. Cecilia McDonald was a cook in Jack White's at the time. Only once in six years had she been paid by cheque before that day.

Liz Hudson was passing by the old restaurant around 9.50 p.m. when something caught her eye. The dining room curtains were pulled – they were hung for effect and were never drawn. 'In all my time in Jack White's I have never seen them drawn,' she recalled. She could see the track of the dust where they had been moved from their pulled back position. Something else jarred with Liz Hudson that night. Catherine Nevin was not her usual self; she appeared to be on edge. She was also running back and forth to the washing machine which is in a little room at ground level, off the hairdressing salon. There's an exit door from this room out into the car park which has two locks fitted.

Catherine Nevin told the staff that a wash was still on and it had another 15 minutes to run. 'This was most unusual as Catherine Nevin never took an interest in the washing or the washing machine,' said Hudson. The staff suspected she didn't know how to work it. When Liz Hudson and Bernie Fleming went to the laundry room to put on another wash they found the machine empty. There was no sign of steam or water, as though the machine had not been on at all. 'We found this very strange and after she had gone out we had a discussion about it,' said Bernie Fleming. 'I said, "Something is going to happen if she is going to check on it."' Catherine returned from the laundry room about 15 minutes later.

The disco was now just a couple of hours away. Liz Hudson, Bernie Fleming, Jessica Hunter and Catherine McGraynor were talking about it in the kitchen when Catherine Nevin walked into the room. 'Where are we staying tonight?' one of them asked. 'In Jack White's as usual,' someone piped up.

Catherine turned on them: 'There's nobody, and I mean nobody, staying here tonight.'

'Sure there's no problem,' said Liz Hudson 'I have keys, I'll let them back in after the disco.'

'No,' said Catherine, 'there's nobody to stay here tonight, end of story.'

The women thought this strange but they didn't dare question her. Also, somewhat unusually, Catherine Nevin did not drink that day. 'In fact she only had one whiskey which I bought for her on that night. This was very unusual especially when Dominic McElligott was there and she would normally sit up at the counter all night drinking with him,' Liz Hudson remarked. If

McElligott hadn't been there that night, she would sit and drink with the staff – she always did this on bank holidays after they finished work in the kitchen.

Nevin had only the one drink, which she put on the counter with a beer mat over it – indicating that nobody was to add to it or to buy her another drink. She never touched that drink.

Hudson mopped the kitchen floor when business finished and left the place clean and tidy. At 10.30 p.m. she locked the freezer shed and checked the gate and the cold-room door. They were both locked. She then locked the exit door onto the yard from the kitchen. Everything was now locked and bolted. Catherine was hopping between the bar and the lounge. Tom was in the bar throwing darts. Some of the women went upstairs to get changed and put on make-up. Bernie Fleming had noticed that Catherine had put on a lot of jewellery, rings on her fingers and four or five chains around her neck. Normally, she would not wear this amount of jewellery behind the bar.

When the women came down it was almost time to go. The hum of conversation in the bar at that stage was coming from the staff getting ready to leave – it had been almost cleared of customers. Catherine Nevin had started to empty the pub early that night, and coming up to closing time, there were only about seven to eight customers in the lounge and a few in the bar.

Liz Hudson shouted over to Bernie Fleming that they had better get outside; the taxi would soon be here. It was now approaching midnight. Six of them said goodbye to Catherine Nevin and Dominic McElligott and went to stand in the porch outside. It was now 12.10 a.m. Tom Nevin's car pulled off at the same time as the staff were piling into the taxi. He had only a short distance to travel to drop two customers, Frankie Whelan and Johnny Brennan, off at their homes. He waved goodnight to them, turned the car around and headed back towards Jack White's.

Apart from the claim by Catherine Nevin that she saw Tom in the bar after his return, Frankie Whelan and Johnny Brennan are the last known people to have seen Tom Nevin alive.

As the taxi was pulling away from the pub, Liz Hudson got a brief glance at Tom Nevin's car through the blinding rain. Then she and the others sped off in the direction of Arklow.

7

AND THEN THERE
WAS ONE

'I sent my soul through the invisible,
Some letter of that After-life to spell:
And by and by my soul return'd to me,
And answer'd: "I myself am heav'n and hell."'

The Rubáiyát of Omar Khayyám

On Tuesday evening, 19 March 1996, Tom Rowley, news editor with the *Irish Independent*, was on duty in the newspaper's offices in Dublin's Middle Abbey Street. At 6.20 p.m. the phone on his desk rang. When he picked it up an anonymous male caller was on the line. 'About the shooting . . . the shooting in Arklow. Get your facts right, robbery was not the reason, it was a hit man.'

'Can you give me further information?' Rowley asked. The phone went dead.

That morning, 43 miles away, the body of Tom Nevin was still lying on the floor of Jack White's Inn in Ballinapark, deep in the Wicklow countryside. He died where he fell at the kitchen counter where he'd been totting up the night's takings while supping a glass of stout.

As the gunman walked the 20 feet from the kitchen door to the counter where Tom Nevin was sitting the publican never moved off the stool. In the dead of night the killer was able to walk right up to Tom Nevin and look him in the eye without any defensive reaction from the man he was about to blast into eternity.

The killer shot Tom at point-blank range. He used a 12-gauge shotgun, a commonly held weapon, the type that normally discharges .33-calibre pellets. The ammunition fired into Tom Nevin's body is used for hunting big game, like deer. The single shot ripped into Tom Nevin's right side and the trajectory of the pellets was towards his left chest. The blast shut down his heart, the post-mortem would later reveal. He died within seconds of being shot.

At the shot, Tom Nevin fell from the stool, a wooden one with a loose top that had been brought in from the bar as it was considered too unsafe to leave there. He fell onto his back, with the top of his head facing the freezer door at the rear wall of the kitchen. He lay face-up with his mouth slightly open, his spectacles still on the bridge of his nose, his arms outstretched. The pen with which he'd been writing when the killer struck was still in his right hand crooked above the darkened blood that seeped from the bullet wound and pooled underneath his back. The colour had drained from his face and it was now deathly white.

The shot ripped through the multi-coloured pullover Tom Nevin was wearing. His trousers were pulled up slightly, exposing his patterned socks. When he fell, his jacket fell open and his black leather wallet popped out of his inside pocket and lay flat on the lining of the jacket. The cap of a blue biro was barely visible at the top of the pocket.

There was £410 in that black leather wallet. The way it fell out, it would have been staring the killer in the face, but the person or persons unknown never bothered to pick it up.

There were other, revealing, details in the kitchen scene. The counter where Tom Nevin was murdered faced a wall. Inches away from him, at eye level, was an array of steak knives that Liz Hudson had placed for convenience for serving food in the bar. He never reached for the knives as the killer approached him in the night's silence.

There were other, more lethal, weapons beside him at arm level. Tom Nevin wouldn't even have had to bend down to pick up one of the meat cleavers that the chefs used for carving up lumps of meat and fish. They were kept in a basket-like container at the counter and were level with his right knee when he was shot. All he had to do was extend his arm a few millimetres to arm himself, yet he never made such a move.

There are various explanations: one is that the killer crept up behind him without making a single sound, the other is that Tom Nevin knew the person coming towards him that night. He had no reason to feel frightened until they pulled the gun, possibly from behind their back. By that time it was too late.

The proximity of potential defensive weapons to Tom Nevin was never brought to the attention of the jury in the subsequent trial.

Tom Nevin's nightly book-keeping task normally took him 30 to 40 minutes to complete. He would always put loose coins into tubular silver containers and bring them to the bank. The three silver containers were still standing on the counter next to the food steamer when the gardaí arrived. The account books were open on the counter. Everything in that kitchen was absolutely normal except for the bloodied scene on the floor and the upturned stool.

THE PEOPLE VS CATHERINE NEVIN

Money was missing, £16,550 in all. £13,850 was taken from a cylinder-shaped ground safe and the rest was in sterling and other bits and pieces of cash lying around. The total cash was made up of separate takings of £3,000 for Monday to Thursday of the previous week and £5,200 for the four days of St Patrick's weekend. In addition, there was the £4,500 payment from the advertising company, £2,000 in sterling and £1,850 belonging to Catherine Nevin. Included in the £1,850 was £400 taken from her handbag and an old £100 note she had kept for 20 years.

Missing also was Tom Nevin's car, a black Opel Omega, registration number 92D 27918. There was no gunman, no murder weapon, no evidence of a break-in. All had dissolved into the ether. At first it looked like a robbery gone wrong.

Apart from the body on the floor the pattern was eerily similar to a robbery that had taken place at Jack White's several years earlier.

But this time there was also a bound and gagged wife. Catherine Nevin was cowering behind the front door when the gardaí arrived at 4.45 a.m., some hours after the murder. The exact time of death was never established forensically, but other evidential material put it somewhere between 12.56 a.m. – when Tom Nevin had carried out the last till reading – and 4.30 a.m., just before his wife activated the panic alarm.

Garda Paul Cummiskey and Garda Martin McAndrew were on night duty in Arklow in the early hours of 19 March when a call came through from Wexford garda station to go straight to Jack White's. Something was wrong. Wexford had received a call from Bell Communications, the company that monitored the panic alarm system at Jack White's. The computer printout at Bell Communications shows the time at 4.31 a.m. Cummiskey and McAndrew drove the couple of miles to Jack White's and parked the patrol car in front of the building. After a brief check on the outside of the pub they went inside. The front door was slightly open by about six inches and they noticed the light in the hallway shining out through this opening. Cummiskey also noticed a light on in an upstairs window at the gable-end of the house.

When they pushed open the door the gardaí found Catherine Nevin slumped inside it, clad in a nightie. She was moaning; her hands were tied behind her back and there was a gag in her mouth. The black gag was held in place with a nylon stocking tied loosely around her head. When McAndrew loosened the stocking a pair of black silk panties fell out of her mouth onto the brown and cream carpet. Catherine Nevin had been bound and gagged in her bedroom on the first landing but she had managed to free her feet and raise the alarm. McAndrew undid the turquoise dressing-gown belt that was tied around her wrists and it fell to the floor. Her wrists were also secured tightly with two yellow braided headbands, the type usually worn at football matches. McAndrew and Cummiskey tried to untie the bands but they eventually cut them open with a knife. 'Where's Tom?' asked McAndrew.

Catherine Nevin was now shivering with the cold and her shoulder was sore. Garda Cummiskey went to the bedroom to get a quilt and he saw that the centre light was on, although the two pink side lamps were off. He also noticed pillows propped up against the rose-coloured dralon headboard. As he was leaving he saw a newspaper lying open on the bed and he noticed that the yellow phone on the locker beside the bed was off the hook.

Cummiskey and McAndrew carried Catherine Nevin into the sitting room to the right of the hallway, placed her on a couch and wrapped the quilt around her. 'What happened?' asked Cummiskey.

'He came into the bedroom, he had a knife and a hood over his head,' replied the shivering woman. 'Where's Tom?' she moaned, 'Where's Tom?'

She was now babbling almost incoherently. 'He had a woolly mask, he took jewellery.'

'Who? Is there anyone else on the premises?' asked McAndrew. 'Dominic was here, where's Dominic?' she moaned. Garda Dominic McElligott had been drinking in Jack White's the night before but he'd left minutes before or after midnight.

McAndrew and Cummiskey left Catherine Nevin on the couch and went looking for Tom Nevin. When they walked into the pub they saw a trail of jewellery leading from the stairs in the hallway to the lounge. The scene was reminiscent of the Grimms' fairy tale, *Hänsel and Gretel*, where the two heroes left a trail of crumbs behind them. The two gardaí spotted a gold necklace lying in the hallway in front of the floor-length rust-coloured curtains. Another few feet into the lounge they found a wooden jewellery box minus its drawers. A few feet from the jewellery box lay the drawers and a couple of gold trinkets scattered on the carpet.

They followed the trail down to the kitchen. It was then they saw the lifeless body of Tom Nevin lying in a bloodied mess on the floor. McAndrew and Cummiskey radioed for help. They called the local doctor and then rang the station for back-up.

When they got back to the sitting room, Catherine Nevin knew from McAndrew's face that something was wrong. She asked if she could see Tom. 'No,' the gardaí advised.

A local GP, Dr Nick Buggle, arrived at Jack White's at 5 a.m. He was taken to the kitchen where he carried out a cursory examination of the body. Buggle pronounced him dead at 5.05 a.m. The State Pathologist, John Harbison, was sent for.

Dr Buggle went into the sitting room where Catherine Nevin was lying on the couch. She was shaking and tearful and she complained of a pain in her shoulder. When Buggle examined her he noted that there were no red marks on her neck where the nylon stocking had been tied.

There were no marks on her ankles either but he did notice red ligature marks on the back of both her wrists where they had been bound with the yellow braids. He saw that her right shoulder was tender but she could move her arm. The doctor advised her to go to the hospital. 'No,' she said, 'I want to stay here.'

While Dr Nick Buggle was examining Catherine Nevin, Superintendent Pat Flynn arrived with Detectives Joe Collins and Jim McCawl. By now the stillness of the March night had been shattered: people were starting to arrive, cars were pulling up and the ambulance was speeding towards Jack White's.

The pace of activity around the pub was quickening.

By this time, Catherine Nevin was almost incoherent but she steadied herself sufficiently to be able to give the gardaí some details of the events of the previous hours. The interview with the new widow was taken down in note form at 5.40 a.m.:

'Dominic left the same time as the bus, twelve o'clock. (I) did the cash and went to bed at twelve-thirty.' She saw the raiders, there were two of them, but they were masked.

One raider 'put a pillow over my head, one man had a knife . . . had something wool on his head and face . . . was looking for jewellery. Someone shouted and I heard a noise like saucepans falling. There was another fellow throwing things around. He tied my hands and put something on my mouth and feet . . . the man in the bedroom had a knife, he said, "Where's the fucking jewellery?"'

Still shivering, Catherine told Collins how she got free and came downstairs to press the panic button. Close to tears she asked: 'Where's Tom? Tom's mother is very old; I want to see him, is he really dead? Tom did the lodgment . . . busy weekend; the amount is in the books. Is the money taken? He kept saying where is the jewellery. I told him it was in the press. I don't know if he took it all . . . We have a gun, Tom had hid it in the store . . . two cars drove off. He told me he was going to kill me . . . he tied me up so quick. I heard somebody else throwing everything around in the bedroom, but I didn't see anybody except the fellow who tied me up.'

She was now babbling breathlessly: 'I thought he was going to kill me. He woke me up out of my sleep. He seemed big, aggressive. I don't know how long I was asleep when he woke me up. He put something into my back. I just saw a blade, a small blade. He never looked for money – about £400 in my handbag. All the cheques were in the safe. I want to see Tom before I go to hospital, I want to talk to him. Did you see him? Did he suffer?'

The newly bereaved woman never did go to hospital. Despite pleas from her family and the gardaí – they argued strongly against her staying as the pub was now a crime scene – she refused to leave Jack White's. The first time she left was on 21 March, the day her husband's body was removed from the morgue at Wicklow Hospital to the old stone church at Brittas Bay a few miles up the road.

News of the murder was carried on RTE's 8 a.m. news bulletin. It was from this, and not from the gardaí, that the Nevin family heard Tom had been murdered:

'We heard it on the radio,' said Mary Nevin, Patsy's wife. 'Sean heard it at eight o'clock. It said a pub in Wicklow and a black Omega car, and sure, Tom had a black Omega car and we said, "Could there be another person with an Omega car"? I rang Arklow garda station that time, and told who I was, and they told me Tom was dead and his wife was tied up. And I went out to tell Patsy out in the milking parlour and I came back in and I rang again, just in case I was hearing things, and the same guard answered again.'

Catherine Nevin had given the gardaí Margaret's number in Craughwell, but as there is no garda station there, official notification took longer than it should have. 'That was the way my mother heard it as well,' Margaret recalls, 'she heard it on the radio. She saw Mary (Glennon) crying when she came in, and she said to me, "Mary, what happened up in Jack White's?"'

At 9.15 a.m., Assistant Commissioner Jim McHugh arrived at the scene. McHugh is now Commissioner of Dublin Metropolitan Area but in 1996 he was in charge of the Kilkenny region. It is highly unusual for an assistant commissioner to become involved that early on in what seemed like a botched robbery. It is clear that from the time news of the murder broke, the gardaí were keeping an eye on this at a very high level.

At 11 a.m., RTE's Pat Kenny had a reporter live outside Jack White's. Tom's family still did not know for sure what had occurred. 'Nobody had officially told us yet,' said Patsy Nevin. 'We thought that was very poor, now.'

By now, Jack White's was the scene of frenetic activity. John Harbison had come and gone, but detectives, ballistics, forensics, and police photographers were now crawling over every inch of the pub. Relatives and friends of the dead man and the staff of Jack White's were arriving shocked and ashen-faced to pay their respects to the grieving widow. Catherine Nevin was busy writing out a verse that would be used on his memorial card. When her step-aunt, Patricia Flood, arrived at the pub, she saw the verse propped up on the mantlepiece. Catherine was still complaining about the pain in her shoulder but still she refused to go to hospital.

At 2 a.m., she rang Willie Nevin, another of Tom's brothers. She told him she knew nothing about funeral arrangements. He offered to take care of everything: the family wanted Tom brought home to Tynagh. She agreed.

Catherine was in the front room when Tom's family arrived the next morning. She had changed her mind about Tom going home to Galway: 'I'm not letting anybody take Tom away now,' she informed them. She wanted him buried in Wicklow and she wanted it all over in the one day, Thursday. Willie Nevin protested that they would prefer to have the funeral over two days, 'like everyone else'. 'Oh, Tom is not going to stay in a cold church overnight,' she replied.

It struck some of those who were there that day that Catherine Nevin was curiously detached from the horrors visited upon her and her husband in the early hours of that morning. She regaled mourners with the gory details while playing the part of the grieving widow but there was a slight crack in her performance. 'She was a little too calm; there were tears all right, but she didn't appear heartbroken to me,' said a close family relative on her side. 'She was playing the drama queen.'

Catherine Nevin may have overplayed the part. She refused to clean up the pool of blood on the kitchen floor where her husband had lain hours before. When she was eventually exhorted to clean it up, the newly widowed woman knelt down, rubbed the stain with a face cloth and brushed the blood across her face. It was a macabre act, eerily reminiscent of Lady Macbeth's threat to gild her grooms' faces with the blood of the murder victim.

In the middle of the chaos, Catherine remembered that she should ring her old friend, Cathal Goulding.

Around midday, detectives said they wanted to interview her for a second time. This interview took place at 12.55 p.m. It was informal, but it lasted until 3.25 p.m. She would later say that she refused to make a statement at this time, on the basis that any statement handed in to Arklow garda station would be 'doctored'.

But she did talk, this time, to Detective Sergeant Fergus O'Brien, who had joined Joe Collins. At the outset she gave them a list of people who were on the premises up to closing time. She said the staff had left on the bus at 12.10 a.m. and that Tom Nevin had given someone a lift at the same time.

At this juncture, Catherine Nevin began waving the finger of guilt at other people. She mentioned that the man convicted of robbing the former owners of the pub was now out of jail. He was going to rob the place again, and Tom knew this, she volunteered. Then there were the tenants that Tom had evicted from the Dublin flats; the sacking of an employee by Tom; then there were two young men who had called to the pub and about whom she was suspicious. She was very specific about these two, describing them as 'slightly cultured knackers'. Catherine Nevin was now throwing around the names of possible suspects like snuff at a wake. If that wasn't enough for the gardaí to be going on with, there was the time that Tom Nevin thought somebody high on drugs was following him, she remembered. The gardaí would check all these people and rule them out as possible suspects.

At 2.10 p.m., the hearse arrived to take the body to the morgue at Wicklow Hospital where John Harbison was on his way to perform the autopsy. It began at around 6 p.m. and con-tinued late into the evening, ending at approximately 10.30 p.m.

An incident room had been set up in Arklow garda station that morning and a murder investigation, led by Superintendent Pat Flynn of Gorey, was now underway. All news bulletins were carrying appeals for information and the registration number of Tom Nevin's missing Opel Omega was circulated to garda stations countrywide.

At 5 p.m. on the day of the murder, Eamonn Cosgrave was taking his usual evening stroll along Grand Parade in Dublin. His route takes him from his home at Dartmouth Square along the Grand Canal near Leeson Street Bridge. He was strolling along listening to the 5 p.m. news bulletin on his Walkman – giving details about the murder of Tom Nevin and details of the missing car. As he reached Dartmouth Square he saw a black Opel Omega. The registration number, 92D 27918, matched the number he'd just heard on the radio. He went straight to Harcourt Street garda station and reported it. Two gardaí went back with Cosgrave to check out the car. It was Tom Nevin's.

The gardaí arranged for its removal to the garda compound at St John's Road where it was checked in at 6.30 p.m. The first piece of potential evidence was now being examined for finger-prints and other clues to the killer. None were found, and there was still a long way to go.

Jack White's was protected by D.J. Alarms, Lucan, Co. Dublin. The alarm system had a 'panic' circuit linked directly to a 24-hour monitoring station run by C.P. Bell in Killester in Dublin. Activating any of the five push buttons fitted at various locations, including in the kitchen where Tom Nevin had lain, could trigger this panic alarm. There were also two mobile panic buttons designed to activate the panic alarm, one hidden on a ledge behind the bedroom curtains in Catherine Nevin's room;

the second in the octagonal table in the same room. Of the six fixed units, one was on the frame of the front door, three feet six inches above floor level. This is the one she pressed.

The day after the murder, Alan Fitzsimons, a service engineer with D.J. Alarms, arrived at the pub to examine the alarm system. He found it was working perfectly.

That same day, 20 March, Detectives Collins and O'Brien arrived for a third interview with Catherine Nevin. This time she made a lengthy witness statement and was able to provide meticulous details of events in the hours before and after her husband's murder.

Catherine Nevin's countdown to the murder began just before midnight on the 19th. At closing time there were only about ten customers in the bar, watching television and playing darts. Liz Hudson was upstairs changing her clothes; the staff were off to the disco in Arklow. Bernie Fleming, Jessica Hunter, Catherine McGraynor had gone upstairs ahead of her. At 12 midnight, Jessica, Catherine, Bernie and her boyfriend, Jim Fagan, went outside to wait for a taxi.

It was now 12.05 a.m. and everyone was getting ready to leave the bar. Nevin knew that was the time because a film had just ended on television. Liz Hudson went to the phone and rang the taxi company to check that a cab was on its way. Dominic McElligott was still in the lounge, chatting to Catherine. When the tax arrived Liz Hudson waved goodbye and hopped in with the others. Tom Nevin locked the bar and took the keys with him as he got ready to drive a few customers home. Tom, the bus, and the taxi, were all leaving at the same time. Everyone disappeared together into the rainy night. It was now about 12.10 a.m.

Tom Nevin wasn't long driving Johnny Brennan and Frankie Whelan home. He returned about ten minutes later and hung up the keys in the bar. His routine at lock up time was that he would lock up the lounge first, then check the bar, the ladies and gents toilets and put out the lights. He'd then check the windows to make sure they were locked (they were not alarmed), before walking through the bar and pulling the bar door shut.

'Are the trays done?' he asked his wife that night. She heard the ring of the till as Tom did a read. 'I'm going to bed and I'm letting Dominic out,' she told him. 'I won't be long after you, I'm going to Dublin early tomorrow,' he called after her. They were probably the last words Tom Nevin ever spoke.

Catherine told Collins and O'Brien that she spoke to Dominic McElligott for a few moments and she walked with him to the hallway of the private quarters where he let himself out the hall door.

In her statement she said: 'I closed the door after him, it latched closed. I then went to bed. As far as I was aware there was nobody else on the premises at that stage. Liz Hudson would have locked the sheds, the beer store, the outside gates, the back door and bolted it. Before Tom would go to prepare the lodgment he would check to see if the beer store was locked and to see if the back door was bolted.'

She went to bed about 12.30 a.m. 'I was asleep almost immediately. I had brought up the drink I was having with Dominic, it was Scotch and a splash of Seven-Up. I know I didn't finish it.'

She had taken a sleeping tablet, as she did every night. 'I was wrecked . . . the next thing I knew was I was awakened by someone pressing my face into the pillow . . . the bedroom light was off. It was a man, he was shouting, "Fucking jewellery, fucking kill ya." He repeated that several times. To me he was very big. He was wearing something woolly over his face. He wore gloves. They were dark and cold. It wasn't wool or cloth. He had a knife.'

Catherine Nevin's version of events was that she was held down by his right hand and the knife was in his left hand. She pointed to where the jewellery was and when he took his hand away she saw the knife:

'It was a long knife. I just saw a flicker, a reflection. I know it was a long knife . . . everything in the room was coming down around. It was being ripped apart by someone else in the room. The first person was tying me up at this stage. He tied my wrists first, then my ankles . . . I could feel my shoulders being dragged. He tied my ankles to my wrists. While this man was tying me up I heard a noise downstairs like a saucepan dropping on the floor. I heard a shout from downstairs . . . I have no idea what was said. I don't know how long after going to sleep this happened. I know I felt dopey when I wakened up.'

When Garda Paul Cummiskey had gone up to her bedroom to get the quilt, minutes before he discovered the body, he noticed a newspaper open on the bed and the pillows neatly propped up as if someone had been reading. If Catherine Nevin's face had been pressed into the pillows the way she claimed, it would have left an indent, or, at the very least the pillows would have been disturbed. The bedclothes were pulled back on one side only and the glass of Scotch was still standing upright on the floor, inches from the bed and next to a pair of her pink bedroom slippers. None of this is consistent with Catherine Nevin's account of a violent struggle and two intruders, one of whom was pulling the room apart.

Her bedroom is a large room that was always extremely untidy. It had dated, pink floral curtains, pink floral wallpaper and row upon row of clothes and shoe racks. A large brown suitcase was on the middle of floor that night and three drawers were removed from a cabinet; two were sitting neatly on the floor with some of the contents disturbed. The third drawer was resting at an angle on top of the other drawers and some of the clothes had slid out onto the salmon-coloured carpet.

The gardaí noted that her description of the knife used by her assailant changed from a 'short blade' to 'a long knife' in the course of the interviews. By now alarm bells were starting to ring, but Catherine Nevin continued telling her story to Joe Collins and Fergus O'Brien.

When the intruders finished tying her up, they left her on the bed, she said. 'I didn't hear them leaving the bedroom, I didn't hear a door opening . . . It didn't seem like a long time they were in the room, to me it was an eternity but I know it wasn't long . . . the next thing I heard were two motors starting up. One started up before the other. I have no recollection of them moving away.

'The person who was shouting at me spoke in what I would say was a country accent. It wasn't Cork or something like that. It was a flat country accent and the man was nervous, I sensed that. It seemed to me an hour before I got my ankles free. I didn't think of Tom. It didn't enter my mind at that stage. Tom had his own bedroom in the old part of the house. He wouldn't have been in the same room as myself. My hands had been tied crossing each other. I was trying to straighten my hands to get them moving, but as I did this they got tighter, they were very sore. My hands had been tied behind my back.'

After she managed to free her ankles Catherine Nevin got out of the bed. 'I felt as if I had no legs. I have no recollection of coming down the stairs but when I got down, the first thing I noticed was the door wasn't closed fully. The Yale lock was in its normal position, but the door wasn't fully closed. I still had my hands tied. I turned my back to try and prise it open with my fingers. It was spilling rain. I had intended to try and stop a car if

Tom Nevin behind the bar in Jack White's Inn ROBERT MULLAN

Tom Nevin's confirmation. Tom is at the far left in the second row

Tom and Catherine on their wedding day

Cathal Goulding DEREK SPEIRS

*Catherine Nevin as a young married woman, in a photograph
taken for her modelling school*

Tom Nevin with Jack White's Inn in the background ROBERT MULLAN

Tom photographed with customers in Jack White's ROBERT MULLAN

Inspector Tom Kennedy ROBERT MULLAN

Tom Nevin, photographed shortly before his death ROBERT MULLAN

Judge Ó Buachalla and Andy Cullen, retired court clerk,
Wexford District Court

Tom Kennedy's retirement party in the Grand Hotel, Wicklow.
A second party was held in Jack White's Inn ROBERT MULLAN

The kitchen where Tom Nevin met his death

The funeral ROBERT MULLAN

Catherine Nevin following her husband's coffin ROBERT MULLAN

The hearse ROBERT MULLAN

Tom Nevin's coffin ROBERT MULLAN

AN CHUIRT DUICHE   THE DISTRICT COURT

DISTRICT COURT   DISTRICT NO. 23
AREA OF ARKLOW

THE LICENSING ACTS 1833 TO 1988

Re; Licensed Premises at Ballinapark, Kilbride,
     Wicklow

I, being the Licensing judge for the Court Area and District
above-mentioned in which the above premises are situate and which
said premises in the immediately preceeding year had attached to
it a Spirit Retailers On-Licence (commonly called a Publican's
Licence (Ordinary) in the joint name of **Thomas Nevin** who died on
the 19th day of March, 1996 (the Deceased Joint Licencee) and
Catherine Nevin (the Surviving Joint Licencee) AND both of whom
had already obtained from this Court a Certificate by way of
Confirmation of Transfer to them of the said Licence AND the
renewal of the said Licence not being affected by any of the
circumstances detailed in Section 4 (5) of the Courts (No. 2)
Act, 1986 CERTIFY that the said **Catherine Nevin** of Jack White's
Inn, Brittas Bay, situate in the Townland of Ballynapark
(otherwise Ballinapark) Barony of Arklow and County of Wicklow is
entitled (subject as hereunder mentioned) to receive from and
have issued to her by the Collector, Customs and Excise,
Waterford for and on behalf of The Revenue Commissioners a Spirit
Retailers On-Licence (commonly called a Publican's Licence
(Ordinary) in her sole name in respect of the premises at
Ballinapark, Kilbride, Wicklow for the year ending 30th
September, 1997 and accordingly I ORDER the said Collector of
Customs and Excise, Waterford, for an on behalf of the Revenue
Commissioners to grant the renewal of the said Licence in the
sole name of the said **Catherine Nevin** and to issue the said
Licence to the said **Catherine Nevin** subject to production of Tax
Clearance Certificate provided for by and the payment of the
excise duty payable under the provisions of the Finance Act,
1992.

                 Dated this 29th day of September, 1997.

         Signed; _____
                       (Judge of the District Court   )

*A copy of the court order made by Judge Ó Buachalla transferring the
licence for Jack White's into Catherine Nevin's name ROBERT MULLAN*

Tom Nevin's grave ROBERT MULLAN

I got onto the road. I was unable to get the door open. I then went to the panic button which is beside the front door. I kept pressing it. The guards arrived very quick.'

The reason she came to the front door, she said, was because she 'just wanted to get away. I wanted to run. The guards cut my hands free and went to look for Tom. One of them, I think it was Martin McAndrew, went upstairs. A short time later he told me Tom was down in the pub.'

She told Collins and O'Brien that some time after gardaí Cummiskey and McAndrew arrived at the pub she asked them the time. They told her it was 5 a.m. Dr Buggle was there at that time. 'The doctor told me he'd be honest with me. He told me that Tom was dead, that he had a knife wound. I was later told that Tom had been shot. This surprised me, as I did not hear a shot or the noise of the shot. I am familiar with shotgun noise.'

Nevin's interview with Joe Collins and Fergus O'Brien was broken intermittently by offers of cups of coffee. Friends, relatives and neighbours were still arriving at Jack White's. The funeral arrangements had to be made and there was a myriad other practicalities to attend to. One of them entailed buying a new suit in which to bury the murdered man. Two gardaí offered their help in organising the suit. But Catherine Nevin wouldn't accept any help from the Arklow gardaí. She arranged for someone else to do it.

At this stage, 20 March, the autopsy had been completed and Tom Nevin's body was lying in the morgue at Wicklow Hospital awaiting burial.

The funeral itself was a huge affair; members of the gardaí stood shoulder to shoulder with mourners paying last respects to the 'gentle giant'. A large press corps turned up; this was a murder that, from day one, engendered huge publicity. A sombre

Catherine Nevin carried a single red rose up to her face as she walked behind her husband's coffin as it was carried shoulder-high by his brothers into the stone church at Brittas Bay.

The cortège made its way to the cemetery near Barndarrig, an old burial ground at the top of a winding road. It is an idyllic, peaceful location, overlooking the surrounding countryside. As the cortège was winding its way up the lane, a loud wail went up. Catherine Nevin had spotted a photographer from *The Star* standing in the bushes at a tiny cross in the road with a long-lens camera. 'What are you doing here,' she cried, 'my husband has been murdered.' Another photographer who was there on the day described her verbal assault on the *Star* photographer as savage. 'She kept shouting, "My husband has been murdered," at him. I was standing a good bit away at the time but you could hear her all over the place. It was desperate.'

8

'YOU HAVE THE RIGHT
TO REMAIN SILENT'

⁂

Thursday, 9 April 1996. An entry in Catherine Nevin's diary reads:

> 'Went from the sitting room to the lounge of my premises
> with my insurance agent at 3.05 p.m. I was approached by
> a female who produced an identification card and intro-
> duced herself as Veronica Guerin. She asked for an inter-
> view. I told her that she had some cheek to come into my
> premises after doing a scandalous and scurrilous character
> assassination against me, my family and my business. I
> informed her that I would see her in court with my legal
> team. I said that I would prefer to work as a prostitute than
> do what she did for a living. I ordered her to leave my
> premises and never to return.
>
> 'When leaving the premises she jeered at me and gave
> me a two fingers sign. She left in a red car, 94KE 2645.'

Catherine Nevin had never liked the press and the press, it seems,
had never liked Catherine Nevin. Shortly after Tom Nevin was
murdered, crime reporter Veronica Guerin wrote an article in the

Sunday Independent about the killing and the murder investigation. It didn't exactly show Catherine Nevin in a glowing light. Rumours had already begun to circulate around the Arklow area that she may have had some involvement in her husband's murder. Now things were appearing in print. Catherine was incensed.

Shortly after the encounter in Jack White's, Veronica penned another article. In it she told how Catherine Nevin had shooed her off the premises with threats of legal action ringing in her ears. Two months later, Veronica Guerin would be shot dead by a drugs gang as she sat in her red Calibra at the traffic lights on the Naas Road.

The month after Tom Nevin's murder was a busy one for his widow. The 'month's mind', a traditional Catholic service for the dead, was held in Tynagh that April. Catherine Nevin and Tom Kennedy drove down in a black Mercedes. A friend of theirs, Mervyn Sutherland from Kilpatrick in Wicklow, drove the car. She sat in the front passenger seat and Kennedy sat in the back. He got out and had a look round the yard before he went into Patsy Nevin's house. Superintendent Bill Ryan arrived separately. The family weren't surprised to see him there, because he knew Tom Nevin, and had served in the Loughrea area, close by.

The month's mind was held on a Wednesday night. That Saturday, Catherine Nevin held a separate one in Jack White's. The Nevin family travelled down from Galway.

That evening, they dropped in to the garda station in Arklow to check on how the investigation was getting along. Catherine Nevin rang the garda station to see if they were there. When eventually they got back to the pub, one of the first people they saw there was Tom Kennedy. He was sitting in the corner of the lounge with Ms M (a trial witness who cannot be named for legal reasons) and Ms M's mother and father.

Jack White's was packed with relatives, local people and friends of the dead man. Judge Donnchadh Ó Buachalla was there with his wife, Therese, and his youngest child, a daughter. Catherine Nevin introduced the judge to Tom Nevin's step-aunt, Patricia Flood. When she came to introduce his daughter, she informed Flood that the youngster 'was into ponies, she is very good with ponies'. Flood saw Therese Ó Buachalla from a distance. The judge's wife, a slim, attractive woman with short blonde hair, was chatting away to some of the other guests. When it was time for the Ó Buachallas to leave, Catherine turned to the judge and said she had a salmon for him. She went to the kitchen and gave him a whole salmon to take home.

It is a truism that most people in Wicklow don't have many kind words to say about Catherine Nevin. On rare occasions when they do, they say she was a generous enough woman. Whenever there was a death in the locality, Catherine Nevin would be among the first to help. She'd invite the funeral party back for 'soup and sandwiches' but when they arrived they would find a full meal prepared for them, free of charge.

Janice Breen, who worked at the hair salon at Jack White's two days a week, recalls the kindness Catherine Nevin showed to her during a family bereavement:

'When my father died she organised all the food, she wouldn't take any money for it. She kept asking if there was anything else she could do or anything we needed.' Janice Breen is one of the few people who liked her former employer. 'I got on all right with her. I got on all right with Tom as well, he was an easy-going man. And I knew Mr Kennedy. I used to cut Mr Kennedy's hair when he was there, he was always very nice to me.'

Breen said the Catherine Nevin the country knew from the trial was not the woman she knew. She questioned some reporters who said they had spoken to hundreds of people and found not one who had a good word to say about her. 'Well, I had. I would have, if I'd been asked.'

There is another hairdresser who would have had positive things to say about Catherine Nevin but Nevin herself prevented her from doing so. Noeleen Hynes-Gorman, a stylist in Peter Mark in Crumlin, was a friend of Catherine's for more than 20 years. She agreed to be interviewed for this book with one proviso: Catherine Nevin had to give the go-ahead – Ms Hynes-Gorman insisted on this out of loyalty to the jailed woman. Nevin, through her solicitor, Garrett Sheehan, said 'no'.

'That was one thing about Catherine,' Liz Hudson said. 'She could be very generous. When Cecil's father died she took care of all the food, nothing was too much trouble for her.' Cecil Hudson is Liz's husband. 'And when my daughter was having her baby, she went out and bought loads of baby clothes for her, and she bought her a baby walker, she was very good like that.'

On 12 April, three days after Veronica Guerin's visit and the entry in the diary, Catherine Nevin was in the sitting room at Jack White's when two other visitors pulled up in a car, Detective Sergeant Fergus O'Brien and Detective Garda Joe Collins. They exchanged pleasantries for a few moments before the detectives began asking questions relating to the murder inquiry. In the course of the conversation, Catherine stood up to leave the room for a few minutes. On the coffee table in front of the detectives was a diary, a little wine coloured one with pages for telephone numbers and addresses. It was open at a certain page.

During her absence from the room, the two detectives took a peek at the diary. They saw the name 'Heapes' written down beside a Dublin telephone number. The name rang a bell with the two detectives and they jotted down the number.

'It's been said that we suspected her from day one, we didn't,' said a garda source. 'But after finding that name in the diary, it was decided to look further at the possibility that she was involved.' On 18 May, Superintendent Pat Flynn issued a search warrant under Section 29 of the Offences Against the State Act. This section is activated where there is 'reasonable suspicion' that evidence, or 'sufficient material' is to be found on the premises for which the warrant is sought. That warrant was to lead to the first breakthrough in the investigation. Hard information on the person – or persons – who did the actual killing would continue to elude the gardaí.

When the search party arrived at the pub on the same day, Catherine Nevin was there. Her antipathy to the Arklow-based gardaí was well known; she was now openly hostile when Garda Brian Duffy and other gardaí landed on her doorstep armed with a warrant to search the premises. Once inside, they conducted an exhaustive search of the house and pub and seized an array of documents. Among them were her diary and bits and pieces of paper with a car registration number and telephone numbers on them. When they were leaving, the gardaí asked if she had any complaints. 'No,' she replied.

Back at the station, Joe Collins and Fergus O'Brien had a look at the diary. It was the same one they had seen on Catherine Nevin's coffee table on 12 April. Inexplicably – it later transpired in court – among the scores of names and addresses in it was the name and number, 'Pat McCartan,' of Smithfield, Dublin. It was the registered office of the former solicitor Pat McCartan, now a circuit court judge, who lived in Wicklow. Judge McCartan told these authors he has 'absolutely no idea' why his name should be in that book. 'I have never met or heard from that woman in my life,' he says.

Now they had the diary in their possession, Collins and O'Brien were able to examine the little wine-coloured book in more detail. But this time they saw that the name 'Heapes', which had been clearly written in on 12 April, had been scribbled over back and front. To Collins and O'Brien it looked as if an effort had been made to erase the name. However, tests established the name as Gerry Heapes, the former IRA man from Finglas. The telephone number beside his name belonged to William Adams, Heapes's former employer.

18 May was to prove a crucial date in the investigation, as decisive as the murder date itself. What gardaí came up with that day was the investigative equivalent of gold.

An old phone number was jotted down on one of the scraps of paper found in Catherine Nevin's bedroom. The number pre-dated the seven-digit era, suggesting that it had been written down in the mid 1990s or before. When they ran a check, the gardaí traced the number to John Jones, the Finglas republican who ran the TV shop Channel Vision with Dessie Ellis. It was his home number at his address in Balbriggan, Co. Dublin.

Other, more recent documentation led them to Pat Russell, alias the mysterious John Ferguson, the source of the clandestine calls to Catherine Nevin.

The other vital discovery made on 18 May was the note of a car registration number DIL 5206. This led them to Catherine Nevin's old lover, Willie McClean. The question now was what was the link between the four men, three republicans and a small-time criminal? The investigation team decided to round the four men up.

First on the list was John Jones. Jones, Heapes and Willie McClean had been solicited by Catherine Nevin to kill her husband, and Patrick Russell, while not solicited himself, was aware of it. When they learned of the murder, it must have struck all four that there was at least a reasonable chance that she was behind it. Not one of them volunteered information to the gardaí: the gardaí had to come to them.

Jones was later to admit that it was 'perfectly obvious she had done it'. Still he didn't go to the police. Instead, he contacted Pat Russell. Russell was one of the two republicans Jones told about Catherine Nevin's efforts to get the IRA to kill her husband. And it was to Russell that he turned when Tom Nevin turned up dead.

Two days after the murder Jones went to Russell's office at 11 Merrion Square. 'If the guards want me, they'll find me,' he told Russell. They did. In 1996, John Jones was working for Crossan Transport at Dublin Airport as his television business had failed. It took a couple of phonecalls and two trips to Jones's new place of work before the republican agreed to co-operate with the murder investigation. On 16 July, Jones was interviewed by Garda Joe Sullivan and Detective Gerry McKenna. He told them that Catherine Nevin had approached him in 1989. She had asked him if the IRA would be interested in staging a robbery and killing Tom in the course of it. She mentioned a fee.

In a second statement on 28 July, Jones gave detectives further details of his contact with Catherine Nevin between 1989 and 1990. She told him she 'had to put up with the effects of Tom's drinking after closing time', implying that Tom abused her when he was drunk. She also mentioned her big plans for the pub. Jones told detectives that it was apparent to him that she wanted her husband dead so she could take full control of the business.

In his statement Jones said: 'I can recall an occasion either before or after the initial proposition . . . she had bandages on both wrists and she had a black eye which she shielded with sunglasses.' Detectives now had something to go on. The next step was to get Catherine Nevin's hospital records. If they matched the dates in question, it would provide some corroboration of John Jones's account.

The next in line was Patrick Russell. On 26 July 1996, detectives raided his Merrion Square office. After searching the offices, they arrested Russell under Section 30 of the Offences Against the State Act and took him to Enniscorthy garda station. He was held for 48 hours. It was put to him that he was the mystery man John Ferguson. Initially he denied it but then he came clean. He told detectives that his contact with Catherine Nevin had been solely business-related. He gave the name John Ferguson at her request, he said.

During the course of several interviews with Detectives John Melody and John Fitzpatrick, Russell admitted that John Jones had told him about Catherine Nevin's efforts to get the IRA to murder her husband. He said he wasn't aware of the full details of the approach, but the organisation with which he was then involved wouldn't sanction the killing. He would not name the person who was approached but he implied that this person and John Jones were one and the same. Russell was released without charge at 10.21 a.m. on 28 July.

Gerry Heapes was next on the list. Detectives swooped on Heapes's home at Harristown Lane, St Margaret's, north Dublin, in a dawn raid on 28 July 1996 – three hours before Patrick Russell was released from custody. They put the family in a bedroom while they turned the rest of the house upside down. They found nothing incriminating. At 7.50 a.m. the same morning,

Detective Sergeant Fergus O'Brien arrested Gerry Heapes under Section 30 of the Offences Against the State Act and he was driven to Enniscorthy garda station for questioning.

Gerry Heapes had no intention of making a statement. He wouldn't co-operate at all, but back then, republicans never co-operated with gardaí in any shape or form. His wife pleaded with him – if he knew anything at all, tell them, she warned him. Breda Heapes had played this scene at the time of the cash and carry robbery in 1977. She wasn't about to do so again. 'She said she did not want any more of this,' Heapes would later tell the jury at the trial.

During questioning, Gerry Heapes told detectives how and when he met Catherine Nevin, how he came to be involved with her and the relationship that subsequently developed. He was released from custody without charge on 30 July.

The following day, with his wife's threats ringing in his ears, Gerry Heapes returned to Enniscorthy and spoke to Detective Garda Pat Mulcahy. He now wished to make a statement. This time he was a bit more specific. Catherine Nevin had told him she was having trouble with Tom and he was 'making life hell for her'. Then she asked Heapes to get rid of him. She wanted him shot dead. They discussed money – ten grand up front and the pub takings of £25,000. Heapes said he told Nevin to leave it for a few weeks 'until he could time Tom on his runs'.

Gerry Heapes made a statement, but he refused to sign it. 'I'll have to get clearance from my people first,' he said. Detectives took it that he was going to discuss it with Sinn Féin/IRA personnel in Dublin and he'd be back if and when he got 'clearance'. On 3 August Heapes came back. He still refused to sign the statement but he offered to give the gardaí a guided tour of all the locations where Catherine Nevin suggested to him that her husband could be shot.

He took Detective Pat Mulcahy to the Grasshopper Inn (where Tom was supposed to die in her arms), the meat factory in Clonee, the flats on the South Circular Road and the Phoenix Park. All places, apart from the Wellington Monument in the Phoenix Park, were locations on Tom Nevin's weekly route. Heapes could not possibly have known this unless someone had pointed them out to him.

Things were now beginning to fall into place.

There was one more man to go – Willie McClean. The car registration number found in the search of 18 May was traced to a car owned by a woman named Anne-Marie Connolly. Connolly was driving to work one day when she noticed a car following her. She didn't know that there were detectives in the car. Anne-Marie Connolly is now married to Willie McClean. Shortly after they put the tail on the car, the guards found Willie McClean. On 3 August, he was interviewed by Sergeants Joe O'Hara and Brian Duffy. McClean didn't beat around the bush. Yes, he knew the Nevins, yes, he had had an affair with Catherine Nevin. And yes, she had asked him to kill her husband. Why she had kept a record of his car registration number was never explained. McClean is a different kettle of fish to the other two in that he has no republican connections, but that apart, his story was remarkably similar to that of Jones and Heapes.

In his statement McClean said: 'She rang me from St Vincent's Hospital, it was about evening time . . . she was in a private room.' Here was another trail for the gardaí to follow. If it checked out that Catherine Nevin was in a private room on a date approximate to the one Willie McClean had given them, it would help to corroborate his story.

Gardaí had a major problem with the three men – their credibility as potential State witnesses. The three had criminal convictions of one sort or another and their backgrounds were, to say the least, murky. It was highly probable that any jury would look upon them as unsavoury characters. Corroboration was going to be vital if their evidence was to have any chance of getting past a jury. If the hospital records checked out, it would help.

All in all it was going okay. McClean's story was another piece in the jigsaw.

Catherine Nevin was now the prime suspect in her husband's murder. Superintendent Pat Flynn and the rest of investigation team felt that by this stage they had sufficient evidence, at least on the soliciting, to arrest her for questioning. The decision was made: 'Bring her in.'

On 27 July 1996, Catherine Nevin was out walking in the evening sun on the roadside near Jack White's when a patrol car pulled up alongside her. It was 8.20 p.m. Garda Joe O'Hara got out of the car and said he was arresting her on suspicion of possession of information relating to firearms offences at Ballinapark, Arklow on 19 March 1996. Like Heapes and Russell, it was a Section 30 arrest. The garda read her her legal rights. She nodded that she understood what she was being arrested for.

She arrived at Enniscorthy garda station 50 minutes later. She refused to sign the custody records acknowledging that she understood the caution and had the right to remain silent.

The first of the interview sessions started at 9.20 p.m. It ended at four minutes to midnight. In all that time Catherine Nevin hadn't uttered a single word. The following morning a second interview began. Nevin sat staring at the wall, ignoring the questions.

Her sister, Betty White, arrived at the station half-way through the second interview and was allowed in to see her. That interview concluded at lunchtime, again without Catherine Nevin saying a word.

At 3.36 p.m., they began again. This time, Detectives Joe McElligott and Bernie Hanley came into the room. Almost two hours elapsed and still she had not opened her mouth.

Another session followed, again with no response from the prisoner. During the last of the interviews that night, Catherine Nevin was fingerprinted and photographed by Detective Garda Jim McCawl. She remained silent throughout. When asked to sign notes on the questions that had been put to her she shook her head as if to say, 'no'.

This interview ended just after 10 p.m. Catherine Nevin had another visitor – Garrett Sheehan, the solicitor who would represent her at the trial. He was ushered into a room in the garda station. At the end of the consultation, Catherine Nevin handed two prepared statements to the gardaí. In her first, she said she had been continually questioned about the murder of her husband Tom and had nothing left to say. She was referring to the statements she had made in Jack White's on 19 and 20 March immediately after the murder. It was in the second statement that she dropped the bombshell. She alleged she had been subjected to serious assault and verbal abuse by the gardaí. It was one minute to midnight when she was brought back to her cell for the night.

Next morning, just after breakfast, the merry-go-round of 'interviews' began again. Joe Collins and Fergus O'Brien walked into the room. They were the two detectives to whom she had given a statement on 20 March and who had later spotted the crucial diary. Unlike previous occasions, there were no pleasantries exchanged this time. When the two put certain questions to her, Nevin ignored them.

It was a pattern that was repeated throughout the day and for the remainder of her time in Enniscorthy garda station. The memos of garda interviews show a litany of 'no replies'. Her behaviour, gardaí would later note, 'was more like that displayed by a terrorist'. But this wasn't a paramilitary-related offence. It was an 'ordinary' domestic murder.

At 4.50 p.m. Catherine Nevin asked for her solicitor. The gardaí rang Sheehan's office but he wasn't there. They left a message with his secretary. They also rang his home number and left a message on his answering machine. At 4.55 p.m. Catherine Nevin alleged she had been assaulted. She did not ask to be examined by a doctor. The assault complaints were investigated by the Garda Complaints Board and would later be found to be without foundation.

That afternoon, Sheehan arrived at Enniscorthy. Another round of interviews followed with different sets of detectives. She still said nothing. At 7.45 p.m. Superintendent Flynn came into the cell. She was being released, he told her. She was free to go. Flynn asked if she had any complaints to make. 'No,' she replied. As she was leaving the station, the gardaí asked her to sign the custody record. 'I'll sign nothing,' she responded frostily.

She walked past them out into the warm summer night.

9

LIES, DAMNED LIES –
THE PERJURY OF
ANTHONY DOYLE

I t was the day before Christmas Eve 1988 and Larry Darcy was
working behind the bar in Jack White's Inn. The pub had
been packed all day with revellers and many of them were still
there late into the evening. As a result, the staff were a bit behind
in finishing up for the night.

At around 1 a.m. an argument broke out between Darcy and
Tom Nevin. It soon turned nasty. Darcy later claimed that Tom
Nevin had punched and kicked him while Catherine egged him
on. The next morning, Darcy went down to Arklow garda station
and reported the assault to Garda Mick Murphy. Larry Darcy was
asked if he wanted to make a statement. He said 'no'.

Instead he took a civil case against the Nevins seeking
damages for assault. Tom and Catherine Nevin denied the assault
charge. It came before Judge Sean Magee at Arklow District
Court on 7 September 1989. When the case was called, a man
named Anthony Doyle swore that it was he, and not Tom Nevin,
who had assaulted Larry Darcy. Doyle claimed he assaulted Darcy

in the pub garden because the barman had barred him from Jack White's. Darcy's case was thrown out. The judge ruled in favour of Tom Nevin.

William Early, the solicitor acting for Darcy appealed the decision to Wicklow Circuit Court.

On 29 April 1991, Larry Darcy, Anthony Doyle and Tom and Catherine Nevin all arrived at the Wicklow courthouse. Catherine Nevin turned up perfectly groomed and in a smart suit. This time there was a different outcome. Judge Smith rejected Anthony Doyle's evidence in its entirety, saying Larry Darcy could not have been assaulted by him, it had to have been Tom Nevin. The judge ordered the publican to pay damages of £2,500 to Larry Darcy, along with legal costs.

Two years later, on 5 February 1993, a local man, James Breen, walked into Arklow garda station with some revealing information. Breen told Detective Garda Jim McCawl he had information that Anthony Doyle had been paid to commit perjury. Jim McCawl relayed the information back to Superintendent Pat Flynn. Flynn ordered an immediate investigation.

A few weeks later, Doyle finally came clean. He made a statement saying that he had been offered money to give false evidence. In return for taking the assault rap for Tom Nevin he was paid £300. The woman who prepared this false evidence was Catherine Nevin.

'She asked me would I say it was me who hit Larry Darcy,' his statement reads. 'I would not agree to do it but she convinced me. She said she would give me £100. I said I would not give false evidence. She then said she would give me £200 and I would not be barred out of the pub, I could drink away.'

On 25 May, McCawl and Inspector Gerry Dillane travelled out to Jack White's to talk to the Nevins about Doyle's admission.

As McCawl and Dillane sat in the lounge waiting for Catherine Nevin, one of the staff put two cups of coffee in front of them. McCawl thought the coffee smelled of whiskey. 'What's this, Irish Coffee?' McCawl asked. The staff said Catherine had instructed them to serve her special coffee.

When she sat down beside them, McCawl asked her about the perjury allegations. 'I discussed that case with no-one, only my husband and my family solicitors,' she said. She then took a piece of paper and scribbled down the name and address of her solicitor and handed it to McCawl: 'I had no conversation with Anthony Doyle about my husband's case. Watch my lips, I had no conversation with Anthony Doyle.'

That September, Catherine Nevin made a statement in which she made several unsubstantiated allegations about both Doyle and Jim McCawl. She apparently found the conduct of the gardaí as a whole 'despictable [sic] and unacceptable to business people'. She was thinking of selling the business as a result. 'Over the years I have given every possible assistance to the gardaí in Arklow . . . I regard this as harassment,' she stated.

McCawl subsequently served a writ for slander seeking circuit court damages against Catherine Nevin. This case has not yet to come to court. A subsequent report on Catherine Nevin's complaints about the manner in which Detective Jim McCawl and other gardaí had handled the investigation into the perjury allegations completely exonerated the gardaí: 'The allegations made against the gardaí in Arklow are not supported by any evidence and do not stand up to investigation,' the report by Superintendent Eamon Coffey concluded.

As for Anthony Doyle, a file on the perjury allegations was sent to the Director of Public Prosecutions. The DPP directed that no criminal charges be brought.

The perjury of Anthony Doyle is significant in the murder investigation in so far as it showed that Catherine Nevin was a woman of questionable character and a manipulator. But bribing someone to take the rap in a minor civil case is not in itself a capital offence. The gardaí needed to broaden the picture.

When they began digging into the suspect's recent past they discovered a few interesting skeletons in her cupboard. They found that Catherine Nevin had received insurance payments for stolen jewellery and other items. The jewellery had not, in fact, been stolen. Also, cash books and lodgment slips for the pub, which were among the items seized in the May 1996 search, proved very revealing.

One cashbook, covering the week 10–16 November 1991 records lodgments of £4,083.26. This was the amount Catherine Nevin claimed had been stolen from her car in the robbery at Dolphin's Barn Bridge. A bank statement from the AIB on Lower Drumcondra Road, for the current account of Tom and Catherine Nevin, shows the lodgment had been made on 18 November. While there was evidence that the fly window of her car had been smashed, the bank documents suggest that she did not have the money in her car as she had claimed to the insurance company.

Tom Kennedy, in an interview with the gardaí after the murder, recalled Catherine brandishing her wedding ring in front of him. 'The ring was stolen and Tom recovered it for me,' she had told Kennedy. This was among the items of jewellery she claimed had been robbed from her bedroom sometime between 2 p.m. and 2 a.m. on 4–5 December 1993.

Gardaí questioned her about this during one of the interviews that took place after Tom Nevin's murder. Her story was interesting. She said her husband had been concerned about the loss of the wedding ring and vowed he would get it back. She added that he was late back from Dublin one day and when she asked him what had kept him, he said he was trawling the pawnbrokers and auction rooms on the quays. Just before Valentine's Day 1996, Tom returned carrying the missing ring – he had found it in one of the flats. 'He said, "That is the one I gave you 20 years ago, wear it now. I said I would get it back for you,"' she told the gardaí. Enquiries at the pawnbrokers revealed that Tom Nevin was never there, nor did they return any item to him in February 1996. Detectives suspected she had concocted the story and that she was attempting to give the impression that she and Tom Nevin were getting along fine.

The stolen jewellery and the missing cash episode were filed under questionable incidents involving Catherine Nevin. But all that it really amounted to was that she was an inveterate liar who was capable of cheating on insurance claims. More was needed.

Hard evidence pinning her to the murder lay in what Gerry Heapes, John Jones and Willie McClean had to tell. It also lay in her own conflicting accounts of what happened in Jack White's in the early hours of the morning of 19 March 1996.

In her story to the first gardaí on the scene – Paul Cummiskey and Martin McAndrew – Catherine Nevin mentioned only one intruder. Later she spoke of two and of hearing noises from down-stairs while they were in her bedroom. She said she was in bed asleep when intruders had broken in so it is reasonable to assume the bedclothes were covering her. How then did the intruder tie her hands behind her back, and then tie her wrists to her ankles without disturbing the bed? How did he tie her legs and arms behind her back as she lay on her right side while he held a knife in his left hand? If she were lying on her right side, she would have seen the outline of the person who was supposedly taking the room apart. Her story was looking increasingly implausible.

If Catherine Nevin's account was true then the two raiders were in her room tying her up – in the dark – while a third person was downstairs. Also in the first interview shortly after the murder, she said there was one man with a small knife who put the pillow over her head. She subsequently changed this to say that he had pushed her head down onto the pillow, yet the pillows were not disturbed.

If, after freeing her legs, she had got out of the bed on the left side to walk around to the phone, how did she manage this in semi-darkness without knocking over the glass of whiskey, the electric wire connecting the electric blanket to the wall socket while also avoiding the newspapers and slippers, none of which were disturbed? Either she was amazingly agile or she was lying. And why did she not call Tom unless she knew he was dead?

In her statement, Catherine Nevin describes how she struggled for more than an hour to free herself. Her efforts to undo the knots would undoubtedly have caused her to twist and turn on the bed given that she was trussed up. Yet Dr Nick Buggle, who examined her on the morning of the murder, found no marks on her legs consistent with her story.

Her refusal to allow gardaí access to her bedroom to conduct tests as to whether the sound of a discharged shotgun could be heard between the bedroom and the kitchen was hardly the action of an innocent person.

At 5 a.m. on the morning of the 19th, Catherine Nevin remarked to Detective Garda Joe Collins that her husband was doing the lodgment in the books when she retired for the night: '. . . busy weekend, amount is in the books, is the money taken?' At that point she was apparently not aware of the circumstances of Tom's death. How then, gardaí wondered, did she know Tom had entered the amount in the books – even if it was normal practice – unless she had been in the kitchen at the time of the shooting or immediately afterwards? At the time of that interview she had no knowledge of what bank books or lodgments were written up.

Her story just wasn't adding up. Later comments by Catherine Nevin to Assistant Garda Commissioner Jim McHugh were damning: the smell of the incense at Tom's funeral Mass was the same smell she had got from the kitchen the night he was murdered, she remarked.

Catherine Nevin had at all times insisted she never went beyond the hallway when she came down the stairs that night. If that were true, she would be unable to make any comparison between the smell of incense and the smell from the kitchen, because the powder used to propel the fatal shot is nitro cellulose which is smokeless and leaves very little smell on discharge. It certainly would not linger very long. In fact when Cummiskey and McAndrew arrived at the scene they found no trace of a smell from a discharged firearm.

Catherine Nevin's remark to Jim McHugh was an unguarded one, but highly significant for the investigation. In the early hours of 4 April 1996, the gardaí test-fired six shotgun cartridges in the kitchen of Jack White's. The six shots left very little smell. They concluded that there was no way Catherine Nevin could have noticed a smell like incense unless she had been around the kitchen at the time of the shooting or immediately afterwards.

There were other inconsistencies in her story, other things that didn't quite add up. She gave conflicting accounts of what time Sergeant Dominic McElligott left the pub on the night of the murder. She told one set of gardaí that McElligott left the same time as the bus taking the staff home. Yet in her written statement she said: 'I let Dominic out. He was last out, Tom drove

Johnny Brennan home and the only person (sic) left was Dominic McElligott and myself.' In yet another account to Liz Hudson after Tom Nevin's funeral, Catherine maintained that she had left Tom and McElligott in the lounge and had gone up to bed. Dominic McElligott denied this. He maintains he has no idea whether Tom Nevin was on or off the premises when McElligott was leaving.

In her written statement, Catherine Nevin said: 'While the man was tying me up I heard a noise downstairs like a saucepan dropping on the floor. I heard a shout downstairs. I thought it came from the hallway near the hall door . . . when they tied me up they left me on the bed.'

What she is implying here is that, having heard the sound of the fatal shot, she heard someone shouting from the hall door. It was after the shot was fired that the raiders left her room, carrying with them the hoard, including her jewellery box and jewellery. Then having gone downstairs and headed for their escape hatch – the hall door – they chose to go back into the pub in the direction of the shooting, despite the warning shout from the other raider.

In her various accounts she made no mention of the portable television that was found dumped on the landing. This was normally kept in her bedroom. It is almost unimaginable that armed raiders looking for cash and jewellery – and who were willing to kill for it – would attempt to steal a cheap portable television worth less than £100. These were the same raiders who made no effort to open a second safe which contained £4,000, neither did they take the float of £240 which was clearly visible in the open tills and they didn't even bother to bend down to take Tom Nevin's wallet containing £410 even though it was staring them in the face.

Catherine Nevin's erratic behaviour on the night of 18 March was now assuming an even greater significance. Why had she been hopping in and out of the laundry room like a cat on a hot griddle the night of the murder? Was it to allow the killer into the pub through a side window or the door of the hair salon and hide him there until everyone had gone? It certainly had nothing to do with the washing machine as the staff found no sign of a wash in progress. Also, for some strange reason the curtains in the dining room were drawn that night, making it impossible for anyone inside to see a person approaching the side entrance of the pub.

Catherine Nevin had told the staff that the keys she normally hung up in the hallway were missing, inferring that someone had taken them. After the killing she identified keys taken from Tom Nevin's inside pocket as her missing keys. At the time she identified them, she wasn't aware they had been found on his body.

All this accentuated suspicions that Catherine Nevin may have played a role in her husband's murder. By now, the investigation team was looking very closely at the grieving widow. But everything they had so far was speculative and purely circumstantial. In fact the case against Catherine Nevin was to remain almost entirely circumstantial.

Getting any kind of evidence – circumstantial or otherwise – on the gunman, or gunmen, would prove infinitely more difficult. Immediately after the murder, local detectives, with the help of the Garda Special Branch and the National Bureau of Criminal Investigation in Harcourt Square, looked at a number of individuals who might be considered capable of carrying out a contract killing. Among the list of possible suspects was Patrick Eugene Holland.

Holland, nicknamed 'Dutchy', is now serving a 12-year sentence in Portlaoise Prison for drug trafficking. Gardaí named him in court as the man they believed had shot dead Veronica Guerin. Patrick Holland is a serious criminal and as such, was viewed as a possible suspect for the Nevin killing. Back in the mid 1990s he lived in Brittas Bay, a couple of miles up the road from Jack White's, and in 1994 he was seen once or twice having a coffee in the pub.

But there is not a shred of hard evidence to link Holland to the killing of Tom Nevin, gardaí say privately. Despite the lack of any evidence, Holland was identified – although not named – in newspaper reports as the chief suspect in the killing of Tom Nevin. 'When we were looking at suspects, he was in the frame. But there is nothing to suggest Dutchy did it, nothing at all,' says a senior Dublin security source.

A former INLA man from the North was also a suspect, but again, there is nothing to suggest he had any involvement. A third suspect, an anti-drugs vigilante from south Dublin, whom Catherine Nevin would have known, was listed also. Again, there was not a sliver of evidence that would allow gardaí to even arrest him for questioning. It seemed the triggerman had dissolved into the ether. Efforts to come up with a likely suspect were running into the sand.

Gerry Heapes, John Jones and Willie McClean were becoming increasingly important if the gardaí were to crack this case. Without them there was no case. On 4 November 1996, four months after they had tracked them down, Detectives Joe Collins and Fergus O'Brien called round to Jack White's to talk to Catherine Nevin. Specifically, they intended to put to her what they had learned from the three men. When they walked in to the bar, Catherine Nevin was sitting on a stool at the counter talking to Tom Kennedy. Collins told her they wanted to talk to her. 'No problem,' she replied, without making a move off the stool. Kennedy just sat there.

Collins suggested that she might like to talk in private. 'No,' she responded, she was quite happy to talk in front of Kennedy. Collins was left with little choice. He explained the nub of the allegations made by Heapes, McClean and Jones, how she had approached the three on different occasions and asked them to kill her husband. He cautioned her that she didn't have to say anything, but if she did, it would be taken down in writing and may be used in evidence.

It was at this point that Catherine Nevin got down off the stool. Without saying a word, she walked behind the counter and wrote down the name of her solicitor, Garrett Sheehan, alongside two telephone numbers. Without uttering a word she handed the piece of paper to Collins. 'Does this mean you don't want to comment?' Collins asked.

'Yes, thank you very much – see my solicitor,' she retorted. Collins jotted down her comment and the two detectives left.

By this stage, the staff at Jack White's had made written statements to the gardaí. Some of them had made more than one; it was something Catherine Nevin was acutely aware of. One Saturday afternoon, a month after the murder, Liz Hudson was working in the kitchen at Jack White's. A young staff member, Jessica Hunter, was working alongside her when Catherine Nevin buttonholed her. She called Hunter into the store just off the kitchen and questioned the youngster at length about speaking to Garda Paul Cummiskey. What exactly did Hunter say to Cummiskey, Nevin wanted to know, who did she talk about, what did Cummiskey want to know, what was in her statement?

'I want to see a copy of your statement. I'll sue anyone who says anything about me,' she warned Hunter. Nevin turned to Hudson and said she knew that Cummiskey was trying to get Jessica Hunter to talk. Then she called Hudson and Bernie

Fleming up to her bedroom. 'She asked us if we knew what Jessica had talked to Paul Cummiskey about. We said we did not know and she asked us to try and find out what she had said to Paul,' Hudson later recalled. Catherine Nevin was clearly worried about what the staff might say.

Hudson wondered why, if she had nothing to hide, she was so anxious to find out what transpired between Jessica and Paul Cummiskey. Apparently it wasn't the first time Catherine Nevin got the jitters about the staff. A week or so after the murder, Liz Hudson took a few days off and travelled to Dublin for a few days to stay with relatives. Catherine Nevin didn't know she was gone. 'It was a Monday night and myself and a couple of friends were out for a drink in the pub. At about 11.45 p.m., while we were in the pub, my name was called out over the intercom and I went to the phone. Tommy Godkin was on the line.' Hold on, he told Hudson, 'Catherine is waiting to talk to you.' When Catherine Nevin came on the phone, she asked Hudson how she was feeling. 'Fine,' Hudson replied. 'Well you don't sound it,' Nevin replied, 'How are you coming home? If you're coming on the bus, don't come on your own.'

Liz Hudson didn't know what to make of the phonecall, but she was nervous as to how Catherine Nevin knew where to find her that night, as she hadn't told anyone where she was going. Catherine Nevin then asked her when she would be home because she was 'getting a counsellor down to talk to the staff'.

'I have never spoken to any counsellor since and Catherine never mentioned it anymore,' said Hudson. 'I could not understand why she could not have waited until the next day to ring me.'

Apart from her paranoia about what the staff were saying behind her back, Catherine believed the gardaí had the place bugged. Minutes after her release from the Section 30 detention at Enniscorthy garda station on 29 July 1996, she telephoned Paul McGrath, a Fine Gael TD for Westmeath. McGrath had met her and Tom when he was in Wicklow canvassing during the 1995 by-election. These authors contacted McGrath, but he refused to shed any light on the mystery call. We have since established that Catherine Nevin was looking for his brother, Michael McGrath, a private investigator and former garda.

'She was convinced the guards had the place bugged, that's how they were getting their information,' said an informed source. 'She wanted McGrath to do counter-surveillance.' Michael McGrath, whose work is in the area of insurance claims, refused to play ball.

In the humdrum world of Jack White's, life continued on much as normal. Except that with Tom out of the picture, Catherine Nevin was now ruling the roost.

During all this time, gardaí were digging away to gather up as much information as possible to build a *prime facie* case against the sole proprietor of Jack White's Inn. In January 1997 Superintendent Pat Flynn sent a file to the Director of Public Prosecutions for his consideration.

The lengthy file contained 18 main summary points. It covered:

- The bitter and acrimonious relationship that existed between Catherine Nevin and the deceased;
- The soliciting of various people, i.e., Gerry Heapes, John Jones and Willie McClean;
- Catherine Nevin's obsessive greed and desire to be the sole owner of the entire business;

- Her delaying tactics on Friday, 15 March 1996 to prevent Tom Nevin making the bank lodgment;
- Her refusal to allow the staff to return to the pub on the night of the 18–19 March;
- The fact that she paid two members of staff by cheque instead of the customary cash on the weekend of the murder;
- Catherine Nevin's erratic behaviour on the premises from 10 p.m. onwards;
- Her damning comment that 'the amount is in the books' and her comparison of the smell of incense with the smell from the kitchen at the time of the murder;
- Her refusal to respond to questions in custody and by providing false and misleading information;
- The erasing of Gerry Heapes's name and telephone number from her diary sometime between 12 April and 18 May 1996.

The file came back from the DPP in the second week of April 1997. The DPP recommended that Catherine Nevin face trial on indictment on four charges: three counts of soliciting to murder and one count of murder.

At around 1 p.m. on 14 April, Catherine Nevin was driving through Ballybough in Dublin's north inner city when Detectives Fergus O'Brien, Pat Mulcahy and a female garda pulled her over. O'Brien told her that he was arresting her on charges relating to the murder of Tom Nevin at Ballinapark, Arklow on 19 March 1996. The scene was now set for what was to become one of the most sensational murder trials in Irish legal history.

10

THE PEOPLE VS
CATHERINE NEVIN

꧁❀꧂

'CC 1-2-9 of 1998: The People at the suit of the Director of Public Prosecutions and Catherine Nevin'.

The registrar's voice barely reached the back of Court 2, Central Criminal Court, Dublin, but the case number he was calling created a stir along its oak benches. The show was on.

It was Wednesday, 12 January 2000, 10.37 a.m. Barristers on the senior benches leaned back to glance at this latest 'accused', their expressions of studied disinterest betraying a sense that they had seen it all before. Reporters scanned and scribbled, mobile phones switched off but in hand.

Dozens of wondering faces lined the public benches and packed tight together around the perimeters, straining to hear through the rows in front of them. It was a lottery and they had been chosen. Plucked from the electoral register, they were in Court 2 clutching a dull green form that had arrived, out of the blue, in the post – a summons to attend for jury service.

The accused was seated near the top of the court. Tight-lipped and self-possessed, she looked like a middle-aged teacher doing her best to conceal her affront at being accused of the misdemeanours of a schoolgirl, and at now having to wait her turn in the staffroom to answer for them.

It was noted that she was neatly dressed in a navy-blue skirt suit and white scarf, her blonde hair set in a chignon. Behind her sat two Cork men accused of murder, and a separate pair of suited males accused of rape.

The Central Criminal Court is the criminal wing of the High Court, involving the trial by a jury of your peers for the most serious crimes in the book: murder, rape and even the rare possibility of treason or genocide.

DPP v Catherine Nevin had been listed for over a year. After she was charged in the Bridewell Dublin District Court on 14 April 1997, Catherine Nevin had her first taste of prison in Mountjoy. Four days later, she was granted bail in the High Court after she gave an undertaking that she would not interfere with witnesses, and that she would not apply for a new passport. She was released on her own surety of £5,000 and an independent surety of £20,000 put up by her brother-in-law, Betty's husband, Patrick White.

After the sale of Jack White's, on Christmas Eve 1997, she moved into a front bedsit on the ground floor at 17 Mountshannon Road. Her favourite furniture and much of her personal property from Jack White's were transported to a flat in the other red-brick house around the corner, 6 Mayfield Road, and she divided her time between the two places. Her bail conditions were changed in April 1998, allowing her to reside at the Kilmainham address, on the edge of Rialto.

As her case wound its way through the courts, Nevin again appeared before Mr Justice Carney on Friday, 26 February 1999. It was clear there wasn't a hope of fitting the case into that year's list, already stretched with rape trials and a number of what promised to be lengthy and difficult murder trials. There was also a scarcity of judges because of a delay in appointing new members to the High Court. A date was fixed for 12 January 2000 and Catherine Nevin was sent home.

Now, back in Court 2 before Mr Justice Carney, she stood up when the registrar called her case. Peter Charleton, the senior counsel representing the DPP, rose to inform the court that he agreed with the defence that there were further legal issues to be discussed before the matter could go further. He asked that the accused be arraigned on the first count on the indictment only.

On Count 1 – murder contrary to Section 4 of the Criminal Justice Act, 1964 – Catherine Nevin was charged that on the 19th day of March 1996 at Jack White's Inn, Ballinapark, Arklow, Co. Wicklow, she murdered Thomas Nevin. 'How do you plead, guilty or not guilty?' she was asked. 'Not guilty, your Honour,' she replied.

The clipped efficiency of the judge's voice took over. A jury of six women and six men were sworn in, having been warned that they were taking on 'the burden' of a four-week trial.

The case was adjourned to Court 3 before Ms Justice Mella Carroll, who was to be the trial judge. The defence team, laden with red and green document storage boxes, crossed the Round Hall to take up positions. Paul Cummiskey, now a Detective Garda, and in charge of exhibits for the trial, stood arranging large brown evidence bags next to the witness box, ticking off a clipboard list as he checked the numbered bags.

Outwardly calm, Catherine Nevin took her place near to him on the benches facing the jury box. Further along, reporters gathered.

In the public gallery, members of Tom Nevin's family sat waiting, the tall frames and open faces of the Nevin men instantly recognisable from newspaper pictures of Tom.

The original garda file on their brother's murder had run to 2,000 pages and seven volumes, including hundreds of statements. 'You could lay it out from one end of O'Connell Street to the other,' said one officer. The documents had been condensed into the 200-page file sent to the DPP in January 1997, eight months after the shooting. The prosecution counsel, Assistant Commissioner McHugh and the former DPP, Eamon Barnes, then held consultations in the DPP's office, poring over the case.

The officer who handled the file, Detective Inspector Liam Hogan, was now in court, a dapper but anonymous figure, sitting unassumedly on a back seat. A colleague describes Hogan as a recognised expert in the preparation of files for the DPP in major criminal investigations. In the Nevin case, he was the Incident Room Coordinator, handling the processing of thousands of queries and all incoming information. His analysis of the many threads of possible evidence was seen as crucial in persuading the DPP and counsel that a case could be made against Catherine Nevin.

With Hogan was another Corkman, Detective Garda James B. (Bernie) Hanley. The pair had worked together for 20 years, and were members of the Investigation Unit in Garda Headquarters at the time of the murder. They had teamed up with Assistant Commissioner McHugh before, including in the Brendan O'Donnell triple murder inquiry. Hanley's name has figured in most of the biggest criminal cases of recent years. But in this trial, he was not to give evidence, as his questioning of Catherine Nevin in custody had revealed nothing but her silence and facial gestures.

On the senior benches, Peter Charleton, SC, unfolded his wooden bookstand, a prop to hold up the legal tomes he quotes from. A former Trinity College law lecturer and author of a number of leading criminal law textbooks, he is described as 'a born teacher' in the foreword to one of the books by its general editor, Patrick MacEntee, the barrister now seated across from him in court. Charleton's finely tuned sense of justice, combined with a will to bring what is taught into practice, make him one of the fairest advocates in the Irish courts. Said one barrister, 'He doesn't bluster, he doesn't bellow, but he is always streets ahead of the question he is putting now.'

Opposite Charleton was the Chief State Solicitor's representative, Michael Kennedy, and behind him, the junior counsel, Tom O'Connell, BL. 'His ability to analyse evidence has meant he has the knack of turning up in some of the biggest criminal prosecutions in this State,' one legal observer said of O'Connell.

His opponent on the junior benches was Paul Burns, BL, a Belfast-born lawyer whose direct style and keen eye for detail have gained him a reputation for closely guarding the interests of his clients. Garrett Sheehan, who heads a top Irish criminal law practice, was instructing Burns and MacEntee. Alongside Sheehan was his colleague Ann Fitzgibbon, who returned to join his practice after working as an Assistant District Attorney in the United States.

Patrick MacEntee, SC, QC, was opposite the solicitors, his barrister's wig lop-sided on his head, its obvious signs of use a mark of his seniority. The Great Defender of the Irish criminal courts, he sat stooped and concentrated, surrounded by a somewhat deliberate air of infallibility. 'Let Justice be done for my client, even if the heavens fall,' could be his version of an oft-quoted legal mantra. Over the years, MacEntee had defended double murderer Malcolm McArthur, Australian criminal Robert Trimbole, republican Dominic McGlinchey, and Norma Cotter, whose conviction for killing her husband was overturned on appeal.

'His is a confrontational style,' said a member of the Bar who has come under MacEntee's glare in court, 'but he cannot be faulted for how he serves the interests of justice.'

Catherine Nevin had got what was probably the best defence team available in Irish criminal law.

The paths of 63-year-old MacEntee and his chief protagonist in this trial, 43-year-old Charleton, had crossed a number of times before. On the swings and roundabouts of legal casework, Charleton had served as junior counsel to MacEntee on a few occasions. In recent years, they had more commonly appeared on opposite sides of the court. MacEntee defended triple murderer Brendan O'Donnell in the longest single murder trial of recent times, while Charleton appeared with former senior counsel, now Judge Kevin Haugh, for the prosecution. In 1998, MacEntee and Paul Burns appeared for one of Veronica Guerin's killers, Paul Ward, while Charleton prosecuted.

Now there was the case of the murder of a former pub landlord by his wife to be prosecuted and to be defended – apparently nothing too remarkable at all.

'Silence please. All rise,' announced the tipstaff, as senior High Court judge, Ms Justice Mella Carroll, took her place on the top bench.

The 66-year-old judge had not sat in the Central Criminal Court for some time, but she was no stranger to it. Carroll was the first woman to head the Bar Council in Ireland, and in 1980 was the first woman to be appointed to the High Court. As a barrister, she specialised in conveyancing and company law; as a judge she is credited with a balanced and deft touch in criminal and civil law. Her broad knowledge of the law and its place in society has ensured that she has constantly been called on to serve extra-judicial functions both in Ireland and abroad. In the words of one senior member of the Law Library: 'She is an extremely sound lawyer, who has a way of doing it without vanity and shows of scholarship. If you read constitutional law books, the name Carroll, J. crops up again and again. She is not the intellectual's lawyer, she is the lawyer's lawyer, in the sense that she comes to a decision by the shortest possible route, and she invariably gets it right.'

Now Carroll, J. was being called upon to chair what appeared from the cover of the book of evidence to be an ordinary domestic trial. The People, through the Director of Public Prosecutions, a judge and jury, were to have their day in court, calling on one of their number to answer to the charge of murder.

But this one was already different. The accused was a woman.

In May 1996, two months after Tom Nevin's murder, David Murphy had strangled his wife Patricia in their Glasnevin garage in Dublin and then dumped her body in a skip. The horrific crime was first reported as the deed of an unknown killer, but soon suspicions turned closer to home. Murphy sat back as his children gave video-link evidence about 'a monster in the garage' in court. On 23 December 1998, a jury despatched wife-murderer Murphy to jail for life, just in time for his 37th birthday on Christmas Eve.

Murphy's heinous crime was out of the ordinary, but the fact that he was a man accused of murdering his wife was not. Male murder trials were the weekly diet of the Central Criminal Court, and stories of the murder and manslaughter of wives and girl-friends were common.

Trials of women for murder were very rare, and the circumstances were usually very different.

Nevertheless, Catherine Nevin was not the first Irish woman accused of plotting to kill in recent times. On Friday, 26 February 1999, the day Nevin was told she would have to wait another year before her trial could begin, another woman accused of the pre-meditated murder of her husband was unanimously acquitted by a jury after just 80 minutes' deliberation.

Twenty-two-year-old Anna-Maria Sacco walked free from the Central Criminal Court when the jury in her second trial cleared her of the murder of her husband, Franco, at their home in Coolamber Park, Templeogue, Dublin, two years previously. The 15-year-old girl who had shot Franco Sacco was acting alone, the jury decided. They rejected the prosecution case, led by Peter Charleton, that the teenage girl who had killed him with his own hunting rifle was 'put up to it' by his wife.

A month later, in March 1999, Patrick MacEntee was defending a 36-year-old Galway woman, Kathleen Bell, accused of the murder of her common-law husband, Patrick Sammon. She admitted stabbing him six times after they rowed on the night of 20 June 1997, but she denied intent to kill. On 23 March 1999, *The Star* relayed the jury verdict: 'NOT GUILTY: MANSLAUGHTER MUM IS GIVEN SECOND CHANCE'. Kathleen had been provoked by Sammon, who insulted his late wife – her sister – and taunted her about her childhood sexual abuse. She 'freaked out' and stabbed him, 'pushed just too far' after a horrific history of abuse, alcoholism and self-mutilation. The prosecution and defence were united in accepting alternatives to jail for Bell.

DPP v Catherine Nevin was different. A woman who apparently set out to kill her husband, plotting to do it for at least seven years, a well-heeled schemer waiting for her chance.

However, from Day 1 it was clear this was going to be no easy trial. As the first set of jurors waited in their room to try Nevin, her counsel rose to argue that the charges of soliciting to murder should be kept separate from the murder charge she had just pleaded not guilty to. MacEntee also announced an application to stop the trial. He claimed that pre-trial publicity since Tom Nevin's murder had prejudiced the minds of potential jurors against his client. And he sought discovery of Special Branch files on Jones, Heapes and McClean, as well as on Patrick Russell. The defence were opening with an attack.

Catherine Nevin sat up straight, her right leg crossed over her left, her right palm placed on her lap, and her left hand resting across the right. Gold rings on tanned skin. It was a restrained and ladylike posture and she was to maintain it for much of her time in court over the next 60 days. Had she been instructing young girls in deportment as she had in her classes 25 years before, she might have suggested this very pose, perhaps for an interview, or if they ever found themselves the centre of attention in unpredictable circumstances.

Her head was slightly forward, and set within a frame of Barbie-doll blonde hair that changed style almost daily. Her face was made-up, with clear, sharp eyes that looked straight ahead, or occasionally darted to a target.

She was the visiting dramatist who would sit sidestage for most of the show, watching the players come and go, knowing that soon she would take centre stage.

'It is inconceivable that there are not further files in relation to these people,' her counsel was saying of the Special Branch files. 'They have to be relevant; we believe they are relevant.'

The jury was eventually sent away until morning, while the battle lines continued to be drawn in court.

'The first I heard of Special Branch files was at 11:30 this morning,' said Peter Charleton. 'The reality is that all of this could have been done a great deal of time ago, rather than an attempt now being made to adjourn or delay this trial.'

He was not going to ask An Garda Siochána to pass over to him matters that were confidential, and which might have relevance for national security, he said. The Attorney General might also take a view. He was adamant that he had fulfilled his duty to disclose what he had to for the defence.

Patrick MacEntee said the defence had been seeking discovery with great diligence. Only the previous Friday, the entire contents of a filing cabinet had been sent to them. 'Ms Nevin's filing cabinet was requested last week and we gave it back last week,' Charleton countered shortly. But Patrick MacEntee insisted on his basic point: 'The duty of discovery doesn't end with what the Garda Siochána see good to send to the DPP.'

The issue was postponed, but it was to re-appear as a constant legal jam, interrupting the flow of the trial.

MacEntee then handed in a file of press cuttings to Ms Justice Carroll, asking her to carry out an inquiry into 'systematic leaking by An Garda Siochána to the press in relation to this case'. Sifting through articles by crime correspondents in the days and months after the murder, he claimed that the police were using the press to favour one interpretation of what happened – that the murder was a contract killing made to look like a botched robbery.

The pre-trial coverage, he said, was 'calculated to prejudice the jury' and 'reported gossip' about Catherine Nevin's associations with a legal person was there 'to titillate and do damage to her reputation'.

As the afternoon wore on, the defence moved to the third prong of its attack on the prosecution case. The alleged soliciting of Jones, Heapes and McClean had happened so long ago and had no relevance to the murder of Tom Nevin, it was claimed. Therefore, the evidence of the three was prejudicial and should not be admitted to shore up the murder case.

But Peter Charleton argued that there was a nexus between the statements of the three men and the actual murder. 'There is little or no difference between that which she suggested to them and that which happened,' he claimed. Location was the only thing that had changed, and that only because Tom Nevin had changed his banking arrangements.

By 11.20 a.m. the next day, Charleton was citing the notorious English murder trial of Fred and Rosemary West to argue that, irrespective of pre-trial publicity, once a trial begins, 'the facts take over'. The jury had already been sent away again, being told only that legal applications were continuing.

When the jury returned the next day, Catherine Nevin was wearing her hair down. The jurors were sent to their room while Ms Justice Carroll dismissed the two defence applications.

She ruled that all four counts should go to the jury. She also found that there was no real or serious risk of Catherine Nevin not getting a fair trial and that the allegation of conscious and deliberate leaking by gardaí was 'far-fetched'.

When she called the jury in, Ms Justice Carroll told them not to read any newspaper comments or articles on the trial and not to discuss it with anybody. 'You will have to be your own censors,' she said. The jurors could see that since they had last been in the jury box, the press had been moved farther along the benches opposite, away from Mrs Nevin, and there was fresh, clear distance between her and everyone else.

It was now Friday, 14 January. Catherine Nevin was re-arraigned and pleaded not guilty to all four charges. In addition to the murder count, she denied Count 2, that on diverse dates in or about 1989, within the State, she solicited John Jones to murder Thomas Nevin. She denied Count 3, that on diverse dates in or about 1990, within the State, she solicited Gerard

Heapes to murder Thomas Nevin, and she denied Count 4, that on a date unknown in 1990 at St Vincent's Hospital, in the city of Dublin, she solicited William McClean to murder Thomas Nevin.

The prosecution case opened and the show, it seemed, was finally on.

That jury was to hear 60 witnesses over nine days of prosecution evidence, but it was all in vain. On Wednesday, 26 January, the first trial collapsed after jury discussions were overheard from the public balcony upstairs.

For the first time since the trial began, Catherine Nevin was wearing the same suit – a black short jacket with a velvet collar along with a cream blouse, pearl brooch and discreet gold cross necklace. By her feet was the shiny black leather briefcase with a zip top that now accompanied her almost every day to court.

Tom Nevin's family was also in court, as were Catherine's sister Betty White and her brother Vincent Scully.

The prosecution case was only entering its crucial phase. Neither Heapes, Jones nor McClean had yet been called to give evidence.

Cross-examination of Detective Sergeant Fergus O'Brien was continuing when a recess was called for lunch. At 2.15, when the court was due to convene again, something was astir. A queue for the public balcony upstairs had been halted at the foot of the stairs, and a court guard was upstairs signalling to the registrar. There were sightings of the defence and the prosecution outside in the Round Hall, but then they disappeared. Speculation festered on the press bench.

At 3.35 p.m. counsel for the prosecution entered, looking glum. Two minutes later, the defence team came in with their client, Patrick MacEntee grinning broadly at a remark of Paul Burns.

Five minutes later, the jury was called down to court. Ms Justice Carroll discharged them, the secrecy of their deliberations more important than any inconvenience to the court. Catherine Nevin reached for her briefcase and waited to go.

Afterwards, sources suggested that another judge's tipstaff had overheard the jury as he stood beside a fire exit door that led from the jury room to the balcony. The tipstaff concerned was said to have made a statement to an internal inquiry by the court authorities, but he declined to confirm his involvement or to make any comment to these authors.

The balcony in Court 3 had rarely been used in recent years. Larger murder trials requiring the opening of the upstairs public gallery, had tended to be held in Court 2, so it was not surprising that the Nevin jury was the first to fall foul of the poor soundproofing in the other court. However, the judge's choice of the word 'deliberations' to describe the jury's discussions might suggest that there was more to their leaked voices than casual talk about the trial.

In any case, the trial was off, temporarily at least. But the battle between the prosecution and the defence was not. Between the lines of what could be reported in the press, trench warfare was breaking out between them.

The issue of the Special Branch files had rumbled on, and it continued in pockets of legal argument throughout the first trial, culminating in the second, when the head of the Crime and Security Branch, Detective Chief Superintendent Dermot Jennings, came to court to hand them over to the judge.

By the time Nevin had moved from a Barbara Taylor Bradford novel to the *Collected Works of Rudyard Kipling* as her choice of reading material in mid-January, the Garda Commissioner and the Attorney General had already been roped into the argument about the mysterious files.

It was to be another first. 'The first time in the history of the Irish nation that anyone has ever sought Special Branch files is in this case, here and now,' said Peter Charleton.

On Monday, 17 January, Barrister Feichin McDonagh, SC, appeared to put some distance between the Commissioner and the Attorney General on the one side and the Director of Public Prosecutions on the other about access to them. Showing secret files was something that wasn't going to be lightly done.

Charleton was in turn asserting the DPP's independent rights and was concerned that what the defence was after was 'a general trawl' of files containing nothing but the suspicions of gardaí and of 'low-grade informers' about meetings and events that had nothing to do with the case. Could the defence be specific?, he asked. After all, Jones, Heapes, McClean and Pat Russell had the right to the presumption of innocence as much as Catherine Nevin.

'It's not realistic to ask us to say what's relevant when we haven't seen the files,' was the reply from Paul Burns. And he added the name of Tom Nevin to the list of files being sought.

Counsel for the Garda and the Attorney General retreated, returning to propose that his clients examine the documents with a view to finding anything that might aid the defence. This was rejected by both the defence and Mr Charleton, who insisted that, by law, the DPP was independent in the exercise of his functions.

Ms Justice Carroll ordered that the files be made available to Charleton to decide whether or not they were relevant for disclosure. The next day, a worried McDonagh was back again to tell the judge that Attorney General Michael McDowell and the Garda Commissioner were at that moment in consultation about her order. They wanted to avoid an appeal to the Supreme Court, but if they had to, they would. The judge granted a stay on the order.

The following morning, 19 January, Garda Commissioner Pat Byrne and the head of the Security Branch, Detective Chief Superintendent Jennings, were in court. McDonagh now told the judge that the documents were in fact Security Branch files, and not Special Branch files, and he said that the evidence would be 'that there are no relevant documents in relation to the matter'. His clients would be claiming State privilege on the grounds of lack of relevance and of national security.

If there was no relevant information, what was the need for claiming privilege?, the judge asked. Because there were fundamental issues at stake, was the reply. The State was afraid of setting precedents.

But by the following day, an accommodation had been reached between the arms of the Irish State. A senior officer from the DPP's office was to examine the files and report to Mr Charleton. The judge was to read them herself if a problem arose. And no precedent was being set by the arrangement, she said.

That might have been the end of it, but the defence persevered. In the middle of the second trial, before Jones, Heapes or McClean gave their evidence, it was revealed that Catherine Nevin's lawyers had written to the Chief State Solicitor asking if there had been an agreement entered into in the course of the investigation between the DPP, the Gardaí or Attorney General and any of the men.

The Chief State Solicitor replied that there had been none, and attached a letter from the officer in charge of the investigation, Superintendent Pat Flynn, to that effect.

The defence then asked that Ms Justice Carroll herself examine the Security Branch files. There was no opposition from the prosecution, with Peter Charleton informing the judge that in fact the secret files had since been read out to himself and Tom O'Connell and their contents had been 'debated at some considerable length'.

At 4 p.m. on Tuesday, 22 February, after the jurors had been sent home, Detective Chief Superintendent Dermot Jennings arrived to hand over the files. When he was sworn in, the prosecution counsel asked, 'Now if you could just tell us what your position is –'.

The head of the Security Branch looked at the judge, a slow smile appearing on his face. Patrick MacEntee quickly rose. 'I have no difficulty with this person's position,' he said. The detective confirmed that he was the custodian of the documents and they were handed to the judge in a black leather briefcase.

Two days later, Ms Justice Carroll ruled that the privilege relating to the documents could continue; and, in a dismissal of their bearing on the case, she said that nothing further should be disclosed to the defence on the basis of relevance, and that suspicion of involvement in crime or subversive activities should not be disclosed. At lunchtime, again in the absence of the jury, the Security Branch chief returned to collect the briefcase.

Close to the end of the second trial, the judge had another look at the files. This was in the aftermath of Catherine Nevin's evidence. On 29 March, she said that having reviewed them, there was nothing to support evidence given by the accused that there was a purchase proposed of the Killinarden Inn by Tom Nevin with John Jones that was to be financed from Northern Ireland. There was also no evidence of any meeting in the Green Isle Hotel. The defence had got their answer: there was nothing in the files to verify their client's allegation.

But the judge went further. In a voice that hinted at her growing disquiet at the allegations being levelled at Tom Nevin's door by his wife, whose name she by now knew had featured in the Security Branch files, the judge said: 'I would also say that there is absolutely nothing to suggest in any way that Tom Nevin was a member of the IRA or that he had any sympathy for its views.'

The jury knew nothing of all this. The suspected activities of suspected IRA members or associates and their links with Catherine Nevin were a diversion from the case at hand. The argument over the secret files could not be reported until the trial was over. But as this book has already revealed, Catherine was herself mentioned in those files. And there was no file on Tom Nevin.

Another detail in the saga of the files reveals the way in which the trial of Catherine Nevin brought former friends and foes into the same frame. In March 2000, Dermot Jennings was the custodian of the files in his role as Chief of Intelligence in the Irish police. But on 13 May 1981, as Detective Garda Dermot Jennings, he had been part of a Special Branch team that had raided a house in Dunsink Road, Finglas. It was the day after the death on hunger strike of IRA man Francis Hughes, and just over a week after the death of Bobby Sands. Inside the house, the garda unit found 19 home-made electronic timing devices, a number of batteries and a circuit board destined for the IRA.

They arrested the occupant, Dessie Ellis, setting in motion a battle of wits between Ellis and the State that was to take the north Dublin-based republican first on the run, then into jail and then on to his own hunger strike, before his eventual extradition trial and acquittal on similar charges by an Old Bailey jury in 1991. It was on that occasion that he named John Jones as the business partner who had talked him into using his skills for the IRA.

If Catherine Nevin was even vaguely aware of any of these in-trial nuances, she did not show it. As the security files were being handed over and discussions were taking place in closed court about whether they should be stored in the safe of the President of the High Court or returned each day to sender, she sat looking on, only occasionally showing signs of impatience at the cautious, deliberate progress of the case.

After her first trial had been aborted after 11 days, she had four days of respite before the retrial was due to begin. On the last day of January, as Court 2 was again packed with members of the public holding dull green forms, Nevin was transferred to Court 3 and her counsel renewed applications about press coverage that took up another week. On Monday, 7 February, a second jury was sworn in, but defence submissions again stepped in to delay the start of the trial. Then, the next day, a second jury was discharged – one of its members had been too shy to say she was pregnant and just couldn't serve at that time. Continuing with 11 jurors for what promised to be a lengthy case was considered to be too risky.

'It's extraordinary how many things have beset this particular trial,' Ms Justice Carroll remarked.

The following Monday morning, 14 February, a third jury was sworn in. Out of 64 called up to the jury box, 13 were excused when they indicated that they did not have an open mind. 'Not guilty, your Honour,' Nevin said again to all four counts.

As they settled into their seats in the jury box in Court 4, the new jury were eyed up and down. Three of them had been on the previous jury that had never got a chance to serve. Now, one of the three had been elected forewoman, a long-haired, thin, intellectual-looking woman in her thirties, who affirmed instead of being sworn. Beside her sat another affirmer, a middle-aged man with cultivated stubble and half-moon glasses. Save for one middle-aged woman, the remainder were in their thirties or early forties. Six women and six men, it was to be left to their judgment whether Catherine Nevin would walk or go down.

Because the judge expressly ordered that the jurors' anonymity is to be preserved, this book can reveal nothing of their origins, but they did match the profile of an ideal jury: they came from all walks of life.

In the public gallery, new faces had been appearing at each attempt to start the trial. Along with the familiar faces of court watchers, more and more people were dropping in, just to have a look.

From the start, The People versus Catherine Nevin was different. Here was no ordinary domestic murder trial. This was a case of pre-meditated murder; a hired assassin apparently put up to murder by a wife hell-bent on control; a whodunnit case, where nobody knew who had pulled the trigger, or if they knew, they wouldn't say. It was a middle-class murder in a rural community, with the added whiff of corrupt goings-on.

If murder trials provide an opportunity for Irish society to examine itself, here was one where there was the chance that it was going to have a good gawk.

11

TEA LEAVES
ON THE BARN

'The facts are very simply these,' Peter Charleton was saying. 'No matter what happens from now on, no-one can ever deny the fact that I addressed you in this court-room, here and now. If it were denied, you would have a number of people saying it did happen and you may have a number saying it did not. You would have to weigh up the evidence, examine the facts and decide in favour or against.'

It was Monday, 14 February 2000 at 2.25 p.m. The retrial was underway. In light of what was to be claimed in the weeks that followed, Charleton's illustration was apt. If the jury didn't get a grip on reality now, there would be no hope for them later.

They were not to read the newspapers and all that was required of them at this stage was to have an open mind. They were to use their 'ordinary common sense, and a blank mind, a slightly sceptical mind,' Charleton suggested to them.

The judge had already directed the twelve not to read the press. What they didn't know was that three hours before, they had risked being sequestered for the entire trial. A proposal to lock them away in a hotel because of fears of prejudicial press coverage came as Ms Justice Carroll again dealt with defence calls to delay the trial.

'I am going to start the trial and ask the jurors not to read the newspapers in the course of it,' she insisted.

'Since that order is unenforceable, I wonder if the court would consider sequestering the jury for the duration of the trial?' asked Patrick MacEntee.

'No, Mr MacEntee, I won't,' came the short answer.

Saved from sequestration, the jurors were now getting their first taste of the language of the courts. The prosecution counsel gave them the definition of murder, explained that you could be guilty of it even though you did not pull the trigger yourself, and he described soliciting as 'a serious-minded attempt to get somebody to commit a crime on your behalf'.

Soliciting, he said, was only a crime on the part of the person doing the asking. It wasn't a crime to be asked, and it was only if you agreed that it then became a conspiracy.

'The prosecution bases its case in essence on a theory,' he continued. It was only a theory until it was proved: that the late Tom Nevin was murdered at the behest of his wife and that the crime scene was arranged so that it might look like a robbery that had gone wrong.

The prosecution intended to provide evidence that Tom and Catherine Nevin's 20-year-old marriage 'was one where Mrs Nevin had a very poor opinion of her husband', and where the 'bond of fidelity between married couples had disappeared'. But he pointedly added: 'That is something from which perhaps no inference can be drawn, because the evidence will be that Tom Nevin knew of this, and had a particular view on it.'

The prosecution was not concerned with ordinary matrimonial disharmony but was arguing that in this case, it had been replaced by animus on one side, leading to 'a state of mind in Mrs Nevin where she wanted her husband killed.' Three men were to be called to offer proof of this, and the crime scene itself was to be dissected in evidence. Everything about the scene pointed to deliberate murder. Tom Nevin had simply been 'despatched into the next world by an intruder'; 'his heart supply shut down by the discharge of shot from one cartridge into it'.

Mrs Nevin was before them 'clothed in the presumption of innocence'. Either the case compellingly led them to one con-clusion only, 'that Mrs Nevin arranged this', or it led to another rational hypothesis. The prosecution case could be weaker or stronger than what he was suggesting – it was up to the jury to decide which.

Counsel paused, and reached for the book of evidence. What was written inside was now to be used by both sides to examine and cross-examine about what really happened. And whatever was said in the witness stand was to hold greater weight than any-thing said in the book of evidence.

The first witness, James Curry, was called and then would come the evidence, to be painted for the jury on 'a completely blank canvas'.

The canvas was first shown to be yellowed with age, in a mild embarrassment for the police. It transpired that the Ordnance Survey map the jury was working off had first been published in the 1950s or 1960s. Some of the buildings marked opposite Jack White's on the map weren't there anymore. But the long-gone buildings were of no consequence. The jury had by now learned that Jack White's is a pub on a .316-acre site, around 35 miles from Dublin city, on a number of alternative routes to the capital, the main one being the dual carriageway that forms part of the N11.

The jury also learned that when Catherine Nevin had been found inside the front door of the house, she was 80 feet from her husband's body. The body itself was 20 feet from the door of the large kitchen. And there was a fixed panic button 14 feet away from where he lay. If Tom hadn't known his killer, they had done well to get to him unnoticed.

James Curry, the controller-operator at the alarm monitoring company, Bell Communications, was adamant that when the Jack White's alarm alert flashed on his computer screen on the morning of 19 March, the time recorded was 4.31 a.m., and he had then rung Wexford gardaí. Garda Sean Whelan said he received the call at 4.27 a.m., and vouched for the accuracy of the digital clock in front of his desk in the Communications Room in Wexford. This glitch in times undermined the prosecution case.

But it was to be short-lived. Detective Garda Paul Cummiskey soon took the stand and said he got a call from Garda Whelan at 4.35 a.m. and arrived at Jack White's ten minutes later. Whichever clock was right, there was a gap of 14 to 18 minutes between the time Mrs Nevin pressed the panic alarm and when the gardaí arrived – what had she been doing, and why didn't she go to try and find Tom?

As Detective Garda Paul Cummiskey relayed his account of finding the accused slumped inside the front door with whispered voice and tied wrists, it was clear that conflicts of evidence were already emerging. One was between Cummiskey and his colleague, Garda Martin McAndrew, whose statement noted that he spotted a light in the second-floor dormer room, not in Catherine's bedroom. However, Cummiskey had total recall that he saw the light on behind closed curtains in her bedroom on the first floor. He again saw it was on when he went up to that room and grabbed a duvet to cover her. The light 'definitely was on', the detective said, as was the light in the hallway.

Then there was the conflict over just how open the front door was. Detective Garda Cummiskey said that he noticed that 'the front door was ajar six inches'.

'I have to suggest to you that the most you reported at the time was that it was "slightly ajar",' said MacEntee.

'Six inches is slightly ajar,' the detective replied. 'It was slightly ajar, slightly to me is six inches.'

The issue was important to the defence because their client had claimed that when she had travelled the 23 feet from her bedroom to the front door, she found the door open but with no gap, in the sense that the lock was disengaged and the edge of the door was resting on the frame. His instructions were that 'she tried to prise it open with her fingers so that she could try and get someone's attention on the road,' Mr MacEntee said.

The door could have swung in or out of this position in the wind, of course, except that the garda mapper, Detective Garda Gerard Scanlon, had already given evidence that it was positioned in a two-foot-four-inches recess, and Detective Garda Cummiskey had just told the court that even though it had been wet and windy earlier that night, by the time he and his colleague arrived at the Inn, the rain had stopped and it was calm.

The claim that Nevin tried to get to the road – already a moot point because she was saying she tried it before she pressed the panic alarm and without checking where her husband was – was further challenged on Day 6, when Detective Garda Joe Collins gave evidence. He had noted Mrs Nevin telling him that she had tried to prise open the door and that at the time 'it was spilling rain'. She told him only hours after the murder, and he had carried out a test that same day. He closed the front hall door until the Yale latch lock met the receiver. Then he put his hands behind his back and made to open the door as if his wrists were tied tightly. Using his little finger, he 'opened it without difficulty,' he told the court.

Another contradiction was in what Catherine Nevin had said to Garda Cummiskey, the first to question her. 'She never led me to believe that there was any more than one attacker,' the detective told the trial. But in later accounts on the day of the murder, she was to claim that a second raider was in her bedroom throwing things around while his companion was tying her up.

And as to the things thrown about, Cummiskey had doubts. 'In my experience the drawers and boxes would have been emptied out, and they weren't in this case, they were just sitting on the floor.' He went on: 'It didn't seem to me to be a ransacked room by any stretch of the imagination'.

Although the rules of evidence and the conduct of trials can often leave juries with little or no explanation of what they are hearing, the effect of the detective's evidence was clear. If he was right about the room, something was not right about the scene. If he was right that her bedroom light was on, then what was all this talk about being awoken in the dark to a man with a woolly mask wielding a knife. And if he was right about the door being six inches ajar within a quarter of an hour of her pressing the alarm, then she could have easily got outside if she wanted to.

The devil was in the detail.

The defence changed tack with the Arklow-based detective. 'The gardaí in Arklow don't generally like Mrs Nevin, do they?' Patrick MacEntee asked, swivelling his portly frame to face the jury.

'I wouldn't say that, I wouldn't say there was any difficulty between the gardaí in Arklow and Mrs Nevin, or indeed with Mr Nevin.'

'Are you not aware that a young 15-year-old relation of Tom Nevin's [*sic*] who worked in Jack White's bar had alleged in July 1991 that two members of the gardaí had given her a lift in the patrol car, and that one of them had been dropped off, and the other one made a sexual advance to her in the patrol car, and that Mr and Mrs Nevin had made statements in relation to it?' Mr MacEntee continued.

What the prosecution was later to call the first 'bogey man' was being introduced into the trial. Bound by his instructions, MacEntee was putting his client's claim to the first garda from Arklow to give evidence. His cross-examination of Cummiskey on what was later described as 'a giant red herring' went on for several minutes. The theme was reintroduced each time a fresh face from Arklow garda station took the witness stand. Mr MacEntee later corrected his mistake that the girl was a relation of Tom Nevin, and told the jury it was in fact 'a distant relative' of Catherine Nevin. Although the accused went on to name the girl in open court, the girl's name has not been published, and the judge ordered that the usual anonymity for persons making allegations of sexual assault be applied to her. Now an adult, she was given the name Ms M for the remainder of the trial.

But the introduction of the allegations so early in the retrial showed that the alleged bad blood between Catherine Nevin and Arklow gardaí was to be used to cast a doubt over the credibility of the evidence of every garda from Arklow. From Catherine's corner, it wasn't The People versus Catherine Nevin, it was Catherine Nevin versus ABC – Anybody But Catherine.

The next witness was vital in countering that. Assistant Commissioner Jim McHugh, who at the time of the murder was in charge of the South-Eastern division of the gardaí, based in Kilkenny, appeared in full uniform, his light voice a foil to his senior rank. He had arrived at the Inn at around 9 a.m. on the fateful morning. It was important for the defence to put a brake on his evidence.

'Apart from what he saw with his own eyes . . . he has only to add his prestige,' Mr MacEntee said, arguing – in the absence of the jury – against the Commissioner being allowed to give his opinion on the state of Catherine Nevin's bedroom. But McHugh was allowed to continue. The jury heard that in almost 38 years in the force, he had spent 23 years in criminal investigation and two years in the serious crime section at Garda Headquarters, and he had visited thousands of scenes of crime.

'One of the golden rules in this type of situation, and particularly for senior officers, is keep your hands in your pockets,' McHugh remarked. His evidence on the bedroom was crucial, his words judiciously chosen. 'Whilst it was in a state of disorder, nevertheless it wasn't apparent that a systematic search of the room or its contents had taken place,' he said.

McHugh recounted the bedroom scene as he had witnessed it. The main light on, the telephone receiver resting on the floor. Three drawers removed from a five-drawer cabinet and lying on the carpet. Two drawers still in position. Items on the top of the chest of drawers untouched and upright. None of the drawers or their contents apparently searched. A glass of spirits standing upright on the floor beside the bedside locker. The contents of a lady's handbag tipped out beside it. The contents of the bedside lockers intact and medications and other items standing upright on them. Cardboard boxes that had been stacked in a wardrobe, seemingly tumbled out, the contents of one of them spilled out on the floor. A clothes rail undisturbed. And his surprise that armed raiders had apparently contemplated taking the portable Philips television that was lying tight against the banisters of the stairs, screen down, seemingly dropped there, damaging two of the balustrades.

Cross-examined, McHugh agreed that one construction of events was that the room was not ransacked because the raiders knew what they were looking for. But his tight frown as he conceded this point was enough to show that he thought things didn't add up. All in all, it was a very strange scene for a break-in.

The Assistant Commissioner had then gone downstairs and had been introduced to Catherine. 'She conveyed the impression that she was suffering from shock and was traumatised,' he said. After she had given her account of what had taken place, he tried to persuade her to stay elsewhere, but 'she was determined that she wouldn't leave'.

On 23 March 1996, the Assistant Commissioner had returned to Jack White's with Detective Garda Bernie Hanley. It was two days after Tom's funeral, and they found his wife sitting in the lounge, in what seems from the evidence to be quite a combative mood. She talked about her husband, telling McHugh that he was a chain smoker, smoking 60 cigarettes a day. 'She also told me that he drank about a litre of whiskey a day,' he recalled. She was determined 'that she wasn't going to be driven out of business by the animals that killed Tom'.

McHugh was not asked about part of a conversation he had held with Nevin in the incident room at Arklow station on 28 March, in which he had questioned her about a scheme to siphon off money from the business and put it into a hit fund, something she had mentioned to Gerry Heapes. This would have made her guilty of deceiving the Revenue Commissioners, something Mr MacEntee successfully argued was 'an extraneous offence'.

In conversation later, Nevin had been anxious to impress upon the senior garda more of her version of life with Tom. The conservatory and renovations in Jack White's had cost £37,000, she said. It had been paid off in one season, contrary to his expectation that it would take seven or eight years.

'She said that he didn't have a great brain, but what he did have he used very effectively. She said he was good businessman, but that he was an alcoholic and could be very violent at times, and that he had assaulted her on more than one occasion, and that because of that, she was hospitalised on one particular occasion.

'She said that about seven years previously, they had contemplated separating, but at the time, Tom had said who would have either of them at that stage of their lives.

'She said that she didn't believe or think that Tom was involved with any other female, any other woman, and that while she herself had many male friends, she wasn't involved intimately with any of them.'

On 3 April 1996, McHugh called again to the Inn to seek permission to carry out test shots to check sound levels and to establish how long the smell of cordite would linger after the discharge of a weapon. Mrs Nevin had given her full support for the tests, he said. He did not say that when it came to the time of carrying them out, that full support was slightly qualified. Nevin told gardaí her bedroom was off-limits and locked, and the hearing test had to be done from the 'blue room' next door.

By this stage of the trial, a whiff of cordite was surrounding the widow herself. But she sat unfazed, a casual disregard for her surroundings interrupted only by an occasional involuntary blinking of her eyelids, such as when Assistant Commissioner McHugh finished his evidence.

It was 3.59 p.m., one minute before the close of court for the day. The next witness, Garda Diarmuid O'Donovan, had just been telling how Mrs Nevin 'appeared very distressed, her eyes rolling in her head', when he arrived at the Inn on 19 March.

Suddenly, a mobile phone went off in the court, its irritating melody insistent the longer it was left unanswered. In the body of the court, there was a panicked rummaging in bags. Ms Justice Carroll looked up from her note-taking. Mr MacEntee had paused in mid-sentence and he now turned towards his client. All eyes followed him. Catherine reached for her handbag and removed the offending item, switching it off. Her lawyer resumed his cross-examination, his gaze remaining fixed on her. Ironically, a few feet from her on the bench sat reporter John Kilraine, who had been sent to the cells in the Bridewell when his mobile had gone off in court some years before.

Now, each day delivered more threads of evidence against the accused. Several of the jury were taking copious notes. The stubble of the middle-aged man who always took his place beside the forewoman in the front row was now a beard. He had been dubbed the David Hanly of the jury, after *Morning Ireland*'s presenter. When he wasn't filling notebooks, he sat with his arms folded, his eyes searching the ceiling for respite. Some had labelled the forewoman an eco-warrior because of her apparel. She sat, drawn and serious, interrupting proceedings only once to ask if a court-watcher asleep at the back of the court could be drawn out of his noisy slumber.

There was a lot of explaining to do. There was Catherine's unexplained removal of the torn-off pocket of Tom's jacket from where it had apparently been left in the kitchen. On the day of the funeral, she had handed it over to Garda Yvonne Foran, who had noticed it 'crumpled up in her fist', bits of dried blood falling off it.

There was a string of garda witnesses who testified that they had found no sign of a break-in at any of the windows or doors at the Inn. It had nine separate entrances, one upstairs leading to a flat roof and metal fire escape stairs, and eight downstairs. None showed signs of forced entry.

There were the floats of at least £80 lying untouched in each of three cash registers that lay open for the raiders to see – £260 in all. There was more float cash made up in bags found by Detective Garda Thomas Carey in the storeroom. There was the second floor safe in that storeroom, containing a number of bundles of money, untouched. And a portable safe, designed to look like an electrical twin-socket, found high up on the shelves, containing two gold rings and a bracelet. There was the fact that no phone on the premises had been ripped out or disconnected. And apart from the phone Catherine said she had tried to use in her room, there was a white phone sitting on a stool outside the bathroom on the same landing.

And there were the alarms. Four external boxes, five fixed panic buttons and two radio remote-controlled buttons. Pressing any of them could activate the alarm, said the representative of D.J. Alarms. The two remote units, small clip-on versions, were found in the accused's bedroom. Detective Garda Thomas Carey agreed that she would have had to, in Mr MacEntee's words, 'pull the curtains back and root around' for the mobile panic unit that was sitting upside down on the window ledge behind the head of the bed.

The second mobile alarm was found in a drawer in an octagonal table on the right-hand side of the bed, near the door. The batteries inside both alarms were working. On the landing outside, there was a fixed remote keypad that could also be used as a panic alarm. You could either press in the code or press two buttons simultaneously. At least the first, it was conceded, was difficult to do if your hands were tied behind your back.

Detective Carey and Detective Garda William Brennan from the ballistics section of the Garda Technical Bureau had fired three rounds of SG-size shot from a sawn-off Ely shotgun and three rounds from a full-length barrel shotgun into a retrieval box in sound-and-smell tests conducted in the kitchen of Jack White's, after midnight, a month after the murder. Other officers were dotted around the house and outside, and tests were fired with a combination of open and closed doors. Their evidence was that a mild smell of firearms residue could only be got in the kitchen and the sound that travelled upstairs was a 'dull thud'.

William Brennan had a view on the red-and-white push-top pen found in Mr Nevin's right hand. The pen was 'tight between the two fingers of his hand', he said, not in the fashion of him writing, but more in the way that he had stopped writing and was retaining the pen in his right hand to be used again.

Detective Brennan had also applied his ballistics expertise to an examinination of the body. He believed Tom's jacket was open when he was shot at a distance of one to four yards from the shotgun muzzle to the body. He was shot with a 12-gauge shotgun, 'the most common in the country'. The shotgun was never found, nor was the cartridge that had been discharged. He believed the cartridge had been taken away by the assassin. It was not possible to say whether a single-barrelled, double-barrelled or sawn-off shotgun had been used. The shot used was SG size, heavy-gauge cartridges with shot pellets 'designed to kill large game, such as deer'. In an area known for its deer, Tom Nevin had been killed with deer-hunting shot.

A cartridge normally contains eight pellets per ounce, but you would expect to find nine pellets in a cartridge of the size used.

To give an idea of the size, a normal clay pigeon shooting cartridge contains 400 pellets, compared to this.

Only six pellets were accounted for: four found in the body, and two shot pieces found on the outer jacket. The detective could not say why the remaining three pellets were never recovered. He said that at the post-mortem which he attended, he noted four exit wounds in the area of the left back. At least four pellets had exited there, but possibly two or three more, since some of the exit holes were larger than others.

It was not speculated whether the missing three pellets had also been removed from the scene by the killers. But as to whether the cartridge was commercially or home-made, Brennan said the fibre and cardboard discharge wad found on and near the body tended to show that it was a commercial cartridge. It was not possible to say the exact make.

Catherine Nevin's right hand, crossed over the back of the left, now tightened around the palm of the left, so that it appeared that they were joined in prayer.

Detective Garda Brennan had taken hand and face swabs off her on the morning of the murder and her nightwear had also been tested, but Forensics had found nothing. When he took the swabs, Mrs Nevin told him she had already washed her hands, something which normally removes firearms residue 'totally or almost totally', he said.

The State Pathologist, Dr John Harbison, was examined closely about a possible time of death. He expressed scepticism; it was an inexact science. He had used two methods to calculate, taking his readings after he arrived at Jack White's at 2 p.m. on 19 March. Taking everything into account, the earliest time of death was the last time Tom Nevin was seen alive, but another method suggested a time between 3 a.m. or 3.30 a.m. and the time when his body was found.

His colleague, the Deputy State Pathologist, Dr Marie Cassidy, was more blunt about the vexed issue of establishing times of death at an international conference on forensic science two months later. 'Time of death!' she remarked, 'I am always surprised that people still believe in it. But then again, this is a good Catholic country, and we believe all sorts of things here.'

Dr Harbison told the Nevin trial that when shot is fired, it spreads out in a cone-like shape, causing what is known as 'satelliting' of the pellets. In the murder of Tom Nevin, the shot did not have time to spread out until it was inside the body. There was no satelliting. 'This placed the range of the shot within two yards, possibly less,' was his evidence, but he 'would defer to the ballistics expert on that'.

The shot went from the front right-hand side to the back left -hand side – the pellets came from lower down and to the right, rising. The shot cards or wads that follow pellets when a shotgun is fired at close quarters had penetrated the body and lay in tissue beneath the wound.

The pellets, almost a third of an inch in diameter, had travelled through the right lung and into the left atrium of the heart, before injuring the two main arteries, the pulmonary and the aorta. 'These were severely lacerated and were not quite cut in two.' The projectiles then scattered through the left lung and exited through the ribs at the back. Four were left in the soft tissue beneath the chest and the right arm. The larger exit holes were from the pellets; bone fragments may have caused the smaller ones.

The former Tynagh hurler had died of acute cerebral anoxia, a lack of oxygen to the brain, as a result of a rapid stoppage to his circulation caused by a massive shotgun injury to his heart, aorta and pulmonary arteries, which had given rise to a large accumulation of blood in his chest. In effect, he lost consciousness 'after thirty seconds or so', and died almost immediately. He died where he fell and there was no sign of a struggle.

There was 1¼ litres of blood – more than half the volume of blood in the body – in the chest cavity. The pathologist could smell the aroma of alcohol off the body, and tests showed a blood alcohol level of 119 milligrams per 100 millilitres of blood, 'somewhat above the amount allowed to drivers'. It would have taken 2–5 pints to achieve that level.

'It would have had a minor effect on the deceased,' Dr Harbison said. He found the liver was 'a bit paler than normal' and consistent, among other things, with an excessive consumption of alcohol. But it was not necessarily due to it.

The next witnesses, Frankie Whelan and Johnny Brennan of Brittas Bay, told the jury that after a film had ended on television, Tom drove them home. Frankie reckoned Tom would have arrived back at the Inn at 12.30 a.m.

Sergeant Richard Dominic McElligott of Avoca was pale-faced when he took the stand. Tall and well dressed, he said he wasn't aware if Tom had returned as he was sitting finishing his glass of Guinness in the lounge, Catherine behind the bar. Allowing for leeway, he was definitely off the premises by 12.30 a.m. There was no question of him staying on to have a drink with Tom afterwards. He left through the hall door and Catherine closed it after him. He knew Tom reasonably well, 'as a customer, as a customer'.

Catherine Nevin was later to claim to Detectives Joe Collins and Fergus O'Brien that she latch-locked the door after Sergeant McElligott and then mortice-locked it. The two detectives' evidence of their interviews with Nevin was next in the trial. On the day of the funeral, they found her in the private section of the dining area with ex-Inspector Tom Kennedy. Apart from her claim about the mortice lock, she also said that when she was trying to free herself in the bedroom, she got a strange smell. 'I got a funny smell, an unusual smell. I thought the place was on fire, and then the smell went away.'

Cross-examining Detective Garda Collins on the discovery of Heapes's name and number in her address book on 12 April 1996, Paddy MacEntee said that his instructions were that Heapes had been in the address book since the time he had telephoned looking for a flat. His client had told him that Tom Nevin was very annoyed when he found out that Heapes had phoned. 'The cheek of him,' she claimed Tom said. 'There was something of a row at the very suggestion, and there and then, the name was scribbled out.'

The problem with the latest claim to come from Catherine was that in order for it to be true, both detectives had to be lying. They spotted that the name had been scored out on the front and back of the page on the second occasion they saw the diary, after the search of the Inn on 18 May. But when they had first seen it, Heapes's name and the number of the warehouse where he had worked were written in bold black pen.

'Where did you say you were stationed?' asked Mr MacEntee. The Arklow gardaí bogey men were back again.

But Witness 25, Detective Sergeant O'Brien was not an Arklow garda. He was stationed in Wicklow. In fact, O'Brien had been attached to the Dublin Metropolitan district for 15 years and knew Heapes's stomping ground in West Finglas very well.

The claim of 'bad blood' between Catherine and anyone from Arklow garda station also did not wash because Mrs Nevin herself had placed an acknowledgment in the *Irish Independent* on 18 April 1996 in which she thanked An Garda Siochána, and included 'a very special word' to O'Brien, Joe Collins and 'Commissioner' Jim McHugh, amongst others.

Detective Sergeant O'Brien's evidence brought the trial into its eighth day. He had taken extensive notes of conversations with Mrs Nevin that serve as a telling insight to the real Catherine. There was one occasion where she rang him to report that a satellite dish had been stolen from the flat roof on the pub. When he went to check, he found no sign of a satellite dish or a connection for it, and nothing but a pair of rusty iron brackets to hint at its absence.

On 25 April 1996, Catherine had told him and Joe Collins that since the murder, her driving licence and passport had been missing, and so had Tom's – they had been in the safe along with his marriage annulment documents. The driving licence was later found on the premises and returned to her.

On 29 April, she told them that another £2,000 had been taken from a cash box in the store-room during the raid. 'She said she felt that some member of staff gave out the information to the raiders about the location of the cash and Tom's routine.'

Then, on 5 May, Catherine told them she had contacted 'an old acquaintance on the Barn'. Her contact was 'a young grandfather' who 'used to be a tea leaf' and still had contacts with the underworld. She had contacted 'a similar person' and offered 'a substantial reward for information leading to a person appearing in court for the murder of Tom Nevin, irrespective of whether they were convicted or not'.

'The Barn' was Dolphin's Barn, Catherine's old playground during Tom's days working with his Uncle Willie as a barman in the Dolphin House. 'Tea leaf' was slang for thief. This was raw Catherine, without the language of, 'Goodness, no,' and 'To the best of my knowledge,' which she was to use later in the trial.

On 31 May, she rang Arklow and Wicklow garda stations, requesting a visit and saying she had 'vital information'.

When O'Brien got to Jack White's, it was back to the Barn again. She had been talking to 'a very valued friend of hers for twenty-five years, a true Dub', whose sons used to be thieves but had now settled down and were in the taxi trade. 'The people on the Barn were disgusted at what happened to Tom,' she said. She had had a private investigator working on the case since two weeks after the murder. She had spoken to Tom Kennedy, 'whose opinion she valued more than anyone else's in the world, and he had advised her to tell the gardaí'. Not Arklow gardaí, though, she insisted, she felt 'more violated by the gardaí than by the raiders who murdered Tom'.

O'Brien spoke to her again the next day. Her private investigator had found that 'information on the street was not forthcoming'. A substantial reward had been put up but she wouldn't say how much. 'I felt that on that occasion she was showing signs of stress. Her eyes were blinking and jumping a lot, similar to the time of the murder,' said O'Brien.

Detective Garda John O'Neill of the fingerprints section of the Garda Technical Bureau had also cast doubts in the jury's mind. While no fingerprints were found at the scene, the meticulous detective had not come empty-handed to court. Marks developed on the sides of the drawers removed from the cabinet in her bedroom showed fingermarks, but without any ridges. The drawers had been lifted out and placed on the ground by someone wearing fine leather or surgical gloves.

The *Sunday Independent* of 17 March lying on the top of the double bed was another source of puzzlement for O'Neill. 'The newspaper didn't appear to have been extensively read,' he said.

Finger marks had shown up mainly on its front page, which was the most exposed, and not on the parts of the page where you would expect a reader to hold it. What was more, the marks did not belong to either Tom or Catherine Nevin, even though she had said she read the paper before falling off to sleep.

But the newspaper story was to fall through further during her own evidence. When she was being cross-examined about what position she was in when the raider attacked her, she let slip that she had put the newspaper down on the floor before dozing off. If that was true, why had it ended up on the bed after she was attacked, bound and gagged?

Witness 29 was truly to demolish Catherine's bedroom stories. Teresa Nevin of Ballyshrule, Ballinasloe, was married to Tom's brother, Sean. Teresa travelled to Jack White's on the day of the funeral, arriving with Sean, Noel and his wife Rose. When Teresa and Rose entered the Inn, they found Catherine in the sitting room having her hair done. It was about noon.

Catherine jumped up and hugged Rose. 'Oh Rose,' she said, but displaying no emotion. Then she hugged Teresa.

'My words to her were, "Mother of God, what happened at all?"' Teresa told the trial.

'Her reply was, "We'll talk about it in a minute," presumably when her hair was finished.'

Catherine then gave them an account of what happened. 'She said she was in her bed, almost asleep, when the bedroom door burst open and two men burst in.' That Catherine was still awake when the raiders burst in was a new twist to the tale. But it was not the last. Teresa couldn't picture how Catherine could have moved, from her description of being tied and trussed up.

'I asked her how did you move at all, and she told me her ankles were tied with her own tights and they weren't hard to free.' The tights were news as well. None had been found where she was claiming to have removed them in the bedroom. The conversation was interrupted and it wasn't until after the funeral that Teresa and Rose were to see Catherine again.

'We talked in the run of the evening but at about ten o'clock that night I went to the kitchen to see where all this happened,' Teresa told Peter Charleton. Catherine Nevin was already there with a group of people.

'She seemed to be talking to one man in particular and she introduced me to him.' It was Gerry Fanning, Tom's bank manager from the AIB.

'She said to this man that she had gone up to bed and that she was reading for a while when again, the door burst in and two men come in and one of them had a knife.

'I remember the man asked her if she saw the raiders and she said it was dark.'

Noel Nevin's wife, Rose, was also in the kitchen and was listening to the tale. 'When Catherine replied to this man and said it was dark, Rose Nevin said to her, "But Catherine, if it was dark, how were you reading?"'

'She looked at Rose and turned her head to the man and continued the conversation with him.'

'The remark was ignored,' Teresa Nevin confirmed to Charleton. 'She went ahead to tell this man the noise she heard from the kitchen on the night of the murder. She took a lid from the saucepan and was demonstrating with it.'

Mr Fanning appeared at the deposition stage of the trial process but he was not called to give evidence.

The jury also did not hear an account by one of Tom's sisters of another incident later that night.

It was around midnight, and many of the people who had come to the Inn after the funeral were still there. Tom's sister, Margaret Lavelle, went to look for Catherine. She found her sitting in the old dining room, Tom Kennedy on one side, the bank manager on the other. On the table in front of them were what looked like account books.

Asked for an assessment of Catherine's condition on the day of the funeral, Teresa Nevin had this to say: 'From what I could see there was no emotion whatsoever and she was in total control all day long.'

12

THE PRESS
AND MRS NEVIN

Photographer Brian Barron had missed the picture of the day, a photograph of Nevin entering court. But when he bumped into her in the Round Hall, she maintained eye contact with him, so he ventured to say, 'Mrs Nevin, you've got me into trouble this morning, because I didn't manage to get a picture of you.'

When she offered a gentle smile, he chanced his arm: 'Would you mind stepping outside so I can take one?'

Without changing her expression, she turned to him and said, 'As it happens, I am going outside in a minute to see if a friend has arrived.'

Barron scampered off outside the courts, and within a minute, Catherine Nevin was outside, her hands raised to shield her from the morning glare, looking right and left along the quays, affording him all the time he needed to get the shot.

That encounter with the obliging Mrs Nevin occurred on the morning of 31 January, as a new jury was due to be selected following the dramatic halt to the first trial. But as soon as the court convened, her lawyers raised complaints about press treatment of her. The legal argument that followed was to delay the start of the retrial for a further week.

Because of the judge's direction to the first jury not to read them, the newspapers 'went to town on Mrs Nevin', Patrick MacEntee charged, opening the fresh defence application. There had been 'blanket coverage' and what had been written went 'far outside contemporaneous reporting of the evidence given in the trial'. It was 'nine days of intensive journalism, building one day on another, and giving rise to the likelihood that there is not the least possibility of Mrs Nevin having a fair trial',

The press had already got off to a bad start. Not only had publicity since the murder been prejudiced, they argued, but also the gardaí had systematically leaked material to certain journalists in a manner calculated to turn The People against Mrs Nevin. Then, when the judge dismissed the systematic leaks theory as 'far fetched', press coverage surrounding the start of the trial became the next source of complaint. 'The easiest way to stop these delays would be for the newspapers to stop publishing inappropriate material,' Patrick MacEntee remarked.

It was then only 14 January, two days into the process. News editors were despatching more reporters in anticipation that the trial would get underway. With no press bench officially set aside, journalists had to make do with what was on offer: they took up seats on the emptiest bench, the one Catherine Nevin was sitting on.

'The other matter that concerns me is that Mrs Nevin is sitting surrounded by journalists without the slightest possibility that she can communicate with her counsel in privacy,' Mr MacEntee told the judge. Ms Justice Carroll asked 'the people sitting on her immediate left to move'. A couple of prison wardens shunted down the bench, and the three reporters closest to Nevin picked up their pens and walked. The rest looked uneasy. An agreed distance quickly emerged. The press was not to move any closer than a position opposite the junior counsel's bench. The boundary definition was clear. It was 'the black nob on the radiator'.

By 31 January, the press were firmly in the dock. 'From the very first day, they were talking about her costume,' Mr MacEntee said, picking up an *Evening Herald* cutting. He objected to headlines, photo captions and 'the immediate descent into triviality' in commentaries on the first trial. Reading from one article in the *Herald*, MacEntee said it portrayed Tom Nevin as a simple country boy – 'everything short of dancing at the crossroads', in contrast to the Dublin sophisticate, Catherine Nevin. The judge had already dismissed the same piece as 'sentimental candyfloss', but the catalogue of press cuttings now placed before her showed less sugar and more spice. Changes to reporters' copy at the newspaper editing stage had also given rise to a serious factual inaccuracy in one day's reports in the *Herald* and the *Mirror*.

The legal eagles were united on two issues: the decision to publish a front-page photograph of Nevin leaving her house was an invasion of her privacy, and the 'colour' pieces – the articles that were published alongside trial reports, adding colour and atmosphere to the account of what went on in court – had gone too far. The *Evening Herald* stood out. Its colour writers had skipped the undercoat and went for high gloss. Daily updates discussed Nevin's 'catwalk credentials', her 'keeping up appearances', her 'shimmering in a bright blue ensemble' or being 'the bottle-blonde queen'. The colour pieces in the *Irish Independent* also came in for criticism, although here, the defence were reduced to nit-picking.

The colour pieces in the *Herald* suggested Mrs Nevin's emotions in court were not genuine, Patrick MacEntee alleged.

'The daily comment on her costume is calculated to depersonalise her and make her into some kind of fashion item, where people on trial are seen as glossy, less-than-human persons, not of the world of flesh and blood. The newspapers clearly didn't think there was sufficient story in the flesh and blood of Mrs Nevin, they had to make her into a fairytale.' *The Herald* was determined to turn the trial into the No. 1 national soap, 'and reduce the jury to soap opera watchers'.

References to her red-painted fingernails were meant to connote talons dripping with blood, Nevin's counsel claimed. (That might have been an overextended use of his imagination, Charleton suggested drily.)

The press were also accused of 'prying' into a book she was reading, noting the presence there of a memorial card for Tom. In fact, colour writers complained, Catherine had placed the memorial card on the bench top in front of her, for all to see.

'Of what was she thinking: of her devotion to her late husband?' Patrick MacEntee read aloud from another *Herald* piece. This was 'snide utter nonsense put there to damage Mrs Nevin', he maintained. The press, he accused, were invoking the Black Widow syndrome: Mrs Nevin was being compared to the spider who kills her male after mating.

The following day, the defence counsel was again brandishing a copy of the *Herald*. It had a front page picture of Catherine Nevin with the title, 'New Look Hairstyle'. 'It's quite clear a campaign is going to be waged against Mrs Nevin come what may,' he said. Even her choice of reading material the previous day, a Rudyard Kipling collection, had led to references to 'the female of the species being more deadly than the male', he complained.

But he had thought about the matter overnight, and he was not going to ask to stop the trial, he said – just to delay it. He wanted 'to put some distance between the campaign that was waged by the newspapers last week' and the start of the retrial.

The prosecution pointed out that colour pieces work both ways. Peter Charleton said that, for example, he was not objecting to reports that Mrs Nevin had been 'weeping' in court. But he, too, was particularly critical of the *Evening Herald*, describing some of its commentary as 'rude and ignorant'.

However, 'newspaper discourtesy' was not a reason to stop or delay the trial, Charleton insisted. He said that what the defence was characterising as 'an effort to demonise Mrs Nevin', was in reality nothing more than comment on her clothing and demeanour, distasteful and discourteous though it was. The evidence fell short of a claim that there had been a systematic attempt to get at the jury. 'The newspapers will do what the newspapers will do,' Charleton said, but juries could be trusted to make up their own minds.

Patrick MacEntee was adamant that there should be a lengthy adjournment: 'No-one has ever been asked to turn straight around and start again while the country is still abuzz with the material circulated,' he said.

In a ruling the following day, Ms Justice Carroll stepped in to muzzle the press. But she was not going to stop the trial. Relying on Supreme Court judgments in other cases, she found that there was no real or serious risk of Mrs Nevin not getting a fair trial which could not be avoided by appropriate rulings and directions.

She said: 'I found the colour pieces, particularly in the *Evening Herald*, but to a lesser extent in the *Irish Independent*, the worst kind of tabloid journalism designed solely to sell newspapers, without any regard to Mrs Nevin's dignity as a human person. Mrs Nevin has been dissected every day by comment on her personal appearance, her demeanour. She is given no credit for her composure in a situation of great stress. Comment on her appearance was made in a particularly offensive way.'

The judge refused the defence application, but announced her intention to ban further comment on Nevin's hairstyle, dress, jewellery, nail varnish, reading material or demeanour in court. She also banned publication of photographs of Nevin until the trial was over. But the restrictions were to apply only to the press, and not to radio or television. And they were to apply even to newspapers that had not offended.

Despite lengthy legal submissions from counsel for *The Irish Times*, and separately lawyers for Independent News & Media and the Trinity Mirror Group, the ban stayed.

Lawyers acting for Nevin then renewed their earlier bid to stop the trial because of alleged systematic leaking by gardaí in the time since the murder. Seven journalists, most of them serving or former crime correspondents, were asked to reveal their sources. Press ethics had just taken a bashing, but now it was the media's turn to take the high moral ground.

In the witness box, journalists Liz Allen, Tom Brady, John Maher, Stephen Rae, Senan Molony, Tony Murphy and Damien Lane all declined to reveal the source of their pre-trial material, citing their professional ethics and duty to protect sources. But any who were asked said that in their view there had been no deliberate leaking by the gardaí. Some said that the guards were downright unhelpful. After a day of interrogating them, barrister Paul Burns applied to Ms Justice Carroll to direct the seven to reveal their sources. The Nevin Seven, as they were now being called outside the courtroom, faced the prospect of jail for contempt of court.

The following day, 3 February, the judge refused to order the journalists to name names. She had heard enough. Giving her reasons later, she said that on the basis of the journalists' own evidence, the defence theory that she had previously described as 'far-fetched', she now regarded as 'unsubstantiated'.

Later, Assistant Garda Commissioner Jim McHugh was cross-examined on the claims during his evidence in the retrial. He could not accept that the leaks came from gardaí. 'With respect to journalists,' he said, 'they have a particularly vivid imagination, and sometimes they attribute things to sources which are not accurate. It's always very difficult to establish the sources of information printed in the media.' Raising the prospect of an appeal based on press coverage, Patrick MacEntee countered: 'I am not talking about that. That may be another day's work, and your concern in another place.'

But the judge's gagging orders had left the print media, in particular, feeling very hard done by. Television crews had free rein to film Mrs Nevin coming and going from court, and radio reporters could describe her demeanour in court, but newspaper reporters, who were there as 'the eyes and ears of the public in court', were being asked to wear blindfolds.

Ms Justice Caroll, though, was not for turning. She refused an application from counsel for Independent News & Media and the Trinity Mirror Group who claimed the right to 'publish and publish now' and who objected to what was in effect a 'blanket ban' on comment. She rejected appeals from counsel from *The Irish Times* that it, at least, should not be included, as it had done nothing to warrant restriction.

In a ruling on 9 February, continuing the ban for the duration of the trial, the judge stressed that the rights of the press fell far short of the rights of an accused person to a fair trial. But she also later made clear that the media had a right to criticise her judgments, and she refused a defence invitation to view an editorial and a court report in *The Star* as an attempt to undermine the authority of the court.

For her part, the judge was leaving no route open to claims of an unfair trial. She accompanied her press gags with a direction to the new jury panel assembled before her on 7 February. If their ability to approach the case with an open mind had been affected by pre-trial discussions or publicity, they should tell her and step down, she said. The third jury heard the same direction when their turn came on 14 February.

But the press were not out of the picture yet. In the retrial, just as Jones, Heapes and McClean were due to give their evidence, lawyers acting for them approached the judge's bench and sought a ban on the press from 'improperly describing' their clients. The bid followed sub-editing errors and changes that had wrongly placed them as the alleged hitmen. The three succeeded in getting a ban imposed that prevented publication of photographs or colour pieces on them in Independent group newspapers or in the *Mirror*.

Then, on Friday, 10 March, Mr MacEntee again applied for the jury to be discharged. The offender was again the *Evening Herald*, this time for publishing an article profiling Judge Donnchadh Ó Buachalla after he had given evidence. Mr MacEntee alleged the article was 'calculated to revive the very matter that the district judge roundly denied'.

'Once again, the *Evening Herald* is publishing a profile of a witness and expressing a view on the character of a witness,' Ms Justice Carroll said. But she was 'very reluctant to abort the trial at this stage'. She called on the editor of the *Herald* to appear before her the following Monday 'to explain what he is at in relation to this trial'. *Evening Herald* editor, Gerry O'Regan, duly appeared in court with his counsel, who did all the talking. Ms Justice Carroll interjected: 'If I had to abort this trial last Friday, how would your client like to have to pay the costs of the trial to date?' The offending article had trespassed on the role of the jury to decide the credibility of witnesses and had brought in extraneous comment on matters relevant to the trial, she said.

There had been no deliberate attempt to frustrate the trial, counsel protested. But the judge said that she was coming around to the view that in a criminal trial, the reporting should be limited to what happened in court 'and nothing else'. Serious consideration should be given to it, she said. 'I have never known a trial where there has been as much intrusion by the newspapers,' she remarked, before pointedly adding: 'A fair trial comes before the rights of the mass media to make money.'

Karen O'Connor, a barrister and former RTE producer, believed the judge had to put her foot down. 'I felt she had no choice. She had to do something, take some stand, otherwise she was looking at a mistrial. The rights of the accused had to be protected. I'm not sure if it was the wisest thing to do, to ban photographs in the print media and allow pictures in the electronic media; I can understand why journalists in the print media would feel that was unfair, and I think perhaps it was a bit unfair. But it was all getting out of hand, so it was appropriate for her to do what she did.

'This murder was a very callous crime, there's no doubt about it. It was carried out in a very cold-blooded manner, so I can see why people were interested in it. But the media shouldn't deliberately degrade and dehumanise the accused. The colour of her nail varnish or the way she looked and her demeanour in court and so on, had very little to do with the issue at hand. The criminal justice system was there to take care of that. And it worked.'

A senior legal source was even more forceful in his view that the judge had done the right thing: 'The media during the Nevin trial was not a normal dog; it was a very vicious dog, it needed a muzzle or it was bound to use its fangs again.'

In truth, in at least one newspaper, nothing was sacred when it came to this particular accused. The presumption that she was innocent until proven guilty was nowhere to be found in articles with headlines like PASSION AND INTRIGUE OF BOTTLE-BLONDE QUEEN. Comments like 'be still her beating heart' and 'at 48, with dyed blonde hair and possessed of matronly curves' were interposed with extracts from the actual evidence in the trial. It was even reported that she may have had surgery to enhance her lovemaking, though nothing was proffered in the way of standing up this claim.

The media had identitified Ireland's answer to the OJ Simpson trial and it was not letting go. For some, it was literally a case of The People versus Catherine Nevin. When Nevin was convicted, an article in *Ireland on Sunday* gloated: 'My only regret is that there are no bars or slop out buckets or locked doors in Mountjoy's new women's prison.' Again, this was not in an opinion piece, but in a straight report on the conclusion of the case – a 'wraparound' it is called in the trade.

'I was very concerned, I thought it vilified and dehumanised the woman,' commented Karen O'Connor on the media coverage in general. 'I felt the system had worked, there was plenty of time given in the courts, the jury had deliberated for a very lengthy period, and she was convicted. When someone is convicted, I am concerned at society getting its pound of flesh.'

O'Connor pointed out that in the Gillane case, a recent trial of a Galway man convicted of soliciting two men to kill his wife, 'there was very little about what he wore to court'. 'Look at the General,' she added, referring to the dead criminal, Martin Cahill, 'He made a virtue out of coming to court dressed in a particular way and I don't remember reading details of his underwear – nor would I like to. In this case, it wasn't so much guilty by association, but guilty by virtue of what you wear. It's pure sexism.'

Dermot Walsh, professor of law at the University of Limerick, was also concerned at what he saw as prejudicial coverage. The details in the Nevin trial 'were what the public wanted to hear' he said, 'It was pandering to the old human interest, anything to do with sex, intrigue, the evil woman.

'We are used to seeing women who kill who are suffering from psychiatric problems,' he said, 'but a woman who cold-bloodedly and in a calculating manner plans to murder, rarely happens. Because it's so unusual, it is like a Little Red Riding Hood scenario; those fears are out there. A woman bears life, protects life and here we have this turned on its head. The media fed the primeval fears that lurked behind this scenario. Better still if you can tie sex into it, then you are into titillation. Newspaper editors, particularly the tabloids, know that titillation captures a broad readership.

'It's all very fine for the media to play this up for what they call the public interest, but in doing so, they also run the risk of biasing a jury against the defendant. It's like seeing the evidence through a long lens, or with a particular focus, even sub-consciously, and that's what starts to create the problems.'

Days after the verdict, Liz Allen of the *Sunday Independent* was interviewed on the Late Late Show, ironically taking the place of Nevin herself, who had agreed to go on if she was acquitted. 'I did not see it as adding anything new and most of it was pure gossip,' said Karen O'Connor, commenting on the content of the interview. 'I felt it was feeding that sense of voyeurism and the kind of vengefulness that was evident from some of the media coverage after she was convicted. In my day you had to have your sources and you had to be able to stand over it; gossip just wasn't good enough.'

O'Connor and others critical of the media coverage noted that female journalists were the worst offenders. Yet, it was editors who were pushing for more and more salacious reportage, and with the recent exception of the Ireland edition of *The Sunday Times*, they were all men. 'They couldn't get enough of it,' confided one woman reporter. 'They sent me down to get more of the juicy bits.'

Ms Justice Carroll herself said that she did not subscribe to the view that Mrs Nevin had been 'deliberately demonised'. The press coverage was 'rather a pandering to the insatiable appetite of some of the media for details about Mrs Nevin, at times cruel, at times titillating and always intrusive,' she said.

Catherine herself might not have cared. The press and Mrs Nevin was a two-faced theme. While her lawyers were fiercely defending her rights inside the court, unbeknown to them, their client's by now regular chats with press photographer Brian Barron had led to the promise of pics of herself and Tom on their last foreign holiday together. 'Don't mention it – any time – just ask,' she said, when he thanked her for allowing him to take a snap.

13

A TRIP TO THE
HAIRDRESSER

❧❧❦❧❧

The staff at Jack White's were no sooner called to the witness box than the defence was trying to keep them out.

Sisters Fiona and Deirdre Lawlor from Co. Carlow had just given evidence that, for the first time ever, on Monday, 18 March, they were paid by cheque, and by Mrs Nevin herself.

Fiona Lawlor said Tom and Catherine's marriage was 'more like a business relationship'. The phrase was repeated by others. So was the description of Mr Nevin. 'He was brilliant, he was really nice,' said Fiona. He was 'really supportive' when she was young and away from home, said Deirdre.

After a lunchtime recess, Patrick MacEntee rose, his brow furrowed. All the staff evidence was highly prejudicial and should be excluded, he argued. Peter Charleton then announced his intent. 'Evidence will be called that Mrs Nevin was in a marital relationship with another man: Inspector Tom Kennedy,' he said, 'and that they were found in bed together.'

From former chef, Alan McGraynor, the jurors heard that Tom and Catherine had separate bedrooms and would talk only business together. He had never witnessed violence between them, 'but arguments, yes'. McGraynor had gone on holidays to the Canaries with Tom Nevin twice, but Tom 'never discussed private matters' with him.

It was Alan McGraynor who was later to become the object of Catherine's allegation to carpet fitter Donncha Long that Tom was having 'sexual affairs with the barman'. Alan McGraynor denied the suggestion that he and Tom had a relationship. The claim that Tom was gay was also dismissed by his first wife, June O'Flanagan, and the members of his own family.

Orla Glennon, a niece of Tom Nevin's, had worked in Jack White's in Summer 1989. Tom and Catherine were sharing a bedroom at the time, she said, 'but they were arguing a lot'.

Caroline Strahan, who was just 15 years and 11 months old when she started as a kitchen worker and waitress at the Inn in 1992, said Tom and Catherine 'used to argue a lot of the time' and that 'they had separate bedrooms'.

Then the first allegation of an affair was out. Catherine had a relationship with someone else, Strahan said. 'Tom Kennedy – the Superintendent from Wicklow.' The jury later heard that in fact, Kennedy had been Acting Superintendent for a time in the area.

'My instructions are that that is not so,' Mr MacEntee said of the alleged relationship.

'Well that's what it seemed like to me, what I had seen when I was working there,' Ms Strahan said.

Peter Charleton rose to re-examine. 'It's been put to you . . . and you indicated what you saw – can you tell exactly what you saw?'

'I seen Tom (Kennedy) and Catherine in Catherine's bedroom a few times,' Caroline Strahan said. 'There was a phonecall for Catherine and I went upstairs to tell her and that's how I seen them.'

'Can you finish the sentence?' Charleton's tone was gentle.

'Catherine and Tom were in Catherine's bed when I went in to tell Catherine about the phonecall. I think it was evening time. From what I seen, Tom didn't have any shirt on him and I can't remember about Catherine.'

'What did he have on if not his shirt?'

'I didn't see anything.'

The next witness, Adrienne Fisher, was so overcome at events that she was close to tears and spent just a few moments in the witness box. A slightly red-faced Catherine Nevin glanced up at her former worker on the witness stand and raised her eyes briefly to heaven.

Eileen Byrne then told the trial that Inspector Tom Kennedy was at the Inn 'every morning' and that it was 'like a second home to him'.

By the time Catherine McGraynor, Alan's sister, gave her evidence, Nevin's arms were crossed in front of her. It was a Friday. Outside, staff witnesses were calling her counsel 'the Rottweiler'.

And then it was Monday, Day 11 of the retrial, and Day 30 of the proceedings. Jane Murphy of Redcross, the former cleaner at the Inn, was asked if she could recall some phonecalls to the Inn.

'Yeah,' she said. 'Mr Ferguson, that's all, and the judge. The judge from Arklow.'

Did Mr Ferguson ever come to visit or stay?, she was asked. 'Not that I know,' she replied.

'And the judge, did he ever come to visit or stay?'

'He did, yeah.'

By 3.30 p.m., the judge from Arklow had featured on every news slot since midday. Down in the Four Courts, lawyers were sniffing at the prurient press.

In the Central Criminal Court, the prosecution was gathering pace. Detective Garda Joe McKenna had told the jury that he first met John Jones on 16 July 1996 in a car park at Dublin airport. Jones was operating shuttle buses there. Their first meeting was 'a confrontation, so to speak'. On 23 July he went there again, and this time spoke to Jones for 20 minutes. On 27 July he rang him at his home number and met him at the agreed venue of Balbriggan garda station later that day. Mr Jones had decided to talk.

'Can I have Mr John Jones, please?,' the prosecution counsel said. A respectable-looking man with a grey beard, grey hair and receding hairline slowly walked to the stand. He was wearing a sports jacket and tie and a yellow shirt, and could have been a school teacher or a civil servant.

'The first time I met Mrs Nevin would have been around eighty-four or eighty-five. She came into the advice centre,' said Jones. This was the Sinn Féin centre run from the upstairs back room of 2a Church Street, Finglas. 'She said that she had been recommended to us by one of our offices in Dublin, either Blessington Street or Parnell Square, and that she was looking for a pub to buy.'

'A very unusual' request to deal with, he agreed. He couldn't assist her, 'not at all'. He later learnt that she had got a lease for the Barry House. And did he see her again? 'Oh, I saw her several times. She allowed us to use the pub for a fund-raiser, and for selling *An Phoblacht*.' The Cumann would have functions there, yes. 'Did she have an involvement with your organisation herself?,' Charleton wondered.

'None whatsoever,' Jones replied.

Then there were the 'propositions' years later. It was around 1989. She had come into the advice centre, and after general chit-chat for 45 minutes or so, she said, 'I have a proposition for you.'

'Go ahead,' he said.

'I want you to get the IRA to shoot Tom,' she said.

'That was it. I just laughed it off at the time, I couldn't believe it.'

Jones detailed the approaches that followed and the promise of the £23,000 to £25,000.

Catherine Nevin had told him that Tom did the bank lodgments 'either in Rathgar, Rathmines or Rialto', he could not remember. 'She would ensure that Tom was on his own and that the IRA could get him en route.'

'I said that I could not contemplate that. I said I couldn't even think about it; it was beyond thinking about at all. It was nonsense.'

Jones said he and Tom had got on well, having met at the Barry House, and that Tom was 'a quiet man'.

Jones was propositioned 'five or six times' over the period of a year, from 'sometime in 1989 to sometime in 1990'. On the last two or maybe three occasions when she called in – always with some excuse – she said, 'Have you thought any more of the proposition?'

'On the final time she came in I said I didn't want to hear the subject ever again and I saw no more of her,' Jones said.

He told the jury of one occasion when Catherine came into the advice centre and revealed a pair of black eyes, sometime in 1990 or 1991. Later, plastic surgeon Dr Michael Earley was to tell the trial that Nevin had a plastic surgery operation on her upper and lower eyelids in St Vincent's Private Hospital in September 1991. She was released from hospital on 8 September with what would appear to the lay person as 'two black eyes,' he said. But he named the venue as Vincent's, not the Mater. In fact it was the

Mater Hospital, and it was the occasion of that admission on 6 September 1991, that she named Tom Kennedy as her next-of-kin. If Nevin came to Finglas with black eyes from plastic surgery, it was in 1991. John Jones had no problem with that date, he simply couldn't remember exactly when it was, but the indictment sheet said he was solicited in or around 1989. In her direction later to the jury, Ms Justice Carroll said the wording of the Count 2 charge could include 1989 and 1990 'but could not stretch to 1991'.

Cross-examined, Jones said that he left Sinn Féin in 1993, maybe 1994, and had not joined any similar organisation. He originally joined in 1969 or 1970, and had not been a member of the Fianna, the republican youth wing, at any stage. His training was in sales and administration. In 1978, he and Dessie Ellis had set up the business partnership, Channel Visions Ltd.

'Tell us about Mr Ellis,' said MacEntee. 'He was a TV repair man,' said Jones. The defence counsel wanted to be told more. 'Well, politically he was involved in the IRA, I believe,' Jones replied.

He had no idea which part of bombs Ellis was convicted of making, and was not sure of the length of his sentence. He was not working for Ellis as such, but Ellis would call to the shop at lunchtimes as he held down his regular job at Kilroys in Santry.

At 4 p.m., Mr Jones's mobile phone went off as he was sitting in the witness stand. He apologised to the court. Catherine Nevin wasn't the only one with a busy social life. As he left the Four Courts, Jones gave photographers the slip. 'There were five of us after him. I don't know how he managed it,' one of them recalled.

John Jones had taken voluntary redundancy to manage the business full-time when Dessie Ellis was on the run. He also helped set up the advice centre in the aftermath of the hunger strikes when Sinn Féin was looking to get into mainstream politics.

When Ellis was arrested in 1981, 2a Church Street had been raided and all the files relating to the business removed. Jones was himself arrested, and 'questioned about Mr Ellis'.

'Were you questioned about perhaps the making of circuit boards at 2a Church Street and your possible knowledge of that?' inquired MacEntee.

'No,' said Mr Jones.

John Jones said he had met Tom Nevin when Catherine introduced him after they took over the lease of the Barry House.

'He was, of course, of republican sympathies,' interrupted Paddy MacEntee.

'I couldn't tell you,' said Jones.

'Well, why do you say that?'

'I am unaware of any sympathies, his political sympathies or his religion for that matter. I know nothing deep about the man.'

'Was it not the case that at the time you sold An Phoblacht there with his consent?'

'No, I am sorry, it was with Catherine's consent,' Jones retorted.

Later, Jones was asked if it was in 1989 or 1990 that she solicited him to murder. 'It was sometime in eighty-nine or ninety, yes, or maybe ninety-one,' he said. 'To be honest, it was somewhere around eleven years ago. It was not something I can look up to recall, I am just going from memory. I know Dessie Ellis was released from England in ninety-one, ninety-two – he had been extradited to England – I know it was prior to that date.'

The jury had already heard that Ellis had been arrested in the early 1980s and had gone on the run. They knew that he was caught in the USA and returned to Ireland where he was convicted of possession of explosives and spent eight years in jail. They now knew of his extradition.

But they were not told that at the trial that followed, Ellis was forced to answer the charge of conspiracy to cause explosions, a charge that puts the onus on the defendant to prove his innocence. On 23 October 1991, the Old Bailey jury acquitted him and he was immediately released and sent back to Dublin.

Ironically, that release date, which was not brought to the jury in the Nevin trial, showed that if Jones's recollection was right, then Nevin's soliciting of him could have occurred right up to October 1991 – a date outside the remit of the Count 2 charge Nevin was facing, which was in or around 1989.

In his evidence, John Jones told the jury that he found Catherine Nevin's propositions bizarre, and even more bizarre was her story to him that when she went into apartments that she owned 'on the North Circular or the South Circular Road,' she was confronted by two SAS men. Patrick MacEntee put it to him that Catherine had brought components back to Jones from those apartments and that she had allowed him use one of the flats, rent free, for five weeks. 'That is not true,' said Mr Jones. 'I have never been in any of her places. I never had the use of anything, ever.'

Patrick MacEntee continued with his client's account: that indeed, two people had passed Catherine as she went into the house and one had broken glass in his hand and cut her with it as he passed. That she had gone into the flat and found what looked like television circuit boards hidden there. That she went to hospital and got stitches, that she told Mr Jones about it and he told her not to go to the police.

'I've never heard such a load of rubbish in my life,' John Jones said. 'She told me that she was confronted by two SAS men; she struggled with them and they got out the window.'

Jones had not told the police about her story because he didn't believe it, and because of what he and his family and friends had suffered under Special Branch harassment, he wouldn't have anyway, he said. 'But you did,' said Mr MacEntee.

'After the fact,' Jones countered. 'After it had happened.'

Any words he spoke to Nevin in dismissing her 'ridiculous' proposition 'would have been quite angry', he said.

'Why didn't you go to the gardaí and say here is a lady who is either bats or a very nasty piece of goods?,' asked the barrister.

'Very simply, Mr MacEntee, the reason was because of our relationship with gardaí. I wasn't sure whether herself and Tom had been asked to do this, to put this to us to discredit us.'

From the moment Catherine Nevin first came in asking for pub advice from Sinn Féin he had felt 'there was something wrong about it,' he said.

When she made the initial approach to solicit him, he had spoken to two members 'in the movement,' one Pat Russell, the other, he insisted he just could not remember.

'Did it ever occur to you to contact some of the people in the IRA you might know?,' enquired MacEntee.

'I beg your pardon? I am not aware of anyone in the IRA. I do not know anyone in the IRA and I would not know how to contact them.'

The point was, said Jones, that Nevin's proposition was beyond contemplation and 'wasn't considered in any way at all'. When Tom was murdered, he felt it his duty to get in touch with the gardaí, but Pat Russell advised him that they would no doubt be in touch with him anyway.

As the details of Catherine Nevin's allegation of a meeting in the Green Isle Hotel with £100,000 promised from the North for the proposed purchase of the Killinarden Inn were put to the witness, he denied all knowledge of it. 'Justice, I know nothing of this at all,' he said.

By the end of the cross-examination, things were getting hot and heavy. Jones was proving a match for the wiles of the famous barrister. 'No amount of bluster' from Mr MacEntee could change the fact that Nevin had asked him to get the IRA to kill her husband, he said convincingly. Then he was asked about his previous conviction.

He had bought a car from an ad in a newspaper and only discovered the papers did not match later, he said. He put it in his garage and bought another one. He was 'considering how to get rid of the thing' when the Special Branch found it and he was hauled before the courts. 'I employed a very prominent barrister,' he said. 'He gave me two options: I could fight it, but because of my republican background, the gardaí would make it awkward. The second was to put my hands up and the barrister would explain the situation.'

He chose the second option, and the car was returned to him by the court. 'It's just that Mr MacEntee represented me,' he said. 'That is so,' said the Great Defender, retreating.

On the first day of his evidence, Gerard Heapes wore a blue denim shirt with a tie, and a black suit jacket. By the second day, the tie had been discarded, and the denim shirt was open at the top. Heapes was settling into the witness box.

He told junior prosecution counsel Tom O'Connell that on his release from prison in May or June 1985, he joined the Finglas Cumann of Sinn Féin for a few months.

He remembered Catherine Nevin, 'popping in and out, once or twice a week' from the Sinn Fein advice centre in the rear room of 2a Church Street. In 1986, he and his wife, Breda, went to the opening of Jack White's. In 1989, Catherine approached him in Finglas and as they chatted in the Barry House, she confided in him that she wasn't getting on with Tom and claimed he was beating her up.

'Then she came out with the bombshell: she wanted to know would I kill her husband.'

Thus began what Heapes asked counsel to understand was 'a long course of events.

'I said like, Catherine, I'll think about it. I don't want to be called a male chauvinist here, but I just thought it was a woman in one of her moods, you know, going off her head.'

Heapes then brought the jury through his 'ten to twelve meetings' with Nevin. Each time she stretched the plans and he stretched the excuses, he claimed. 'I said you couldn't kill him in the pub, there'd be too many people there,' was one example.

'I said I wouldn't kill someone for £25,000, you know what I mean . . .' was another. When he said that, she upped it to £40,000, he recalled.

He detailed his trips with her to the Phoenix Park, to outside the South Circular Road flats and to the Grasshopper Inn in Clonee, Co. Meath. He told of her proposal that the killing be made to look like a robbery, of her suggestion that she would pave the way for a hit on Tom as he made his lodgments in the bank, and of the proposal to shoot him as he collected rents from the flats. She had also twice tried to get him to carry out the killing on bank holiday weekends.

When she told him the Grasshopper plan, and of her wish to die in Tom's arms, Heapes thought that proposal was 'sick' and their meetings ended abruptly, he told the trial.

He had found all of her approaches to him 'ludicrous'; but first 'curious,' and then 'intrigued,' it seemed he couldn't stop meeting her. When she spoke to him first, he thought he was 'better off letting her have a rant about it,' but he eventually said, 'Talk to me again about it, I have to go home.' He blocked each proposal she made, but when he 'knocked one on the head,' she would come up with another.

After the Grasshopper plan, he wanted no more of it, and she was cottoning on to the fact that he was going to do nothing.

It was clear that Gerry Heapes was no angel. In his throwaway style, he admitted that he had gone out to Jack White's some years later, 'To see if she still wants her husband killed and see if we can get some money off her because she wouldn't be able to go the police.' Heapes's attempt to con Catherine failed from the starting post. She marched over to him on his arrival at the Inn and said things had been patched up between herself and her husband.

Heapes, the failed robber, had been foiled again.

'Mister Heapes,' Patrick MacEntee said witheringly, rising to cross-examine. It was during that session that Heapes was to admit to being a former member of the IRA, although his outline of the 1977 heist on the Fairview cash & carry didn't include the detail about the money in his socks.

He was caught straight away, and the siege went on for another ten hours, he said. He was sentenced to ten years for illegal possesion of firearms and robbery, but 'we were also found not guilty of having firearms with intent to endanger life.'

He denied that his attendance at Sinn Féin meetings dropped off because of a difference of views. It was, he said, 'because I felt I had given the best part of twenty years to the republican movement and it was time to give some to my family'.

Heapes said he didn't go to the gardaí when Catherine Nevin solicited him to murder because of 'the treatment' he had received at the hands of the Special Branch in earlier years. 'I'd have nothing to do with the gardaí,' he said. He also, 'didn't think she'd go ahead with it.'

He hadn't 'a clue' when the soliciting had happened, it was the late 1980s, early 1990s, he would say it was later than '87. Did he know even the decade? 'Will you settle for the century?,' he asked.

Redser and Macker, the 'fellas in the pool hall' he spoke to about it thought it was a wind-up. 'It didn't seem possible that someone would keep on coming back when you knocked the holes in it, and yet she kept coming back . . .'

The defence counsel zoned in on the pool hall and read from Heapes's own statement to the gardaí, a statement he never signed.

The statement suggests Redser and Macker weren't just drinking buddies. It says: 'They told me to get more details and keep reporting back to them.' It goes on: 'When I reported back again, from the impression I got then, knowing how serious the matter was, I thought action would be taken to stop it, either by telling Tom or calling Catherine in.' He understood that action was taken. 'A few days later, I heard that some people had either gone out to Jack White's to Catherine or called her into Dublin and told her they had heard about her plans and if they heard anything more about it, they were going to tell Tom or deal with her, or whoever got the contract.'

In court, all Heapes confirmed was that when he was 'down in the pool hall' a week later, 'they said they had looked after it'. But he denied Redser and Macker were 'people of some substance.'

Heapes wasn't giving anything away. Sitting back on the witness stand with his legs crossed and his arms folded, he was already back in Finglas, telling the tale of his showdown with Paddy MacEntee.

William McClean was pernickety. Mr Charleton told him there was water there for him to drink. 'Is that a clean glass?,' he asked, picking up one to examine it. If Heapes's dress sense was sloppy, McClean's was just bad. Neat as a pin, with freshly washed, combed hair, he wore a succession of garish patterned jumpers – his first ensemble a green-knit v-neck with large mustard-yellow stripe, cream shirt and gold tie.

McClean replayed his encounter with Catherine in St Vincent's Hospital, but first he admitted to having had an affair with her. It took in the period when Tom and Catherine moved to Jack White's. Her 1990 request in a private room in St Vincent's Hospital that he get someone to 'do a job' on Tom was accompanied by the promise of £20,000 and the evidence of a motive: that she'd get 'the pub, the insurance money, the lot – everything'.

Under cross-examination, McClean was incredulous when he saw Nevin's counsel was disputing that she had an affair with him.

He was reticent about his criminal convictions. He appealed his three-month sentence for deception from Clogher Magistrates Court in 1973, he said.

But in the following year, at Omagh County Court, the sentence was affirmed, defence junior counsel Paul Burns pointed out to him.

'Well I didn't do the three months, then,' said McClean.

'Well are you wanted up North then to do your three months, is that a possibility?'

'It's a possibility.'

'Tell us about the second conviction'.

'That was apples.'

'Abbots?' Peter Charleton interjected.

'I bought a load of apples.'

'Well you hardly bought abbots,' Burns scoffed.

'I don't speak Ulster Scots,' Charleton mumbled.

'I bought a load of apples and exported them to the South, and didn't pay any duty on them,' McClean continued. 'Then the man I bought them from came after me.'

'Why did he?,' asked Burns. 'Didn't you pay the man you bought them off?'

'No,' said McClean.

'Well, weren't you convicted of a crime, then?'

'I didn't say it was a crime – you did.'

McClean said he had no links with paramilitaries, either loyalist or republican. He agreed he had told gardaí that Catherine Nevin knew he was involved 'in a bit of hookie'. That was just 'wheeling and dealing, that's all,' he said. He used to do 'a bit of smuggling' of cattle and spirits as well.

'Smuggling's a crime, you know that,' said Burns.

'Well, if you're caught it is,' said McClean.

Later, the defence was to call McClean a liar who practised in deception and was 'in the business of peddling false pretences to obtain benefit for himself.'

But McClean's evidence of soliciting got backing from an unlikely source. Sr Mary Baptist, also known as Patricia Summers, the former Chief Executive of St Vincent's Private Hospital, confirmed that Catherine Nevin had been admitted to the hospital twice in 1990. The first admission, 3 May to 11 May, was to a four-bed ward. When she was admitted the second time, between 25 October and 31 October 1990, she was transferred to a single room when one became available.

The judge from Arklow returned to the attention of the trial when he was named by Liz Hudson on 3 March 2000. Her evidence was first interrupted by legal argument over her allegation that 'as far as we could see, Catherine was having affairs.'

'I don't wish to raise the spectre of discharging the jury,' said Paddy MacEntee, when the jury were in their room, 'but if this goes on, I will have to.' But Peter Charleton said there was more concrete evidence to follow – the next-of-kin evidence from the 1991 hospital admission would be 'entered in due course' to prove Catherine's relationship with Tom Kennedy. He recognised the danger of doing it, he said, but he felt that given the defence challenges to the evidence that was so far before the jury, he had no choice.

'I don't want the case to become about Mrs Nevin and people in Wicklow,' he said. 'I don't wish to make this into a case about Mrs Nevin's sexual mores.' However, it was being alleged that Willie McClean was lying when he said he had an affair with Mrs Nevin, and now it seemed Ms Hudson's evidence was being challenged.

Liz Hudson confirmed to the judge that she was speaking from her own personal knowledge, and her evidence was allowed to go ahead. 'There is nothing in her statement that gives the impression she saw anything of this nature,' Patrick MacEntee protested. 'But so be it, if this is your lordship's ruling, I'll abide by it.' 'This is an outrage,' he whispered to his junior.

Back before the jury, Hudson was giving evidence about sets of keys. Catherine asked her for a loan of her set one night, she said.

'And without saying who had the set she had, can you tell us why she wanted them?,' asked Charleton.

'Because somebody else had her set of keys'.

'And I think that was somebody who was well known on the premises?,' counsel asked.

'That's right, Judge Ó Buachalla,' said Liz Hudson.

Bernie Fleming later told the jury that a set of keys normally left hanging in the hall had gone missing six or seven weeks before Tom Nevin's murder. When she asked Catherine Nevin she said, 'The judge has them'.

Later, in her evidence, Catherine recalled conversations with both Bernie Fleming and Liz Hudson about keys, but denied she ever said the judge had them. The prosecution hadn't intended to call the judge, but now they were left with little choice. There was a matter of a set of keys to be sorted out.

By the morning of 7 March, the judge was in court himself, seated beside three uniformed gardaí, waiting.

As the registrar completed a roll call of the jury, Catherine Nevin looked over in the district judge's direction, appearing to try to catch his gaze. If she was, he was ignoring her, turning his head to look at the wood-panelled exit to his left.

When he was called, Judge Donnchadh Ó Buachalla strode up to the witness box, his face firmly set away from the accused as he passed her.

'Yes, indeed I came to know Jack White's very well, and found myself knowing both Tom and Catherine Nevin very well, and had an excellent relationship with both of them,' he said.

Yes, there were times when he would have called in, possibly two to three times a week, and sometimes in the morning, but it would have depended on what was going on in his main functions.

'No, I never stayed overnight,' he told Mr Charleton.

'At no time whatsoever did I have keys, nor did I see any set of keys,' he said.

The last time he had been there in the pub was with his wife and family, 'and indeed in-laws' on the weekend Tom Nevin was murdered. They had a meal at around eight. 'In fact, Tom joined us for some ten to fifteen minutes at that table'. They had talked about 'some very, very general matters.'

'It has been suggested here that you were having some sort of an affair –' began Patrick MacEntee, cross-examining.

'Sorry, it has never been suggested,' Peter Charleton interrupted, rising.

'It has.'

'Well, perhaps if the jury could retire for a moment,' the prosecution counsel said.

The jury safely in its room, MacEntee said he wasn't asking the question on the basis that it was ever said in direct terms, but that it was 'said in innuendo and said in circumstance'. A formula was agreed. It was to be put to Judge Ó Buachalla that it had been implied that he was having an affair.

The jury returned. 'Evidence was given by Ms Hudson and by Ms Fleming from which it may have been implied that you were having some sort of irregular sexual affair with Mrs Nevin,' MacEntee put to Ó Buachalla.

'It is not so. That is totally untrue.'

'Did anything ever happen that may have given rise to that suggestion?'

'No, nothing that I am aware of.' Ó Buachalla's evidence finished shortly afterwards and he strode from the court.

The following day, Liz Hudson was recalled at the request of the defence. She repeated her evidence about her exchange with Mrs Nevin over the keys and said it had happened 'a couple of weeks before Tom was killed'.

From Patrick Russell, the mysterious 'John Ferguson,' the jury heard of the accused's attempts to change accountants in the weeks before the murder. Jack White's existing accountants, Coopers & Lybrand, had slapped on an extra fee for an audit by the Revenue and Mrs Nevin was none too pleased. She rang up Russell and when they met, she asked him if he could take on the accounts. It was too much for him, he told the court, and anyhow, he didn't want to work for her, as he believed her to be 'a hard taskmaster'. In addition, he wasn't qualified to sign an audit.

He didn't find her accountancy quibbles surprising either. These Revenue audits were a common problem in the licensed trade and there was 'a major dispute within the trade over whether accountants should be charging for this as an additional fee,' he said.

Russell's evidence was that at a meeting in the Davenport Hotel in mid-January 1996, Catherine Nevin had told him that Tom 'was drinking heavily and wasn't pulling his weight. 'In passing, she mentioned that she would love to buy him out, but she knew that Tom wouldn't go for it'.

Russell said that they arranged that he would ring about finding her a new accountant, and she told him, 'in the most strident terms to be very circumspect when I phoned the pub'. He came up with the pseudonym John Fergus, though he accepted that John Ferguson is what it transpired to be. Catherine was 'obsessive' about the use of a false name; she didn't trust the staff, and 'wanted all the ducks in a row' before she spoke to Tom about the change of accountant.

Russell said he had begun to detach himself from Sinn Féin in 1987 owing to pressures of time. He kept up his friendship with John Jones, and had occasionally done some accounting work for him.

He held a number of business, accounting and finance, marketing and legal degrees and diplomas from Trinity College, the former NIHE in Limerick, and King's Inns. He was now a financial consultant, working with property developers and 'putting people together with deals'.

After his meeting with Catherine in January, he arranged two meetings between her and a Cork accountant, Noel Murphy. She hadn't turned up for the first, and he made a number of phonecalls to ensure she did for the second. Ironically, Mr Murphy, who was later to meet Tom, was phoning Jack White's Inn on the morning of the murder, unaware of the reason why he was getting an engaged tone.

Cross-examined about his days in Sinn Féin in Finglas, Russell could not recall saying in garda custody that John Jones appeared to be friends with the Nevins, and that there was talk of him going into business with them. But he said: 'I was aware that the Nevins were trying to buy the Killinarden Inn. It was common knowledge in the Finglas area.'

Later in the trial, ex-Inspector Tom Kennedy turned up in court two days in a row waiting to deny the allegations about his affair with Catherine Nevin.

In the absence of the jury, Charleton was adamant that he was not going to call him. Kennedy was essentially a defence witness, the prosecution lawyer felt. He would make Kennedy available to the defence but was not willing to tender him.

Inspector Kennedy was down on hospital admission documents as Catherine Nevin's next-of-kin, Charleton said. The prosecution could not call someone's spouse, 'and while he may not know it, that was her view of him'.

'Is there a reason you don't wish to call him?' Ms Justice Carroll asked Mr Charleton.

'There is, my Lord. If I offer him as a witness, I am not able to cross-examine him, and he is, to use the least term, the closest friend of the accused for ten years. If Mr MacEntee chooses to have Inspector Kennedy say he and Mrs Nevin were not having an intimate relationship, then I want the right to cross-examine him. Mr Kennedy is here. He has spoken to Mr MacEntee, and he can be part of the defence case.'

The following morning, Ms Justice Carroll ruled that 'coming as it does, at the end of the prosecution case, I must find in favour of the defence, so that there can be no claim of unfairness'. Inspector Kennedy was to be a prosecution witness, whether Charleton liked it or not.

'No, M'Lord, never. I am not into that, M'Lord. I value my family and my marriage,' said Tom Kennedy, denying a sexual relationship moments after he took the stand.

He said he sometimes visited Mrs Nevin in her bedroom during her frequent bouts of illness. He would be asked to visit, he said. He would pick up medications in Wicklow and bring them to her. Kennedy claimed it was usually her husband Tom, or members of the staff at the Inn, who asked him to see Mrs Nevin.

He denied staying overnight at 17 Mountshannon Road, and again denied any sexual relationship. His evidence finished, he moved from the Four Courts up the quays, a retired garda in a respectable black overcoat, his large frame pushing an extended belly before it.

It was a Friday. The prosecution case was closed and it was now over to the defence. Legal argument took over. Speculation mounted. Would Mrs Nevin take the stand?

Earlier in the trial, she had complained that someone had threatened her as she sat having a cup of coffee in the Four Courts restaurant. She had also complained of a threatening phonecall.

Erring on the side of caution, it was decided to assign Bridewell gardaí to look after her while she was within the court precincts, while detectives from Kevin Street station were assigned to monitor her away from the courts.

The next day, a Saturday, Catherine was taking one of her regular trips to a Peter Mark hair salon in Crumlin Shopping Centre, where her long-time friend, Noeleen Hynes-Gorman was a stylist. Noeleen had been styling Catherine's hair throughout the trial. Often, Nevin would make an early appointment so that her hair could be arranged before she was dropped to the Four Courts. Her days often began or ended with a trip to the hairdressers.

Crumlin shopping centre is right next to a garda station, around the corner from Dolphin's Barn. For all her concern about threats, that Saturday Catherine tried to lose her garda cover by slipping out of the back door of the salon.

14

ANORAK MAN

'**M**y husband, my Lord, was a member of the IRA.' With a flutter of eyelids, Catherine delivered the latest bombshell shortly after 3.15 p.m. on 14 March. It was Day 22 of the trial, her fortieth day in court, and she was finally centre stage.

Placing herself in the witness box just 20 minutes before, she had pursed her lips and moved the microphone down towards her mouth. A small gold brooch sat on her purple suit. It was the model of a plane, pointing skywards.

The Barry House was 'a very nice pub' but she had 'never been in the Sinn Féin advice centre' in 2a Church Street. John Jones 'was a friend of my husband's so he was in and out quite a lot.'

'My husband had political friends of his on the premises. I wasn't there all the time, my Lord, I wouldn't know everything that happened in the place.'

'When you talk about political friends, what do you mean?' Patrick MacEntee waited. It was then that she dropped the bombshell.

'I heard it approximately three years after we were married, my Lord', she said of her IRA claim. 'Well, my Lord, my husband was coming home three nights a week, very late. When I say late I say six o'clock in the morning, and when we sat down and talked about it, I had presumed that perhaps he was seeing someone else, and it was then that he told me that this was part of his life and it would always be part of his life.'

Bombshell number two was not far away. Her 'intimate life' with her husband was all right, there was nothing wrong, 'for the twenty years of our marriage we were very happy'.

And so she moved on. 'Tom entered negotiations to purchase the Killinarden Inn in Tallaght', she said. 'Tom visited it on many occasions, and I went to see it myself as well.' Tom was to take over the ownership of the premises but £100,000 was to come from John Jones. That arrangement came about from a meeting in the Green Isle Hotel attended by 'myself, my late husband, John Jones, Johnny Deery from the North of Ireland, John Noonan – I think he was from Tallaght – and Dickie O'Neill, I think he was from Tallaght as well.' As these authors have already noted, John Noonan has denied to us that he ever met Catherine Nevin and he said he spoke for Dickie O'Neill also. Under cross-examination in the trial, John Jones likewise denied any knowledge of this alleged meeting. Johnny Deery is now in Moscow, and could not be contacted.

Under the arrangement as outlined by Catherine Nevin, Tom was to hold the title and put up something over £500,000 for it, while the balance was to come from Jones, who was to be the silent partner. Jones was 'to be given it by Dickie O'Neill, who was to take it down from the North from Johnny Deery'.

She claimed that Tom had the £100,000 that came down from the North in a deposit book and had shown it to her. The account, she presumed, was in her husband's name and the loan was being made to him. The three houses, at Mountshannon

Road, Mayfield Road, and her house at 446 South Circular Road, were to be the collateral.

'No, my Lord, the deal didn't go through. Something happened between John Jones and my husband and the deal just didn't go through and my husband was very upset over it.'

Then: 'My husband, God rest him, had a lot of other dealings with Mr Jones, but I don't know what they were about – they were political, so I don't really know . . .'

But she did claim to know of one of them. It was during the time they were in the Barry House, late Winter 1985. A flat became vacant and 'Tom gave it to Mr Jones, rent free.' He had been there five weeks when she passed the house at 2 or 3 a.m., returning from the Barry House, and she saw all the lights on. 'When I went in, I was confronted by two men who came at me with a sheet of glass', she tremored. 'I put up my hands to protect my face and two fingers on my left hand were very badly injured.' Showing her hand, she said she still couldn't straighten one finger and had stitches in the other. The men ran out the back. What she saw in the flat 'disturbed me something terrible'. There were bundles of wires and what looked to her like 'components from the backs of televisions'.

She immediately picked up the phone and rang Tom. 'He told me not to ring the police under any circumstances.'

She had gone to St James's Hospital, got her fingers stitched and received a tetanus jab and a pain-killing injection. She wasn't detained there and did not know who had treated her. No proof of this hospital visit was offered. Three hours after her return home, Tom went with her back to the flat and put the wires and components in a box, telling her 'they had to be taken to John Jones'. She had brought them to Jones herself, and 'just told him what happened'.

Nevin then denied every aspect of the case against her. She had no meetings with Heapes. She had no affair with Willie McClean and to add to her earlier hearsay, she said she knew nothing of him, except what her husband told her, which was 'that he had plates and that he was making £20 notes'.

The gardaí had boycotted the Inn after she and Tom made statements about the alleged sexual assault, and the Circuit Court Civil Bill issued against her for defamation by Detective Garda James McCawl was entered as an exhibit to go to the jury. She had never said her husband was violent, she told the jury.

She and Tom had always occupied separate bedrooms, she said, 'from after we got married'. If they wanted to make love, 'there was always two rooms available'.

'Are you saying you did make love?' – Her counsel appeared surprised.

'Oh yes! Frequently, yes.'

'Evidence has been given that you had a strictly business relationship – what do you say to that?'

'Goodness, my Lord, That's not so. Far from it!'

The last time they made love was on 28 February prior to his death, she said. It was her birthday, and after a meal in Blakes of Stillorgan, Tom had stayed the night with her 'in what was classed as my room'.

It was 'not true at all' that she had a sexual affair with Tom Kennedy. 'My late husband Tom and myself were very, very friendly with Tom and his family.'

Allegations of an inappropriate relationship with Judge Ó Buachalla were 'absolutely rubbish'. 'Judge Ó Buachalla and his wife Therese were again, very friendly with Tom and I . . .'

And, 'Goodness, no', Judge Ó Buachalla would have no need for a set of keys to Jack White's.

She denied ever having anybody with her in the flats on Mountshannon Road. She couldn't remember if Willie McClean had stayed the night of the opening of Jack White's. 'He may have. I was talking with Cathal Goulding for quite a while. Cathal was a very, very good friend of mine and I was talking with him for quite a while.'

The Official IRA man had a room at the Inn that night. She stayed alone in her room downstairs.

And then Tom was hosting monthly meetings after 1 a.m. in the old restaurant with 'two car-loads of people' attending. Tom would have her put on the heating 'and leave plenty of ashtrays and Ballygowan bottles out'. The meetings were sometimes argumentative and 'it was always about money'.

Some sterling and around £5,000 in punts was always kept in the second floor safe, the timelock safe, 'to be exchanged for other money'. A tall man in a long coat with receding, fair hair and a peaked cap would carry a briefcase with money in it and exchange it with money from 'my late husband'.

It was Wednesday, 15 March. Bombshells dropped, Nevin moved on to her account of what happened on the night of the murder. That evening, RTE carried pictures of Mrs Nevin leaving court in a smart blue suit, having completed two days of direct evidence. The following day, she would be cross-examined.

But the Anorak Man got in the way. She had literally tripped over him, Catherine was to say later. It was after she returned to her flat at 17 Mountshannon Road on the Wednesday night. When she went to turn on the side light in the flat she knew someone was there. 'It was then that I fell over his feet. He was sitting on the couch.'

The following morning, Thursday, 16 March, RTE Radio's ten o'clock news reported that the accused, Catherine Nevin, had collapsed at her home and had been taken to St James's Hospital by ambulance.

In court at 11 a.m., her defence team could not explain what had happened. 'I simply do not know', Patrick MacEntee told the judge. Solicitor Ann Fitzgibbon had already been despatched to the hospital bedside. The jury were sent away without explanation. Normal reporting restrictions were imposed, and all that could be legitimately relayed was what was said to the jury and what was already in the public domain. The prosecution was to later complain that 'it was being put about that this lady collapsed'.

St Patrick's weekend followed, the anniversary of Tom's murder. On Monday, his widow was still in hospital, still 'suffering from the effects of the ingestion of noxious substances', her counsel said. She was in the care of the hospital consultant on duty at the time of her admission and had been seen by three consultant psychiatrists, one retained by the defence.

But the prosecution counsel had lost a good measure of his patience. The entire exercise had been engineered by Mrs Nevin to either stop the process or engender sympathy amongst the jury, Charleton alleged. And he raised the possibility that 'soap' was amongst the substances taken. He warned that if necessary, he would apply for a discharge of the jury or a remand in custody.

Later that day, Dr David Breen, medical registrar at St James's Hospital, told the Ms Justice Carroll that a toxicology report on Mrs Nevin's blood showed that three drugs had been taken. Two were significant: Dalmaine, a benzodiazapine or sedative requiring prescription, and Tylex, a painkiller containing paracetamol and codeine, an opiate. The third substance was Spironolactone, a diuretic, used, amongst other things, to reduce fluid and swelling in the legs. He could not say when any of them had been taken.

The level of paracetamol found was 46 micrograms per milli-litre, which could be a toxic level, depending on when the tablets were taken. If they had been taken one hour before detection, for example, they would not be toxic. Twenty to thirty paracetamol would give the level detected after 12 hours, but ingesting two to five would give it after one to two hours.

The hospital was dependent on the account given by Mrs Nevin of what had happened and when. When she was first admitted, they had to look upon her as 'a probable overdose'. Following an injection, her condition was stable and all objective signs were normal. 'We didn't know the level [of toxicity] and we had to treat her,' Dr Breen said. He and the other consultants believed that the accused would be ready to resume her evidence that Wednesday.

Wednesday 22 March came, and with it Catherine Nevin, back in the witness box in the absence of the jury. The judge had demanded an explanation, overruling the plea from Mr MacEntee that he 'wasn't proposing to go into that.'

Eyelids aflutter, Catherine began explaining to a sceptical court why she had been absent for the past six days. Ms Justice Carroll put down her pen and leaned back in her leather chair. She looked like she had already heard enough.

Mrs Nevin said that when the day's session had finished on the previous Wednesday, she had a consultation with her legal team in counsel's offices. Her brother, Vincent, collected her and drove her home to 17 Mountshannon Road at around 7.30 p.m. Vincent could not get parking, so he went on to his own flat around the corner. As she entered her house, the mortice locks on her front and flat door were unlocked, although she had 'almost positively' locked them on leaving that morning.

She opened both doors with the Yale locks. It was when she went to turn on the side light in the flat that she knew someone was there. 'It was then that I fell over his feet, he was sitting on the couch', she said.

When she saw him, she 'just froze', she said. 'I know it's difficult to explain, but I was just terrified. I don't know the man by name but the man was a friend of my husband, a connection of my husband's. He was wearing an anorak with a hood and he had a beard. From what I can remember . . . he would be nearly forty years of age.' She had seen the man a number of times over the years in the presence of her late husband.

'Has this got something to with the reason she didn't turn up in court?' Ms Justice Carroll asked.

'Yes, it has, on my instructions it undoubtedly has,' said Mr MacEntee.

'I was very frightened', Catherine Nevin continued. 'He told me to sit down and he told me I was naming people I shouldn't be naming in court, that I was causing problems for people and I wasn't going to name any more people. I told him that my evidence was almost complete and I was ready to go into cross-examination. He told me that I wasn't going to name anyone else.'

With that, the bearded anorak man made her take tablets, she claimed. The tablets were in a plain white container he took from his pocket. 'I don't know how many of the tablets he made me take, but he gave me something white to drink. It tasted like milk. I remember getting sick. I don't know how much time passed, I remember getting sick a second time and I don't remember anything else until the hospital.'

The trouble with Catherine's tale was that no-one believed her. Amongst those who had sat through it, her credibility had by now dived to near-zero.

These authors have established the details of what happened on the day Catherine went A.W.O.L.

Detective Garda Tom Noonan and Garda Andy Dignan had turned up at 6 a.m. outside the house at Mountshannon Road. At 9.30, Catherine's brother, Vincent Scully, arrived to collect her. He knocked on the front door and then on the window of her front room bedsit. The curtains were closed.

One of the tenants eventually answered the door, and gardaí gained access to the flat. Vincent went in first, along with Detective Garda Noonan. The flat was unlit. Catherine was lying on the couch, half-on, half-off, wearing pink pyjamas, dark-coloured woollen socks and partially covered with a duvet.

An ambulance was immediately called. Detective Noonan found she wasn't responding to any questions. Another tenant, a medical student, said she appeared to be in a deep sleep.

Ambulance driver Colm McCarthy had just come from Our Lady's Hospital for Sick Children in Crumlin when he received a radio call from Ambulance Control at Tara Street.

When he and his colleague arrived at Mountshannon Road, they found the patient had a pulse and was breathing. There was a smell of vomit in the room. Some medications were strewn around and there were half-bottles of spirits on a table.

Once the ambulance men had 'checked her vitals' and found she was responsive to pain, she was lifted onto a stretcher and taken on the two-minute journey to St James's Hospital Accident & Emergency department, receiving oxygen on the way. 'We were under the impression that she was feigning unconsciousness', Colm McCarthy said. 'When somebody is unconscious, basically you can open up the eyelid. We put a thumb on it and there was a certain resistance there when we were doing it.'

Meanwhile, a closer examination of the scene by gardaí suggested that Fairy washing-up liquid might have had a role to play. Samples of the vomit were taken from the floor and examined at the forensic science laboratory. A report from the forensic scientist, Dr John Power, said that the contents had 'a typical vomit odour and I smelt a soap-like odour also'. Tests showed a significant fatty liquid content in the vomit.

But the tests were inconclusive. Although vegetable oil is one of the main constituents of washing-up liquid, he had to allow for the fact that Nevin could have eaten fatty foods on the evening before, and there was also no guarantee the fatty liquid had not already been on the floor from where the sample was lifted.

The tests at St James's Hospital were pored over to see if they could shed more light. If the patient's stomach had been pumped in hospital, perhaps the answer would lay there.

The contents of Catherine Nevin's stomach were not pumped in the hospital. Medical registrar, Dr David Breen confirmed that it is normal practice not to pump the stomach of such a patient as there is a risk of aspiration into the lungs of vomit fluid.

He said that Catherine Nevin was drowsy when she was first admitted to Casualty. When he saw her an hour later, 'with effort she opened her eyes and said something, but with very little response.'

Despite the inconclusive medical and forensic tests, there is more to show that Catherine's story was a fake.

Robert Sinnott, a tenant in the bedsit next door to her, is a sociology and politics student who has written a critical assessment of the media coverage of the Nevin trial. He is adamant that he holds no view for or against her innocence, but he staunchly defended her right to be presumed innocent.

Sinnott had been up studying on the night of the alleged Anorak attack. In his statement to gardaí he said he could not be sure of the exact time, but it was before 7 a.m. when he first heard someone moving about next door. The Paul Power Breakfast

Show, which runs from 5–7am, was on Today FM. He would have usually expected to hear Catherine Nevin get up between 7:45 and 8 a.m., he said, but on that morning he heard her normal sounds sometime earlier.

But the final problem in her story was that two gardaí from Kevin Street Detective Unit were on watch outside the house while she was claiming to have been force-fed drugs inside. They had been put there since her complaints of threats earlier in the trial. 'Out of an abundance of caution,' as one source said.

Tenants at 17 Mountshannon Road regularly heard the radios of uniformed gardaí outside the back of the house at night, and saw their cigarette butts pile up in the back garden each day.

But there are problems in proving no one gained entry to the flat. A number of tenants who spoke to these authors confirmed that although the mortice lock on the front door is supposed to be kept locked, it regularly isn't, as tenants come and go without care. If Nevin locked it as she left, it did not guarantee that it would remain locked for the day.

As well as potential access through the Yale-locked front door, the locks on a bathroom window upstairs had been temporarily removed for painting, and the window could be accessed by climbing up a drainpipe on the outside wall.

However, the house is occupied most days all day. There is very little hiding space in it, and if an intruder wanted to break into Catherine's bedsit, they would risk alerting the tenant just next door, in the next room. None of the tenants who spoke to gardaí on 16 March said they noticed any suspicious activity the previous night, or any sign of someone having been in and around. No signs of forced entry were found.

And the biggest foil to Mrs Nevin's story lay in television news footage. Her blue skirt suit of television news programmes on

Wednesday evening had been replaced by a pink pyjamas when her brother and the two gardaí burst into her flat the following morning.

The prosecution examined the 22 statements made to gardaí in relation to Catherine's 'collapse'. It decided that it was best not to introduce the issue into the trial. They wanted a conviction based on what happened in 1996 rather than what didn't happen in 2000, Charleton told the court.

But after the trial ended and Mrs Nevin's 'collapse' was reported, many still wanted to know why the jury weren't told about it.

The reason was that apart from the inconclusive scientific evidence, there was the possibility that in the remaining section of Catherine's evidence-in-chief, she would claim that she had received threats, and the fact that she was under 24-hour garda protection would be revealed to the jury.

While garda sources insist the measures were only taken to avoid the very claims to which the 'collapse' episode led, there was the worrying possibility that Nevin might succeed in raising a doubt in the jury's minds. If any members of the jury already found tales such as that of the man in the long coat and the peaked cap credible, they might find the Anorak Man plausible too. But worse, they might think that if Nevin was under garda protection, there must be some truth in what she was saying.

And there was another, legal, reason why the prosecution's hands were tied. A legal source familiar with criminal trials said this centred on a rule of evidence that means that once Catherine was asked something touching on her credibility about the Anorak Man claims, the prosecution could not contradict her about it. They would have to take her word for it.

Inside the front door of 17 Mountshannon Road there's an old noticeboard with cards and notes pinned to it. Chief amongst these is a notice covered in plastic, written in the neat hand of the former Catherine Scully. It is a list of house rules for tenants. High on the list appears the line: 'Be of good behaviour and respect the right to privacy of other tenants.' The words, *'This is most important'* appear double underlined beneath the sentence.

On the same list, the final entry reads: 'Keep number of Kilmainham garda station handy at all times.'

The prim notice is ironic in light of the Anorak Man claims. But it is also in stark contrast to what was revealed when gardaí burst into her bedsit on the morning of the 'collapse'.

As bail conditions required her to sleep in Mountshannon Road, Catherine had been returning there every night, while she spent a good deal of the rest of her time in 6 Mayfield Road.

She had been sleeping on a bed-settee in a cramped, old-style bedsit, a cushion and quilt her bedlinen. The conditions inside were 'unbelievable', according to a garda. Dirty dishes were piled up in a small sink built into a wardrobe. Full ashtrays were discarded about the room. Parts of the book of evidence against her were 'left about the place amongst the mess'. Suits and other clothes were draped from the wardrobe or hanging on the back of the door.

For a woman who had posed as a bastion of composure and ladylike disdain during the trial, her private room showed the turmoil that she was actually going through. She may have enjoyed the image of a sophisticated femme fatale, but Catherine was human, after all.

Back in court after the visit from the Anorak Man, Catherine resumed her evidence before the jury with a fresh claim . 'Tom was an alcoholic', she said, 'but a very disciplined alcoholic'.

The conversation with the carpet-fitter, Donnchadh Long, never happened, she said. A direction to the staff not to return to the Inn after the disco 'never even crossed my mind'. It was not unusual for the curtains to be closed in the dining room.

The mobile alarm buttons hadn't been taken out for a long time and it was Tom who had instructed that they be put away. The couple had never contemplated separating, 'Goodness, no', she said. And the money taken by the raiders wasn't £16,550 or £13,000, but 'between £7,500 and £8,000'.

And of course she had never suborned Jones, Heapes or McClean to murder Tom. 'I have no idea who killed my husband, I have no idea at all,' she said.

When she had seen his body the night before the funeral, she said, 'I just wished I was dead as well'.

When Peter Charleton rose to cross-examine, his first question was designed to disarm. He asked Mrs Nevin to describe her husband. 'Tom was a very nice man,' she began. Within five sentences, she was saying, 'He had his interests and his political friends – but he was a decent man.'

Softly spoken and unerringly polite, Charleton's manner of cross-examination concealed a lethal intent. His questions had a tendency to go to the heart of the matter.

Although Catherine was insisting the marriage was happy, it transpired that the pair had not had a holiday together since having been granted the restaurant licence in 1989.

Then the prosecution counsel relentlessly pursued Mrs Nevin across Wicklow, Wexford, Kildare, Dublin and Cork and through countless rendezvous with ex-Inspector Tom Kennedy.

The Horse & Hound Inn, Ballinaboola, was 'one of our favourite restaurants', she was saying. The only trouble was, no one was quite sure which Tom she was referring to, as the questions continued. But finally a creeping admission: 'I did see

Tom Kennedy sometimes when Tom Nevin wasn't there, yes'.

At this stage, it was a trial of the wife, the thief, the lover, the judge, the SAS men, the ex-Garda Inspector, the IRA and the plastic surgeon. Now it was the turn of the cook. She said she would detour to Ballinaboola sometimes when returning from Darina Allen's cookery courses at Ballymaloe, Shanagarry in Co. Cork. But 'Tom' had stayed in one of the chalets at Ballymaloe, she thought. 'Are you going to call Tom Kennedy?' she was asked. 'Well, I am advised by my counsel so I will have to take my advice from them,' she said.

Tom Kennedy's wife, Mary, hadn't been in the pub for quite some time. She thought 1993. 'Could it have been back in the nineteen eighties?' asked counsel. 'Oh no, no way, no,' she said.

She couldn't recollect if Tom Kennedy had gone to darts matches with her. 'I have no recollection offhand of Tom Kennedy, but I do recollect Superintendent Bill Ryan coming with me one night Tom was away.' Catherine was proving to be a bit of a name-dropper.

The prosecution counsel switched to the IRA allegation, what Charleton called her 'gross defamation and character assassination of your husband'. She denied that it was. 'I didn't support the IRA. I explained to Tom what I felt about it and he assured me that I was in no danger and he was in no danger,' she said.

By her account, there was never a mess left when Tom hosted late-night meetings with bottles of Ballygowan and ashtrays. She never had to take out the Hoover to clean up by morning. They were 'exceptionally tidy', the men who attended, suggested Charleton.

'I am here to tell the truth,' she said to the charge that she was 'spinning a gigantic yarn' to deceive the jury.

She had never shown John Jones black eyes, and her conversation with Assistant Commissioner McHugh was 'slightly different to the way Mr McHugh recollects it. I cannot account for what other people say or how they interpret things', she said.

The next day, her third of cross-examination, was replete with more denials. Her husband and Tom Kennedy were 'exceptionally friendly together'. Did she accept that she was having a long-term affair with Kennedy, she was asked. 'I was married to my husband for twenty years and I never committed adultery,' Catherine said.

There was a plethora of people she had lined up as suspects for the murder in the course of the garda investigation, she was challenged. Yet she didn't mention the IRA once to gardaí at the time. Charleton wondered why.

Then the jury heard of Catherine's 'solemn promise' to Tom that she wouldn't tell a soul. 'I suggest to you that the only thing your husband was a member of was the GAA,' said counsel. 'And I am not putting that to you as a joke, but as a fact.' Tom was in the IRA, repeated Catherine. She was 'deliberately putting lies into the mouth of a dead person', countered Charleton.

'I love my husband and my husband was in the IRA,' the widow said.

The SAS story had been her way of ingratiating herself with John Jones, Charleton suggested. The accused said she had no idea who the two men were, if they were SAS men, 'or who the SAS are' but that was what happened.

And she blamed Tom for crossing out the name and number for Gerry Heapes in the back of the address book. 'I definitely crossed it out in front. What Tom did afterwards I don't know.'

As to why she hadn't thought of Tom as she was trying to free herself after the raid, she said: 'Tom always said if anything ever happened, not to worry about him, he'd always take care of himself.'

'But Mrs Nevin, he could have taken care of you,' said Charleton. She had no answer for that save to repeat her last one.

On 28 March, the seven surviving brothers and sisters of Tom Nevin took to the witness stand to rebut the claims of Catherine against their brother. 'One of the most respectable families in Co. Galway', Catherine had called them.

It was oddly one of the most heart-rending days of the trial. After all the allegations and counter-allegations, all the denials and deadly deeds, there were seven sound voices to reclaim Tom Nevin's name. One after the other, they took to the witness box, filling the courtroom with quiet calm. The salt of the earth was unmistakeably there.

Tom had no involvement in the IRA, they said. Hurling was 'the top subject' between them when they met, said Patsy, now the eldest of the family.

Tom's former wife, June O'Flanagan, provided another foil to the unreal air that hung around after Catherine had stepped down. She described him as a hardworking man whose dream was to own his own pub and have his own home.

Ten garda witnesses testified that they had never seen any subversive activity around Jack White's Inn in the course of night patrols past the pub. The only car they saw there late at night was that of ex-Inspector Tom Kennedy, some said.

Nevin's evidence that she and Tom Kennedy were just 'good friends' was now raised again in the absence of the jury. The prosecution wanted to rebut that claim by calling evidence that she had named Tom Kennedy of Wicklow garda station as her next-of-kin on a hospital admission record in 1991.

'What is now being proposed is that this trial should close before the jury with this single document, this magican's trick,' an indignant Paul Burns said. While the prosecution had started the case determined not to turn it into a trial of Mrs Nevin's extra-marital relationships, that very issue was now proving very important in establishing her credibility with the jury.

But the judge agreed with the defence that the next-of-kin evidence was too prejudicial and too late to call it. It was a blow to the prosecution.

Junior counsel for the prosecution, Tom O'Connell, took four hours to make his closing speech. The jury had to choose between the credibility of Catherine Nevin or that of 24 prosecution witnesses, including Assistant Commissioner Jim McHugh, he said. 'Implicitly she is saying that these people are either telling barefaced lies or they are fantasists.'

The prosecution had exposed 'two enormous lies' by her: the first, that Tom was in the IRA; the second, that theirs was a happy marriage and that she wasn't having affairs. It wasn't the affairs that the prosecution were concerned about, 'but the lies'.

For the defence, Patrick MacEntee took ten hours over four days. It was a meticulous, forensic, dramatic and extraordinary performance which seldom lagged, despite a length that suggested endurance of Lough Derg proportions. In his speech, MacEntee asked the jury were Jones, Heapes and McClean men that they could rely upon? He said there was 'a big question mark' over Jones, Heapes was a convicted IRA man and 'liar' and McClean was 'a conman who lives by his wits'. 'At the end of the day, would you buy a second-hand motor car off any of them'? he asked.

And he claimed Catherine hadn't told the gardaí that Tom was a member of the IRA because to do so risked bringing the wrath of the IRA down on top of her.

They were marathon speeches for a marathon trial. Then, in her summing-up, Ms Justice Mella Carroll directed the jury to consider the soliciting charges first, before they went on to consider any verdict in the murder charge. They must 'compartmentalise their minds' and decide each of 'four trials' separately.

And, in a crucial part of her charge, she told them that it was not necessary to believe everything a witness said. They could 'pick and choose' from the evidence of any witness, 'accepting it in whole or in part'. The witnesses were presented 'as they are, with all their faults'.

On Friday, 4 March, the jury retired at 3.10 p.m. As the weekend wore on, they were still locked in discussion. Catherine Nevin had turned to Seamus Heaney's translation of *Beowulf*.

On a sunny Saturday afternoon, the court was packed. For the first time since the start of the trial, Catherine's brother, Vincent, and sister, Betty, were sitting with her.

On Sunday, at 12 noon, the jurors were asked if they had reached a verdict on any of the counts on which they all agreed. The reply was no. The judge immediately directed them that she would accept a majority verdict.

Assistant Commissioner McHugh joined the long wait. Ever more curious onlookers were turning up, some replete with tea flasks and foil-wrapped sandwiches – an alternative Sunday picnic.

By evening, waiting-room fatigue was setting in. The court was 'grossly overcrowded', said Peter Charleton; a sample of the public should be allowed in, 'not the entire country'.

The wait was only beginning. Surpassing every record in the book, the jury were sent to their hotel four nights in a row, until Tuesday, 11 April.

Each day, as speculation circled around the Four Courts, returning to be rehashed again with different faces and different angles, the jurors put their stamp on the trial.

They had sat through 42 days and 182 witnesses. They deliberated for five days, officially taking 26 hours, 36 minutes. Their knock came at 6.25 p.m. on the Tuesday. All assembled and their pale, drawn faces returned to the jury box. At 6.40 p.m., registrar Joe Brennan took the issue paper from the forewoman.

'On Count 2 [the soliciting of John Jones] You say the accused is Guilty on Count 2?'

'Yes.'

'Was that a verdict of all of you?'

'The verdict of 11 of us. One dissented.'

'On Count 3 [the soliciting of Gerard Heapes] – You say Catherine Nevin, the accused, is Guilty on Count 3.'

'Yes – the verdict of us all'.

'On Count 4 [the soliciting of William McClean] – You say the accused is Guilty on Count 4.'

'Yes.'

'On Count 1 [the murder charge] – You say Catherine Nevin is Guilty on Count 1.'

'Guilty. Yes. That is the verdict of us all.'

The Count 4 verdict was then clarified. It too was a majority verdict of 11:1.

It was moments later when Catherine Nevin blinked. But for those seconds, there was not a stir. Then a tight, slightly cynical smile gathered around her mouth.

Afterwards, a prayer book lay discarded at the foot of the chair she had occupied. *I Talk to God. He Talks to Me*, proclaimed the title. The book was new.

15

'ALL HELL'S
BREAKING LOOSE'

I t was almost nightfall when RTE's Mary Wilson went live on air. 'Catherine Nevin has begun a mandatory life sentence after being found guilty of murdering her husband, Tom, at their Co. Wicklow pub, Jack White's Inn, four years ago . . . In passing sentence, Ms Justice Mella Carroll addressed Mrs Nevin: she told her she had had her husband assassinated and then tried to have his character assassinated. Mrs Nevin stood and looked calmly at the judge as sentence was passed.'

By 9 p.m., Catherine Nevin had been admitted into the healthcare unit of Mountjoy, a small unit just off the main section of the women's prison. She had £170 in cash on her on arrival. The cash and jewellery were taken from her. She was in shock that night and was put under heavy sedation.

The Four Courts, earlier the scene of frenetic activity by hundreds of barristers, witnesses, gardaí and journalists, was now locked up and deserted. Superintendent Pat Flynn and his team of detectives headed off down the quays like the Magnificent Seven. The barristers, the victorious and the vanquished, slipped quietly back to their chambers.

As soon as the verdict was announced there was an immediate rush from the press gallery and a near stampede for copies of a prepared statement from the family of Tom Nevin, before the scores of reporters began jumping into taxis, cars and outside broadcast vans and heading back to their respective media organisations to get the news out. This was pure OJ.

The next day's papers would be full of it. Stories like the Anorak Man that had to be kept under wraps unless and until the jury returned a 'guilty' verdict, could now be told. And after the next day's papers, came the Sundays and many thousands of words more. And that would have been more or less it.

Except that there was one more story waiting to be told. It concerned Judge Donnchadh Ó Buachalla and the transfer of the pub licence into Catherine Nevin's sole name in circumstances that has given rise to a judicial inquiry under Supreme Court Judge Frank Murphy.

It was a story that almost didn't get told. It was written by Liz Walsh for the current affairs magazine, *Magill*. The magazine had already been put on hold for two weeks pending the verdict. When it did not come by 7 p.m. on Monday, *Magill* went to print without the Ó Buachalla/Nevin story. Its alternative cover was a story about Charlie Haughey and the National Lottery. The subs, the production staff, designers and the editor, Harry McGee, had put huge effort into the 16-page Nevin article. Everyone went home deflated that night.

At 6.30 the following morning, this author got a call from *Magill* publisher, Mike Hogan: 'We're going to get that Nevin story out. I'll get a printer somewhere – I'll try everywhere. Give Harry a call and tell him to get back in to the office. We're back on track.'

Hogan's wife, Mari O'Leary, had come up with the idea of getting a supplement printed and attaching it to the main magazine. He tried two printers without success; they were fully booked. The third time he struck lucky. Hogan arranged to deliver the 16-page supplement to a Drogheda printer at dawn, and have it rushed back to Smurfit's where he had a slot on the binder booked for 4.30 p.m on Wednesday.

Binding is a process that entails putting the main part on the binder and the supplement on top and the two are bound together in the form of a wrap-around. 'I stood there watching Mrs Nevin going over Charlie. Thousands and thousands of times. It's the first time anyone has ever knocked Charlie off the front page of anything,' Hogan recalls with a grin.

The next morning's news bulletins carried the story from 6 a.m. At mid-morning, the Minister for Justice, John O'Donoghue, announced he was setting up a major three-pronged inquiry, involving the Garda Commissioner, Pat Byrne, the President of the District Court, Peter Smithwick, and the Chief Executive Officer of the Courts Service. Judge Ó Buachalla had holidays booked and was due to depart for Tenerife four days later. He was told to make himself available for the enquiry. He had to shelve his holiday plans.

The nub of the pub licence controversy is the deletion of Tom Nevin's name and the transfer of the main publican's licence into Catherine Nevin's sole name on 29 September 1997, when she stood charged with murder.

Catherine Nevin, the joint licensee, did not obtain an 'ad interim' transfer on the death of her husband. The licence fell due for renewal at the annual licensing court on 1 October 1996. It wasn't renewed, because Customs – the body responsible for issuing the licence – required a court order, because one of the licensees was now dead. In effect, Jack White's, a pub frequented by the great and the good, was trading as a shebeen from that date.

On 13 June 1997, Judge Ó Buachalla issued a certificate authorising Customs to delete the name of Tom Nevin from the licence. Customs refused. On 1 September, lawyers acting for Catherine Nevin made a three-fold application to Arklow District Court for an early hours licence, an exemption for Sundays and St Patrick's Day opening and a restaurant certificate. There was still no main pub licence in force. On 12 September Inspector Peter Finn informed Catherine Nevin's solicitor, Donnchadh Lehane, that he would be opposing the application on these grounds. It came before Arklow court on 26 September and was adjourned to Gorey on 29 September.

Time was running out. If 30 September passed without a main licence having been issued, it would no longer be open to Catherine Nevin to seek a transfer or renewal. It would have lapsed entirely. On 29 September, hours before it was due to lapse, Judge Ó Buachalla issued a court order directing Customs to issue the licence in Catherine Nevin's sole name. Seamus O'Tuathail, Nevin's barrister, told Finn it was an *ex-parte* (one-party) application to have Tom Nevin's name deleted. Customs accepted the judge's order.

This was done not in open court, but in the judge's chambers. The gardaí were not put on notice and neither were notices published in the newspapers.

A copy of the internal garda file on the controversy was obtained by this author. Inspector Finn raises 11 main points of objection. These include:

- the failure to put the superintendent in charge of the area on notice;

- the application was held in chambers and not in open court;
- the ex-parte application was an incorrect procedure;
- the court, having apparently accepted the application as an ex-parte application, effectively denied a right of legal audience to Inspector Finn;
- there was total disregard for the statutory requirements essential to legalise the licensing position in respect of Jack White's.

Dawn was breaking when journalists began pulling up outside the judge's house in Stillorgan Wood on the morning the story broke. First to arrive was INN, then RTE. A reporter pressed the buzzer on the intercom: 'Hello, hello,' the judge said. At 8.15 a.m. the door opened. Judge Ó Buachalla emerged with a prepared statement and offered it to the reporters. 'Do you want it?,' he asked, 'I've nothing further to add.' It was a short, terse statement, neither signed nor dated and headed simply 'Judge':

'A renewal certificate cannot be granted to a dead person and the licence had been in the joint names of Tom and Catherine Nevin. This difficulty was brought to the attention of the court in September 1997 and Inspector Peter Finn of Gorey station attended all discussions in relation to the matter. It became necessary to amend the existing licence so that a renewal could take place. When the matter came before the court as the annual licensing court there was no objection by the gardaí to the renewal of the licence in the name of Catherine Nevin solely. This application was made in open court with Inspector Peter Finn confirming that the gardaí had no objection.'

Judge Ó Buachalla was due to sit in Bunclody court at 10.30 a.m. He was late. He arrived at the Meadowlands Ballroom, where the court was sitting, a little after 11 a.m. and was flanked by two uniformed gardaí on his way in. By now, an RTE camera crew had set up outside. The Meadowlands is an average size ballroom and the judge was sitting at an ordinary table at the top of three steps. The media pack was hanging over shelving used for holding drinks when the ballroom is not being used as a courtroom. 'He heard forty-five cases in forty-two minutes, then at 1 p.m. brought the local media out for lunch,' one reporter recorded.

The following Tuesday, the media, including an RTE cameraman, were again camped outside the judge's house. At 8.40 a.m., he peered out the door to pick up the milk from the doorstep. He was wearing a green-and-black striped dressing gown that stopped at mid calf. He spotted the RTE van and quickly shut the door.

He emerged a little later. 'Have you anything to say about the licence controversy? asked INN's Emma Counihan. 'I can confirm that I have spoken to Peter Smithwick and he enjoyed my full co-operation,' he replied. He headed to Wicklow Court pursued by the meda posse and went around the back door, past an old firing cannon left over from other battles. All he said was – 'I welcome the inquiry.'

The judge's statement of 13 April did not specify which court on what date. Either way, the balloon was up. Judge Ó Buachalla endured embarrassing publicity in the Nevin trial. He was being openly taunted outside the courthouse with chants of, 'Catherine, Catherine, Catherine'. Now, there were more awkward questions to answer.

The *Irish Independent*'s Miriam Lord was at home that morning. Because of the purgatorially-long deliberation of the jury, journalists covering the case were owed a tonne of time off.

Around mid morning, Lord got a call from the office telling her 'to get down to the Dáil, all hell's breaking loose.'

She ambled down to Kildare Street. In the chamber, John O'Donoghue and his old sparring partner, Nora Owen of Fine Gael, were going at it, hammer and tongs. 'When will the minister come to the House to explain the circumstances surrounding this case?' Owen pleaded.

'All the time he was sitting across the floor from her with his chin stuck in the air and a huffy expression on his face. Three times she called on him not to let the matter fester and three times he looked the other way, letting Bertie Ahern get on with the order of business,' Lord wrote.

The licence affair came as no surprise to John O'Donoghue. He'd known about it since early 1998. That was the year Finn's report landed on his desk. In fact, shortly afterwards, the Department sent three senior officials to Wexford to speak with a number of court clerks present during the various hearings who had expressed misgivings about the procedures used.

The pace of events in the Dáil quickened. At 4.30 p.m., Jim Higgins, Opposition spokesman on justice, got up from his seat waving a sheaf of papers in the direction of the minister. 'I have in my possession a covering report,' he said. It was Finn's report. 'The decision to grant an application for the transfer of a liquor licence was no ordinary decision. It was a bizarre decision taken in the most unusual and questionable circumstances. This was no ordinary application.'

'I accept that some serious issues have been raised in this case to which answers will be required,' responded the minister. 'We are, in fact, dealing with a judicial decision handed down by a judge in the exercise of his judicial function. It is well-established practice . . . that the Minister for Justice, Equality and Law

251

Reform does not comment on the correctness or otherwise of a judicial decision.'

How the judge could consider it appropriate to hear the case in the first place, given that Catherine Nevin had been charged with murder and he was likely to be called to give evidence at the trial is something the Department of Justice should have taken an interest in before now, retorted Higgins.

The minister defended the two-year lack of official action on the grounds that:

'. . . it would have been totally inappropriate to do so against the background where parties centrally involved in the matter were also centrally involved in different ways in an extremely serious criminal case . . . there could be no question of formally conducting an in-depth examination of the kind now underway and thereby running the risk of damaging the processing of the criminal proceedings referred to.'

The minister did not explain why, after the verdict, it took *Magill* to galvanise him into action when he was already in possession of the facts. *The Irish Times,* in an editorial, described O'Donoghue's statement as 'sounding like a self-serving argument by a minister under severe pressure'.

That week, John O'Donoghue announced that he was appointing Supreme Court Judge Frank Murphy to head a statutory inquiry into the licence affair. The minister also announced he was extending Murphy's terms of reference to include the un-substantiated allegations of judicial bias against Mick Murphy, Vincent Whelan and other gardaí. They were now going to come under the judicial microscope.

It was clear, because of the complexity of the issues involved and the need to interview a number of people, including

Donnchadh Ó Buachalla, that this was going to take some time. Initial expectations that the inquiry would be complete within weeks were beginning to look very optimistic.

Events took another twist. O'Donoghue's address to the Dáil made no mention of a flurry of correspondence between his department and Tom Nevin's family dating back to January 1999. Crucially, he did not refer to the fact that his private secretary had written to Patsy Nevin the previous August saying the transfer of the licence was all above board.

If that was so, and the Department of Justice had this information before O'Donoghue went into the Dáil, what was the reason for setting up a formal statutory inquiry? The import of what the minister told Dáil deputies was that the department had carried out preliminary investigations, but more substantial inquiries were effectively stymied pending the conclusion of the murder trial. If the preliminary investigations showed that everything was in order, why did O'Donoghue deem it necessary to move to phase two? The Nevin family were mystified.

They had first contacted the department by phone in 1998. They received no answer. Several more calls followed in quick succession. Still no response. On 15 January 1999, Patsy, William and Sean Nevin wrote to the Minister for Justice looking for answers to the following questions:

Was an ad-interim transfer of the licence made to Catherine Nevin and if so, on what date and in what court? Was there a subsequent confirmation of transfer and if so, on what date and in what court? Was the confirmation of the licence made on notice to the gardaí and advertised in a newspaper?

On 16 February, the department supplied an acknowledgment.

On 30 March, Justice acknowledged a second letter from the Nevins.

On 19 April, Tom Nevin's family received their first detailed reply. It stated:

'As the surviving joint licensee, Mrs Nevin was automatically entitled to be registered as the sole licensee of Jack White's Inn and could simply apply under Section 16 of the Licensing (Ireland) Act 1874 to be registered as sole licensee . . . no parties are required to be notified (under Section 16).'

The Nevins were still deeply unhappy. Even if the department was correct in its interpretation of the use of the legislation that had been invoked, the procedures were flawed, they insisted. In May, Patsy Nevin wrote to the department saying:

'Even if the minister's advice is correct . . . then it is clear the application must be made in writing, must be on notice to the gardaí and must be dealt with in the local district court . . . I further understand that when the matter was dealt with in Wexford District Court it was dealt with in the judge's rooms, rather than open court.'

The department sent back another holding letter. It took until 16 August for the Department of Justice to confirm that Judge Ó Buachalla had issued the order for the licence in his chambers – not in open court. 'In this regard Section 16 of the Licensing Act is silent as to the formal and notice requirements of such an application.'

The Nevin family were still deeply unhappy and sent correspondence until November 1999. They were coming up against a brick wall.

The Murphy inquiry hinges on the use of Section 16 of the Licensing (Ireland) Act of 1874 versus the Licensing (Ireland) Act 1833, the one normally used in licensing applications.

Section 16 of the 1874 Act deals with changing the name of the owner of a licensed premises on the register, not with a change in the licence itself. Because it's a technical change of a register entry, it does not demand that the gardaí be notified.

The findings of Mr Justice Frank Murphy had not been completed by the time this book went to press. It may well be that, by the time of publication, the Murphy inquiry will have concluded that the procedures adopted by Judge Donnchadh Ó Buachalla in the licensing affair were absolutely correct.

EPILOGUE

✦✦✦✦✦

What the People got, after three juries and two separate trials calling over two hundred witnesses and comprising approximately nine million spoken words, was a version of the truth. This perhaps is inevitable in an adversarial system where there is a jury to be swayed and two opposing sides with much to gain and a lot to lose.

The truth could have embraced a whole series of events, conspiracies, actions and sub-plots leading inexorably to the discovery of Tom Nevin's body on the floor of Jack White's Inn on 19 March 1996. It could have embraced all this and more. We could have heard more about the relationship between Tom Kennedy and Catherine Nevin, but because the strict rules of evidence intervened, we did not. All that can be said with certainty is that Tom Kennedy's account conflicts totally with that given by his wife in another forum. More crucially, Kennedy's sworn testimony is wholly irreconcilable with that given by a number of the staff of Jack White's. Whose version of the truth will ultimately prove to be the correct one?

Then there is the – as yet unexplained – role of the IRA in the Nevin saga. The IRA, privately, tried to brush off the significance of republicans becoming State witnesses by claiming that John Jones and Gerry Heapes were republican 'has beens'. However, Catherine Nevin's claim that the IRA had sent £100,000 down from the North to co-finance the purchase of a Tallaght pub, the Killinarden Inn, has been supported by a key IRA source in this book, who confirmed that that very figure had been set aside for the Killinarden. Then, documentation that came to light after the trial showed that Jack White's figured on a list drawn up by the Garda Anti-Racketeering Unit.

And then there's the killer. We are no nearer to finding out who actually slayed Tom Nevin on his wife's behalf. The file is not closed. Gardaí are still hopeful of getting that vital break that will allow them to bring to justice the person, or persons, unknown, who pulled the trigger. Perhaps they will get lucky. Perhaps they will never find who did it.

The one person who knows who shot Tom Nevin – apart from the killer – is Catherine Nevin, but she's not saying.

And what of Catherine Nevin herself? Women who murder are extremely rare; that's a universal phenomenon and not peculiar to Ireland. Some studies suggest that male biochemistry ensures that, in general, males have greater potential for aggression than females. A 1995 study on homicide in Ireland by Enda Dooley of the Department of Justice gives a national homicide rate of some 10 in a million. Males constituted 90 per cent of the perpetrators and 70 per cent of the victims. Roughly a quarter of the victims were spouses and other relatives.

The study appears to offer compelling evidence that women who kill usually do so in self-defence or as a result of cumulative provocation by an abusive partner – impulse killing. This type of female killer, the kind society can just about comprehend, are rare enough. Premeditated murderers, women who trawl gangland for hired killers, are not even on the scale, which partly explains the phenomenal interest in Catherine Nevin and the self-affirming synergy that accompanied her conviction.

At this stage, millions of words have been written about her but no-one, apart from herself, knows just what it is that makes this woman tick. She has become something of an enigma. She was consorting with 'the crims' in Dolphin's Barn, the Provos in Finglas and the establishment in Wicklow.

It may well be that Catherine Nevin herself does not know what it was that drove her to do the things she did, or why she acted as she did. Her behaviour is so detached from the norm as to be verging on the insane: lack of guilt, inability to cry, lack of conscience, pathological lying – traits that run down the spine of behavioural or personality disorders. She displays all the signs of a ruthless, narcissistic sociopath and is undoubtedly a manipulator and an exhibitionist. But is she evil? She was described as such in a plethora of publications, but sociologists and others involved in the human psychology argue that very few people are inherently evil.

However, some, relatively few people, commit evil acts, a point made by Max Taylor, Professor of Applied Psychology at University College Cork:

'I'm reluctant to use words like evil, but people behave in a particularly bad way. She very coldly, very calculatingly, set about planning this terrible deed. She has very little moral scruples. It's something we often see with paedophiles: they believe they are not causing anyone any trouble so they put the blame somewhere else. And we saw this with Catherine Nevin.'

Taylor maintains that in the absence of a clinical psychological evaluation, his comments must be viewed in a general context. However, observing her from a distance, he said that aspects of her behaviour are consistent with someone who is very much into control:

'She seems very much a manipulator, very much engaged in that type of behaviour, used to control and controlling others. Then, take an issue like the trial, she couldn't control that, so what did she do? She stood back from it. The idea that you can disassociate yourself from things, almost as if it is an inconvenience and not central to you. Yet it did not affect the imagery she created around herself, the way she dressed and so on. She seemed to have a fixed view of the world and where she was in it, and that somehow she's not to blame for what happened. It's all about keeping things in a rigid compartment.'

Catherine Nevin's exhibitionism and her by-now infamous capacity to have several lovers on the go at once can also be linked to the control factor, Taylor said:

'You often find that with particularly sexually active people, they have no emotional involvement with people. With a lot of women who are reasonably sexually active there is an element of control. The argument is often made about men who are sexually active – this concept of the stud male – that it's as much about control as it is about sex. Well, that might work the other way around. Take that and turn it on its head and you have the stud woman. Her exhibitionism, showing herself off to people, the lack of effect the trial seemed to have on her, it's all part of that. It's all about control.'

The need to get one's own way, an inflated sense of self-importance and self-obsession are base characteristics found in the general population and yet most people resist the urge to murder their spouse. So what was it that about Catherine Nevin that not only caused her to self-destruct but by doing so, destroyed so many, many lives in the process?

Dr Richard Blennerhassett, Consultant Psychiatrist and Clinical Director of Psychiatry at Beaumont and St Ita's Hospitals in Dublin, again looking from a distance, identifies in Catherine a 'psychopathic personality make-up.' He makes the point that the traits of 'self-obsession, self-absorption, ruthlessness are the ones that are very much admired in our society and will get you to the top in journalism or business or medicine. Narcissism is valued in our society.'

Had she been sitting across from him, Blennerhassett would see someone who needs to have her own way, 'the kind of person who regards herself as one of those special types of individuals who can only be understood by other very special types – as we saw when she wanted to put an ad in the local paper and would only deal with the editor. 'You could point to all kinds of aspects of her behaviour now and ask weren't there pointers to her make-up, but the reality is that up to the murder, there were some people who had nothing good to say about her, while others liked her reasonably well.'

Prison life is something Catherine Nevin will have no control over. For somebody like her, the rigid prison regime will very difficult to cope with. A woman used to having her own way in practically everything, whose wardrobe is now the stuff of legend and whose renowned sexual needs appear destined to remain un-fulfilled for many years into the future.

'It will be very difficult. It's the same for any long-term prisoner', acknowledges John Lonergan, the Governor of Mountjoy Jail. 'The physical conditions are the first thing, the physical control in a small confined area. The second is learning to cope with the actual conviction. They are the two main elements of the penal system, conviction and the realisation that you are not free to come and go. Getting used to the system, phasing yourself into it psychologically, is a huge undertaking, regardless of what crime you have committed.'

Apart from the time spent in her cell, Catherine Nevin will never be by herself for any length of time. 'The visiting room in the new women's prison, while it is modern and bright, is controlled, naturally; it is restricted, so none of the prisoners have complete privacy when they have a visitor. There are two main categories of prisoner: those serving long terms, mainly for violent crimes and the others are run-of-the-mill, mainly crimes arising from drug addiction. There would be women from the lower socio-economic groups, some homeless people, some dysfunctional people who got into trouble and ended up in jail.'

Catherine Nevin was moved out of the healthcare unit after a week or ten days and into a small unit within the prison, housing 12 other women. Her fellow inmates are mainly 'lifers' and drug traffickers serving lengthy sentences.

On 7 June, when she again appeared in court for sentencing on the soliciting charges, Nevin looked tired and appeared to have lost weight, but was smartly dressed and perfectly groomed. Ms Justice Mella Carroll sentenced her to seven years on each of the three counts of soliciting, three short of the maximum. 'I don't intend to give you a lecture', the judge told Nevin.

Immediately, her lawyers sought leave to appeal on over 20 separate grounds, including the judge's charge to the jury and prejudicial media coverage. And Patrick MacEntee SC introduced the first ground of appeal by brandishing a letter sent by the DPP to Nevin's solicitor Garrett Sheehan on 30 May, revealing that Jack White's had been on a list of pubs under investigation by the Garda Anti-Racketeering Unit in 1991 for suspected links with the IRA or IRA suspects. The pub was later excluded from the list after further inquiries turned up nothing. Ms Justice Carroll refused leave to appeal. Nevin must now serve a seven-year sentence concurrent with her conviction for life. As she left the courtroom, she picked up her latest book, *Bread for the Journey*, a religious text.

Under the life sentence, in 2007, when she has completed the first seven years, Nevin will be entitled to apply to the Prison Review Group to have her sentenced reviewed. The review group will examine psychiatric and probation reports and at that stage, may well feel she has paid her debt to society. If they reject her application, she may apply again three years later. Any prisoner may apply for temporary release at any time during their sentence.

When Catherine Nevin was convicted, Tom Nevin's family felt a huge surge of relief. But this dissipated about a week later and was replaced by anger. Anger that the person who fired the fatal shot has never been caught, anger at the manner in which the Department of Justice fobbed them off over the licensing affair and anger at those who, they believed, did not tell the whole truth at the trial.

'At the time (of conviction) we were very relieved,' says Tom's sister, Mary Glennon. 'Then about a week later we realised, sure, this is not completed at all. We didn't do what we set out to do. We just wanted justice.'

Their anger over the way they were long-fingered by the Department of Justice is palpable:

'We were making phonecalls and then it came to us that we were getting nowhere and we had no record kept, so we started writing', says Patsy Nevin. 'The phonecalls were directly to the minister's office number. We phoned dozens of times.'

On top of the grief they had to bear when they buried their brother, this residue, and the fact that the gunman who killed their brother has yet to be brought to justice, is too much to cope with. In the eyes of Tom Nevin's family there are too many unanswered questions:

'We're looking for justice to be completed. That's all we wanted from the very beginning and we still want it. And it doesn't seem to be completed in our eyes. There's questions. There are still things left unanswered.'